THE POPE'S LEGION

THE MULTINATIONAL FIGHTING FORCE THAT DEFENDED THE VATICAN

Charles A. Coulombe

[handwritten inscription and signature, dated 5 June 2009]

palgrave
macmillan

To His Late Holiness, Blessed Pius IX;
to His Holiness, Benedict XVI;
and to the gallant men of all nations who served
in the Pontifical Zouaves,
this book is respectfully dedicated.

Aime Dieu et va ton chemin

THE POPE'S LEGION
Copyright © Charles A. Coulombe, 2008.

First published in 2008 by
PALGRAVE MACMILLAN™
175 Fifth Avenue, New York, N.Y. 10010 and
Houndmills, Basingstoke, Hampshire, England RG21 6XS
Companies and representatives throughout the world.

PALGRAVE MACMILLAN is the global academic imprint of the Palgrave
Macmillan division of St. Martin's Press, LLC and of Palgrave Macmillan Ltd.
Macmillan® is a registered trademark in the United States, United Kingdom
and other countries. Palgrave is a registered trademark in the European
Union and other countries.

ISBN-13: 978–0–230–60058–4
ISBN-10: 0–230–60058–1

Library of Congress Cataloging-in-Publication Data is available from the Library
of Congress.

A catalogue record of the book is available from the British Library.

Design by Newgen Imaging Systems (P) Ltd., Chennai, India.

First edition: September 2008

10 9 8 7 6 5 4 3 2 1

Printed in the United States of America.

CONTENTS

Acknowledgments iv

Introduction 1

Prelude 9

    I   A Gathering of Heroes 15

    II   The Crusaders Arrive 41

   III Baptism of Fire...63

   IV The Watchful Peace 91

    V   Garibaldi's Last Throw.................................... 115

   VI To the Porta Pia!... 141

  VII Same Foe, Different Field................................. 167

 VIII Viva Il Papa-Re!.. 195

Appendix I: Songs of the Zouaves 219

Appendix II: Zouave Sites 228

Appendix III: Mass in Memory of the Pope's Soldiers.................237

Notes 243

Bibliography..246

Index..249

Illustrations appear between pages 130 and 131

ACKNOWLEDGMENTS

The writing of this book has been quite an adventure, and—as is usual with such work—something of a team effort. So, many thanks to Jake Elwell, my agent at Harold Ober Associates, who was excited when I first told him the Zouaves' story; to Alessandra Bastagli, my redoubtable editrix at Palgrave Macmillan, whom I surely have cost a few years of life in frustration, and to her assistant, Emma Hamilton, who has been similarly treated; to Mrs. Jeannette Coyne of Cleveland for proofing and sage advice; to M. Jerome Discours of Luxembourg who kindly gave permission for the use of images from his formidable collection; to Marijke Zonneveld-Kouters of the Nederlandse Zouavenmuseum in Oudenbosch for similar permission and clarifications on the role of various Dutch Zouaves; to Msgr. Ignacio Barreiro of Human Life International, Rome, for advice and information on Julian Watts-Russell; to Bart Servaes of Belgium for information on the Zouaves of his country; to John Farrell, Dr. Albert Audet, Stephan Baron Hoeller-Bertram, William Biersach, Stephen Frankini, Tequila Mockingbird, and Axel Müllers of Aachen for their encouragement; and to the rest of my friends and family for putting up with my hermitlike existence while writing this book. And last, but first of all, to my beloved late father, Guy J. C. Coulombe, for first telling me the tale of the Pontifical Zouaves.

INTRODUCTION

The Pope is the bishop of Rome, in succession from Saint Peter, chief of the apostles. That is what Catholics believe, and from that simple—if eternally disputed—statement flows all else about the office. Given that the Pope is head of a universal Church, his followers have always felt that, in order to exercise his spiritual role impartially, it was necessary for him to be independent of any earthly power. There is solid wisdom behind this decision, given the papacy's experience with secular rulers. In the beginning, of course, it was simple: the Church under the Roman Emperors was an illegal organization; membership in it was punishable by death, and from Saint Peter to Saint Eusebius, 31 Popes were executed for the crime of holding the office.

Under such circumstances, it would be understandable if the early Church had simply declared human government evil, as other religions have in history. But the Gospel injunction to "Render unto Caesar what is Caesar's" as well as to give God His own forced the Church to wrestle with the issue in a more complex manner. As Saint Justin Martyr wrote to the emperor of his day, "Whence to God alone we render worship, but in other things we gladly serve you, acknowledging you as kings and rulers of men, and praying that with your kingly power you be found to possess also sound judgment."[1] Of course, this sentiment did not save its author from execution, any more than it saved saints Sebastian, George, and Maurice, the Thundering Legion, the Forty Martyrs of Sebaste, or any of the countless other Christian soldiers who fought well for their emperors but paid the ultimate price for refusing to worship them.

When Constantine legalized the Church, and granted it imperial favor, things changed considerably. For a start, he built the first large Christian churches and gave them to their worshipers. In such grand surroundings, the liturgy was able at last to emerge quite literally from the catacombs, and to develop in time the splendor and expressiveness that characterize all the traditional rites of the Church, East and West.

Moreover, it was held for many centuries that Constantine had handed control over Rome and its environs to Pope St. Sylvester I. The traditional version of this story runs that the emperor came down with leprosy; the pagan doctors suggested that he be cured by bathing in the blood of children. Rejecting this repulsive idea, Constantine had a vision of saints Peter and Paul, who told him to seek out Sylvester. This he did, and that Pontiff instructed him in the Catholic faith and baptized him. In an instant, the grateful emperor was cured of both original sin and leprosy. He happily made the "donation of Constantine," which conferred on the Pope and his successors sovereignty over Rome and the western empire—hence he moved his capital eastward.

But the collapse of the Roman empire in the west, various heresies that wracked the eastern half of the empire (often with the help of the emperors), and recurring invasions of Italy by various peoples completely disrupted civil life on the peninsula. In all of this turmoil, the Pope acted, to the best of his ability, as protector of the Romans against the various waves of invaders. Moreover, thanks to the papal estates in Sicily and Calabria, successive Popes were able to keep their city fed. Regardless of the emperor's sovereignty, it was the Pope to whom the people of Rome looked as their leader.

Nevertheless, the Popes remained loyal to the emperors, and the Romans followed their lead. There were reasons for this: On the one hand, the empire was seen as a holy institution; on the other, there were material considerations. Byzantine troops could reinforce the city militia at need against the Lombards, and the Byzantines safeguarded the papal estates in Sicily from which most of the Roman food supply then came.

But this uneasy alliance came to an end when the Iconoclastic emperor, Leo the Isaurian, decided to dragoon Pope St. Gregory II into his heresy in 727. Much had changed since the previous century, however, and Gregory did not fear captivity, the more so since the Roman militia made it clear that they would fight for him against the emperor if need be. Leo did not test them, but he did seize the Sicilian estates and transferred Dalmatia and Greece to the Patriarchate of Constantinople. For a few years, a nominal connection persisted between Rome and the empire, but subsequent emperors, busy with the Muslims, were entirely unable to protect Rome against the Lombards.

The Pope and his city needed a new protector, and in 753 one was found in the person of Pepin III, called Pepin the Short, soon to be king of the Franks. This was the beginning of the relationship between the Papacy and the Franks, culminating in the coronation of Charlemagne as emperor in 800. He in turn guaranteed to the Pope sovereignty over central Italy—the donation of Charlemagne. Thus were born the Holy Roman Empire and the Papal States. The provinces were made up of many little towns that jealously guarded their civic independence, as did the noble houses that tried to dominate them. No less jealous of their liberties and privileges were the aristocratic dynasties of the Eternal City itself that developed through the centuries, such as the Colonna, the Orsini, the Chigi, and the Cesarini (who claimed descent from the emperors).

From a purely temporal view, much of the time of subsequent Popes was taken up with ensuring their own control over Rome and extending it over the rest of the Papal States, as well as securing their independence from various outside powers. It was not, of course, merely a question of protecting them for their own sake, but of preventing the papacy from becoming a mere domestic chaplaincy to the nearest, latest powerful ruler.

These goals, together with those of safeguarding Catholics wherever in the world they might be and of protecting the missionaries who were extending the Church into new territories, were the basis of all papal diplomacy from that time to this. By extension, the Popes would always be leery of any one ruler becoming too powerful in Europe and the world.

Where and when they exercised actual control, successive Popes did what all secular rulers must do. To this day, the papal coats of arms on various walls, forts, roads, aqueducts, hospitals, public buildings, fountains, harbors, and so on carry mute testimony to the concern of Popes for every aspect of their subjects' lives. But since the major papal business—even of the most worldly of the Pontiffs—was religious, so too was that of the state over which they presided.

Such work aside, to the Pontiffs and their curia fell also the task of providing for the defense of Rome and the Papal States, and often enough diplomacy was not sufficient nor was a Charlemagne on hand. Indeed, all too often the Holy Roman Emperor and the King of France, while happy to take whatever privileges over the papacy that may have come their way by virtue of being successors of Charlemagne, were likelier to use those privileges to rule than to defend the patrimony of Saint Peter—that is, when they were capable of acting effectively on the peninsula at all.

So it was that early on, actual command of whatever military forces and fortifications they might be able to garner fell directly to the Popes. From the time of Charlemagne to the French Revolution, papal responsibility for the security of their lands meant inevitable conflict with a wide variety of foes. This was underscored by the raids of Muslim pirates on the Italian coasts, which culminated in 846 when the Muslims landed in force and proceeded to sack everything outside the walls of Rome, including St. Peter's and St. Paul's Outside the Walls. Fearful of a return performance, in 852 Leo IV enclosed the Vatican and its environs with the Leonine Wall; later expanded northward, this wall and its successors enclose the current Vatican City, Borgo, and Trastevere, collectively called the Leonine City. But if the walls were there, men equally strong were needed to defend them.

Over the next several centuries, something strange happened—the first stirrings of what would be called chivalry. Originating in the complex interactions between Germanic warriorhood and Roman civilization, by the eleventh century chivalry had begun to achieve the outline of what we think of when we use the term today. If knighthood was not yet in flower, it was certainly sprouting. Something of its spirit may be seen in the ceremony of knighting prescribed in the papal liturgical manual, the Roman *Pontificale:* "Receive this sword in the name of the Father and the Son and the Holy Ghost; use it in defense of thyself and the Holy Church of God, for the confusion of the enemies of the Cross of Christ and of the Christian faith, and never unjustly to the injury of any man, so far as human frailty will admit."[2]

This sort of chivalry would find its fulfillment in the Crusades; it was in this period that the mailed—later armored—knight on horseback came into his own, supported by infantry. The shock of the initial charge of knights then dissolved into individual combat between the mounted paladins.

While the Crusades are often bemoaned as an early example of imperialism and cultural insensitivity, it is important to remember that they were a response to acts of aggression. No matter how poorly they turned out in the event, they contributed much to the growth of European civilization. For our purposes in particular, they crystallized the institution of chivalry and were at once molded by and helped further mold the papal views of war.

For one thing, the Crusades produced the military religious orders. Like the Catholic orders of Carmelites or Franciscans except that the majority of the brothers were knights, the charisma of each was the military defense of one or another aspect of Christendom. Some orders were multinational, such as the Templars or Hospitallers (later called "of Rhodes," and now "of Malta"). Others, such as the Teutonic Knights and the Order of Calatrava, were more or less confined to one area. But each had a special relation to the Pope, being considered, in a sense, particularly close to him.

The nineteenth-century French writer Leon Gautier, who was very much a part of the culture and attitude that produced the Zouaves, wrote in his *Chivalry* of the mindset of the Crusaders: "Retarded by the political egotism of kings and emperors, the Crusade is at length preached. It is decided upon: our knights depart. What way will they travel? Will they go direct to Jerusalem? Will they proceed to Constantinople, or will they adopt a new plan of campaign and commence by clearing the Infidels out of Egypt, and marching more safely into the Holy Land? No one can tell, and really nobody cares. Assume the cross and go: that is all one thinks about."[3]

From Godfrey de Bouillon as he set out on the First Crusade in 1099 to Claus von Stauffenberg as he plotted to remove the monster who ruled his country in 1944, this attitude has characterized the Catholic military man who has put his faith over all other considerations, private or public. So it was for the Pontifical Zouaves.

PRELUDE

*D*riven by a lust for adventure and travel, C. Carroll Tevis, an 1849 West Point graduate, was soon bored with the opportunities for both that the United States Army offered. He longed for exotic climes and foreign people. Quitting the American service in 1850, Tevis accepted a commission in the Turkish army, rising to the rank of commander in the elite Anatolian cavalry called the Bashi-Bazouks. A few years later Tevis signed up to fight with the French in the Crimean War. He returned to the United States to aid the Union in the Civil War, rising to brevet brigadier general in the Maryland Volunteer Cavalry. After that conflict ended, he acted as adjutant general to the Fenians attacking Canada. Tevis would go on to spy on Indian nationalists in France for the British, become chief of staff in the Egyptian army, return to the Turkish service, and end his military career as a Bulgarian general. But perhaps the most extraordinary time in his extraordinary career was spent in Rome in the late 1860s as a soldier of the Pope. The war that the Pope was engaged in lasted a full decade, from 1860 to 1870; the papal banners attracted as colorful a band of soldiers as could ever be seen outside a Hollywood movie set.[1]

Leopold Louis Joubert joined up immediately after leaving his *lycée* in France at age 18; from childhood, he had wanted to emulate the knights and crusaders of old, a desire that would bring him to Rome. His ten years spent fighting in the same unit as Tevis only whetted his appetite for deeds of bravery in a glorious cause. It also gave him the necessary training to organize a private army for

Catholic missionaries in the Congo, where he fought a two-decade war against the slave traders. In the end, he carved out a massive safety zone for the locals. He always credited his military expertise to his service in the papal army, the Pontifical Zouaves.[2]

Born in England, George Collingridge was 19 years old and attending school in Paris when news came that his brother had been wounded while serving in the Zouaves. For his brother's sake and that of the cause they both believed in, he set out for Rome. After joining up, he was decorated for gallantry at Mentana, one of the most hard-fought battles the force would experience. After hostilities ceased, he emigrated with his brother to Australia, becoming one of the most eminent writers ever to emerge from that country.

Perhaps the most famous American in the regiment, Myles Keogh, owes his fame to one of the worst defeats the American army has ever suffered—the battle of the Little Big Horn, in which Keogh made his own last stand with the troopers of his company, not far from Custer's. When the Indians began their customary mutilation of the bodies of their defeated foes, they discovered proofs of Keogh's prior service with the pontifical army. Hanging around the neck of the fallen Keogh was an *agnus dei,* a wax square blessed by the Pope of Rome; on his uniform was a medal bearing the papal tiara and keys. As many of Sitting Bull's men were Catholic, Keogh's body was spared the humiliation meted out to the rest of his command.[3]

Both medal and the sacramental wax medallion specially blessed by the Pope were witnesses to the fact that before his Indian-fighting days, before his sterling service in the Union army during the Civil War (at Gettysburg and many other hard fought battles), the Irish squire from Clifden Castle in Kilkenny had been a soldier of Pope Pius IX. Along with the other men whose careers are sketched here, he too was a papal Zouave.

As a member of the St. Patrick Battalion of Irish Zouaves, Keogh had, in September of 1860, won a decoration for valor at the siege of the Italian city of Ancona. Eventually, the Pope would knight him. How he and thousands of other Irish, Italians, English, Scots, Welsh, French, Dutch, Belgian, Austrian, Swiss, German, American, Spanish, French Canadian, South American men—and even a Turk and a Chinese—ended up fighting a decade-long war under the papal flag is an epic tale, and one that has never before been told in any detail in English since the nineteenth century.

They say that chivalry is dead. If that is true, it took a long time to die. Centuries after gunpowder drove the last armored knight on horseback off the battlefield, the plumes and ardor of medieval romance burst forth in one of the most remarkable armies the world has ever seen. Never larger than 20,000 men at any one time, it boasted an incredible collection of characters, any one of whom, from private to commander, would seem to merit a biography of his own.

If the twentieth century was the bloodiest in history, the nineteenth surely ran a close second. Conceived in the horrors of the French Revolution, the conflicts in the hundred years from 1801 to 1901 included successive revolutions in Europe and Latin America, the wars of German and Italian unification, colonial conquests (and local counterattacks) in Asia and Africa, and, of course, the American Civil War. Three things distinguished these wars from all those that came before. While in Europe, at least, war had been regarded as the special province of the nobility and armies of professionals that included mercenaries of various kinds, the French revolutionaries invented the notion of a "nation in arms": Conscription, in the modern sense, was born. Second, in addition to king, homeland, and religion, a new abstraction was invoked to justify armed conflict: freedom. Last, the incredible inventiveness that characterized the nineteenth century was not restricted to steamships, telegraph, railroads, antiseptic, and the discovery of new planets thanks to improved telescopes. New technology was used to produce modern weaponry with truly horrifying effects. It is difficult for us in the twenty-first century to comprehend the shock and awe roused in the folk of the nineteenth by, for example, the Minié ball—a small bullet, to be sure, but one that inflicted fearsome wounds as it pulverized flesh and bone, leading almost inevitably to amputation.

The role of the Catholic Church in this era of conflict was a difficult one. The Reformation had sundered northern Europe from her sway. In the British Isles, Scandinavia, northern Germany, the Baltic duchies, and elsewhere, monasteries were closed, millennium-old ways of life were disrupted, and the more vocal supporters of the old faith martyred. Here and there, as in England's Pilgrimage of Faith and the northern and western risings, and in Sweden's Dacke and Dalarna risings, peasants rose in defense of their religion and were slaughtered.

As the eighteenth century wore on and the teachings of the Catholic Church lost their power over many of the educated and upper classes as a byproduct of the Enlightenment, there was an inevitable effect on the governance of the Church in countries that claimed to be Catholic. The suppression of the Jesuits at the insistence of Europe's Catholic kings; the attempts by German prince-bishops to "update" the Church in their lands; and the general disdain of many of the nobility and intelligentsia in Catholic countries all had the unintended consequence of increasing contempt for their so-called betters on the part of the peasantry.

By this time, the French Revolution was in full swing. In 1789, clerical privileges were abolished, and a year later the religious orders dissolved and all their property taken by the state for sale. These lands, together with those of émigré nobility, became the backing for the French republic's new paper money, the infamous and inflationary *assignats*. On July 12, 1791, the National Assembly passed the "Civil Constitution of the Clergy." This measure required all clerics to swear allegiance to the new constitution, and all bishops and pastors were to be popularly elected, with even non-Catholics eligible to vote. The Pope angrily rejected this measure; those clerics who refused to take the oath were dubbed "non-jurors" and were increasingly persecuted. Louis XVI renounced his assent to the measure before his beheading. Eventually, even the mask of the Constitutional Church was discarded by the masters of the government, and in 1793–94, a new, non-Christian Cult of Reason replaced Catholicism as the religion of the state. The parish churches of France were handed over to the Cult of Reason and were devoted to the group's unusual rites, which included such bizarre celebrations as the enthronement of a prostitute on the high altar of Notre Dame de Paris. In time, all of these activities provoked armed counterrevolutionary resistance in the name of Church and king on the part of many of the French. As the tide of revolution swept over France's boundaries, engulfing Germany, Belgium, Italy, and elsewhere, a similar response was sparked throughout Europe. In a real sense, this is where our story properly begins.

CHAPTER I

A Gathering of
Heroes

Do not think that I came to send peace upon earth: I came not to
send peace, but the sword.

—St. Matthew 10:34

$\mathcal{N}$o army is greater than its chief. In the heat of battle, although a man's attention is focused on keeping himself and his immediate comrades alive, the cause they fight for must not only consume them, the leader in whom it is incarnated must—as far as his men are concerned—truly express it in himself. He must be their hero. Fortunately for the Pontifical Zouaves, the ruler they served was indeed heroic.

Given his wide-ranging interests, his unshakeable belief in Providence, and what he had seen in his own life, it is little wonder that Pius IX was not cowed by the forces arrayed against him. Pius IX had seen Pius VII taken captive and exiled from Rome in 1808, only to return in triumph six years later—just as Pius IX would do in 1848 and 1849. He believed that his cause would triumph, regardless of the forces arrayed against it and whether or not he lived to see such victory. The centering of his hopes beyond the grave gave him a strength lacking in his opponents. Napoleon III and Cavour were concerned with their place in history and their present popularity and political standing; Pius cared about none of this. "Beware the man who has nothing to lose," applied well to him. Against the backdrop of the splendors of the papal court and its age-old rituals, Pius lived his life ever with an eye to what he considered most essential, of which elaborate ceremony served as a constant reminder rather than an end in itself.

In return, for the most part, the Catholic world idolized him as few Popes had been until the twentieth century. The contemporary accounts of him—even by non-Catholics—range from grudging admiration to almost embarrassing fawning.[1] In any case, it is easy to see why his cause became so popular among his far-flung flock, and why so many donated millions to him, and why thousands answered his call to arms despite the odds. Remarkably, the vast majority of those who joined his army, having worshiped him from afar, lost little of their reverence after seeing him up close. His men were devoted to him, a sentiment that was returned; their religious devotion and their conscious appropriation of the traditions of the Crusades and chivalry were married to an immense loyalty to a concrete man for whom they would gladly lay down their lives.

Pius IX was a mystery to many of his contemporaries. Liberals and revolutionaries throughout Italy and elsewhere were overjoyed at his election—some because he was thought to be sympathetic to them, others because they thought he was weak and easily manipulatable, still others because they believed him to be both. Those, of whatever stripe, who met him declared that he had an "imperturbable serenity," while being at the same time extremely jovial—especially loving jokes and puns of all kinds. Although watchful over the rights of the Holy See, Pius was eminently approachable, never as happy as when walking among his flock—either in the open or incognito. He was an immensely spiritual man, especially devoted to the Blessed Virgin (he defined the Immaculate Conception and approved the apparition of Our Lady of Lourdes) and to the Sacred Heart. But the Pope also appreciated some of the finer things in life, especially tobacco and cologne (he had a special blend of his own).

The Pontiff's earlier life gives us many clues to the enigma that was Pius IX. Born Giovanni Maria Mastai-Ferretti on May 13,

1792, in Senigallia (a town in the Marches), his early years were of course dominated by the chaos of the revolution in France and Italy. Although diagnosed as an epileptic (a diagnosis that has been disputed), the young nobleman was sent to the Collegio Romano to pursue studies in theology and philosophy. While there, he lodged with an uncle who was a canon of St. Peter's, but the two were forced to flee the Eternal City when Pius VII was taken into exile by the French. Back home, he was summoned in 1812 to Milan; because of his family lineage, the attempt was made to recruit him for the Noble Guard of Napoleon's Kingdom of Italy, but his supposed epilepsy excused him from service. Giovanni stayed in Senigallia until Pius VII stopped there on his way back to his capital in 1814. The young count was presented to the Pontiff and followed him back to Rome. A year later he was rejected for the Pope's Noble Guard and then felt called to the priesthood. But his disease prevented such aspiration until he was cured upon a visit to the Shrine of the Holy House of Loreto.

The life of the Church in Italy had been terribly disrupted by a decade and a half of war and periodic persecution. As one of the missionaries sent out to work among the people under these conditions, the future Pope began his lifelong activities with orphans. In 1825, having been a priest for six years, Giovanni was appointed assistant to the new nuncio in the recently independent South American country of Chile. This stint awakened Giovanni's interest in the Church beyond Europe.

After his return to Rome in December of 1826, Mastai-Ferretti was appointed by Leo XII to run the largest orphanage-cum-trade school in Rome, the vast Ospizio Apostolico di San Michele a Ripa. Wielding a firm but loving hand, this relatively minor command showed the shape of things to come. At least, Leo XII thought so.

In 1827, Leo consecrated Mastai-Ferretti as archbishop of Spoleto, a severely troubled and divided see. He immediately set to work on the town's ills, opening an institution for orphans similar to the one he had just left. He was soon very popular, standing by his people during civil unrest and an earthquake.

The new Pope, Gregory XVI, transferred him in December of 1832 to the diocese of Imola, whose bishop, Giacomo Cardinal Giustiniani, had just resigned. Not only did he build another orphanage for boys, he called on the Sisters of Charity to open one for girls and to run the public hospital. He also built an insane asylum and a refuge for ex-prostitutes. The new bishop also established a special seminary for poor aspirants to the priesthood and two new schools—one for the poor and one for the nobility. All of his efforts were rewarded with the love of his people and, in 1840, the red hat of a cardinal from Gregory XVI.

Mastai-Ferretti was selected as Pope in 1846. His predecessor had been an unyielding defender of the faith; in that atmosphere, many a plotter and revolutionary had found himself in a pontifical prison. But experience had led Pius IX to believe that correction tempered with mercy would inevitably bring the best out of an individual, so he ordered an amnesty. Alas, he would learn that hardened agitators are quite different from orphans. To his death, he always attempted to give people what they wanted, as long as he could square it with his duty. It was in that spirit that he would give the Papal States representative government. But the murder of his prime minister, his own flight to Gaeta, and the murders and profanations of churches (including St. Peter's) in his absence were also part of his education.

Still, he never lost his love of charity, serenity, and good humor. Pius IX carved out a legend for himself as an inveterate doer of good deeds among his people. Many such stories survive today, as with the poor boy who came up to him on the street, having recently been orphaned. "I have no father," he tearfully told the Pope. "I will be your father," was the pontifical reply. And so he proved to be, paying for the lad's housing and education out of his pocket until the boy came of age. Beggars, widows, invalids—all found themselves beneficiaries of the largesse of the Pope who wandered his city incessantly. Moreover, appeals for aid came by post constantly and as constantly were answered. At the same time, his tours in Rome were not merely to seek out the miserable; surprise visits of prisons, hospitals, schools, monasteries, convents, and innumerable other institutions led to rewards, corrections—or changes of leadership—on a regular basis. Moreover, he delighted in bringing the sacraments to the dying and the ill. When a cholera epidemic raged in Rome, he assiduously visited the sufferers: in one hospital, a Jewish woman died in his arms.

But with all this activity and the political and military concerns to be dealt with at the time, he had also to run a Universal Church—and not merely from the standpoint of diplomatic fencing with governments anxious either to control the Church or to persecute her. There were liturgical, devotional, and doctrinal concerns in almost every nation of the world to address, each affected by conditions remote to his Roman experience.

In this work, Pius's foremost assistants were the mutually antagonistic Giacomo Cardinal Antonelli, his secretary of state, and Monsignor Count Xavier de Merode, his pro-minister of arms. Understandably, the ingratiating Italian diplomat and the bluff noble soldier-turned-cleric would clash; but it is typical of Pius that he was fond of both these disparate characters and valued their so-different strengths. It is to them that we now must turn our attention.

Cardinal Antonelli (1806–1876) came of a minor noble family from Sonnino in Latium. Although he intended to become a priest, he never went beyond the diaconate, deciding instead to enter the papal bureaucracy. With a flair for administration, a built-in ability to please superiors, and a smooth—some said oily—manner, he went far. By 1845 he was pontifical treasurer-general; two years later, he was made the next-to-last lay cardinal. In 1848, he preceded the murdered Count de Rossi as papal prime minister. After Pius's return, he was made secretary of state, a post which—then and now—includes in its duties supervision of papal diplomacy. As such, he became the face of the Holy See, at least as regarded the great powers. Since Pius was so popular, those who wished to attack him directed their ire at Antonelli. For his part, in foreign affairs Antonelli believed in diplomacy rather than arms.

Regarding the internal administration of the Papal States, Antonelli's views were rather different. After Pius IX's flight from Rome, he was forced to reexamine his methods of governance. The Pope was well aware that he did not have the native ability to carry out the sorts of hard repressions that would be necessary to prevent a repetition of the horrors of 1848. Pius had the humility to put all such questions into Antonelli's hands.

So it was that, in addition to foreign affairs, censorship and punishment passed under the secretary of state's purview. In truth, he was far more ruthless in these areas than his master could ever have been. He refused to take chances with agitators and propagandists, and was quick to throw them in jail (of course, as the partisans of the Bourbons of Naples would find out after the fall of that kingdom to Garibaldi, the new rulers were also quite capable of brutal repression in what they considered self-defense).

For a long time, however, Antonelli—so clear-eyed with regard to internal threats—had an almost childlike faith in the pro-papal assurances of Napoleon III and Victor Emmanuel II. His strategy was to appeal to the Catholic powers for protection. But Pius, based upon his experience, believed that he would have to mount his own defense. So, once again happy to defer to those whose abilities he considered superior to his own, he turned to Xavier de Merode for help.

Born in 1820, Xavier de Merode was born into a noble Belgian family; his father was an official of King Leopold I. Although intended for the priesthood, the hot-tempered young nobleman would never brook opposition lightly. Merode was no respecter of persons, and in later years he had violent arguments with his generals and even with the Pope himself. But Pius IX put up with this for the greater good.

After attending Catholic schools, Merode entered the Royal Military Academy at Brussels. Upon graduation two years later, he was posted to Liege. But peacetime life in the army of a neutral nation did not appeal. Young Merode, with his king's permission, passed into the French army, serving heroically in Algeria. His valor there won him the Legion of Honor. As a diplomat's wife put it, "He was really an ideal soldier—like one in a chivalrous religious romance—full of courage, and spirit and wit, and yet so deeply devout, picking up the dying Arab child and carrying it on his horse to a spring to baptize it."[2] But in 1847, he decided to follow his vocation in the priesthood and was ordained two years later; at that time he was appointed chaplain to the French troops in Rome. In 1850, Pius IX placed him in charge of the Roman prisons; so successful was he in this position that foreign nations copied his reforms. Thus, when Pius IX felt need of a new leader to reorganize his army, Merode seemed the obvious choice.

When Merode became pro-minister at arms for Pius IX, he inherited an army of less than 10,000 soldiers—for the most part poorly trained, uniformed, and equipped. Apart from civil duties and the 1848 war, the papal army had not fought since 1797, and many of its rifles dated back to Napoleonic days. Some of its artillery was even older, and the arsenal at the Castel Sant' Angelo was a virtual museum. Sardinian and Garibaldian spies had already discovered that the arsenal was freely accessible in the afternoon, when its single sentry took his nap. Undaunted by this apparently hopeless situation, in early 1860 Merode traveled to Brussels for a secret meeting with his distant cousin, General Christophe Louis Juchault de Lamoricière, under whom he had served in Algeria; he offered him command of the papal army.

Lamoricière, a devoted Catholic, had quite literally covered himself with glory in Algeria. Born in Nantes in 1806, he entered the army of Charles X in 1828; two years later he was sent to North Africa, where he would spend most of the next 17 years. He fought bravely, was decorated frequently, and promoted rapidly. In his last year of service there he captured resistance leader Abd-el-Kader, thus effectively ending opposition to French rule.

In 1831, early in their conquest of Algeria, the French had found willing allies in the Kabyles, a Berber people living in the mountains. One of their tribes, the Zouaoua or Zwāwa, was particularly anxious to join the tricolor. One by one, three battalions of them were raised, and in 1838, these became a regiment under the already distinguished Major Lamoricière. Wearing their traditional dress of baggy trousers, short vests, and native headgear, the Zouaves, as the French called them, were an imposing sight. They were soon replaced with Frenchmen who retained the unique uniforms and won a reputation as a crack light infantry. By 1852, two more regiments had been formed, and two years later the Zouaves of the imperial guard were inaugurated. In time other countries would form their own Zouave units.

But Lamoricière did not share their triumph in France. Back in Paris for the 1848 Revolution, he entered parliament and briefly served as secretary of war. But he opposed the rise of Louis Napoleon Bonaparte, and after the coup of 1852 made the president into the emperor he was arrested and exiled. A contemporary described him thusly: "Vigorous of constitution and robust of frame; as insensible to fatigue as unconscious of fear; keen of vision, Quick of comprehension, and ready of resource; collected in the worst hour of difficulty; calm and cheerful, even gay and jaunty, under the deadliest fire."[3] Great gifts, to be sure—and he would need every one of them in his new command.

He was quite aware of the problems he faced, saying to Pius IX shortly after his arrival at Rome on April 1, 1860:

> "Most Holy Father, your Holiness has required my services: your desires are orders, and I have not hesitated a moment. You can dispose of my blood and life. But I ought at the same time to say that my presence here is either an assistance or a danger: an assistance, if I have only to maintain tranquility in your States, and preserve them from revolutionary bands; a danger, if my name be a pretext for hastening the Piedmontese invasion. For it is impossible for me, unless through a miracle, to triumph over an army trained to war, with troops of recent formation, badly armed, and who should have to fight one against ten."[4]

Both Pope and general knew what they were up against, and their first problem was lack of manpower.

Of the enemies that Pius, Antonelli, de Merode, and Lamoricière would face, none was more dangerous than Camillo Count di Cavour. Although he would die in 1861, all of Cavour's successors as prime minister to Victor Emmanuel II followed the policies—and the duplicitous tactics—laid down by the crafty politician from Piedmont.

Although, reviewing Cavour's career, one might think that the count had little regard for tradition, this is not entirely true—at least as far as his own family's traditions were concerned. The Bensi, as the clan were originally called, had supported the pro-imperial Ghibellines against the pro-papal Guelphs throughout the Middle Ages. After the imperial cause was defeated, they became loyal servants of the dukes of Savoy, who became the kings of Sardinia. In the eighteenth century the head of the clan was made marquis of Cavour by his king, and Benso di Cavour—often shortened to Cavour—became the family name.

Despite the favors heaped upon the Cavours by their monarch, when Napoleon seized the mainland and the king was forced into exile in Sardinia, the Marquis Michele Giuseppe di Cavour stayed behind, and became grand chamberlain to Prince Camillo Borghese, brother-in-law to the conqueror. In 1810, the marquis' second son was born, and the Borgheses stood godparents to young Camillo.

Once restored to the throne, the Savoys showed themselves extremely kindly to the clan that had betrayed them. Camillo attended a military academy and was commissioned as an officer in the engineers. Despite the kindness shown him, he expressed liberal ideas even in the army and was asked to leave before his term was up. But the ambitious young nobleman told a friend, "I thank you for the interest you take in the matter; but, believe me, I shall make myself a career all the same. I have a great deal of ambition, an enormous ambition, indeed; and I trust I shall justify it when I am a minister, for in my day-dreams I already see myself Minister of the Kingdom of Italy." Thus, at age 21, Cavour already knew what he wanted to do in life.

A sojourn with Protestant relatives in Geneva weakened his belief in Catholicism, as did his acquaintance with some influential Calvinist clerics there. Cavour imbibed two major dogmas at that time: that the Church should be separated from the state, in the sense of having no influence on public life; and further that, as in most Protestant countries of that time, the Church should function as a department of government, confining its activities to teaching the ignorant basic morality and unquestioning obedience to the rulers.

After studying and traveling, he settled down in 1847 to found with some like-minded noblemen a journal called *Risorgimento*. The new publication called for "the independence of Italy; union between the princes and peoples; progress in the path of reform; and a league between the Italian States." This was moderate enough, to be sure, for it reflected the views of his colleagues, most of whom were members of a group called the Neo-Guelphs. They wished to see Italy united as a federation of her princes under the nominal presidency of the Pope (a prospect made likelier by then-easy-going personality of the as-yet-untested Pius IX), and a removal of French and Austrian influence over the peninsula. Cavour may or may not have shared their opinions at that time—the program advocated by the journal was elastic enough.

The following year, Cavour was part of the group that pressed the king, Charles Albert, to grant a constitution; in 1849, he himself went into the new parliament. In the meantime his king, having allied with the various revolutionary governments in Italy against Austria, was defeated for a second time by the Austrians at Novara and forced to abdicate. His son, Victor Emmanuel II, then assumed the throne, and in 1852 Cavour became prime minister. From then until his death, he was either head of the government or architect of policy without the title.

Even before his accession to power, Cavour had great influence on the affairs of state; one of his most important goals was that of hobbling the Church within the realm of Sardinia and muzzling its internal supporters. This was necessary in order both to achieve his own view of the Church's proper place in society and inhibit one of the major opponents of a unified Italy, and to curry the favor of the anticlerical revolutionaries whom he intended to use as foot soldiers in his struggle to conquer Italy. Much had already been accomplished by the time Cavour came to power.

In 1848, the Jesuits had been expelled by Charles Albert in fulfillment of the revolutionaries' demands; as well, a secularizing education law was passed. Starting in 1850 and gathering strength under Cavour's leadership over the next five years, successive laws were passed in violation of treaties, taking from the clergy their privileges and immunities (including immunity from conscription, which Cavour introduced), abolishing certain Church holidays, governing teaching in the seminaries, introducing civil marriage, and suppressing all monasteries and religious orders in Sardinia (seizing their property for the state). This last piece of legislation received the royal assent on May 28, 1855.

Cavour, who has ever since been trumpeted as the guardian of civil liberties, ruthlessly crushed the opposition to these measures. His opponents in parliament were sidelined, university professors and students who protested were ejected from their places, bishops and priests were exiled and imprisoned, and dissenting journals were suppressed. He also imposed a regime of conscription and ruinous taxation upon the Sardinians for the purpose of creating a modern military that would outgun all the other armies in the peninsula put together. Possessed of this weapon, Cavour led his country into the Crimean War at the side of Britain and France in 1856. This would be crucial in the days to come.

Cavour's sometime ally, frequent tool, and occasional opponent was just as key in the attainment of the Sardinian prime minister's goal—the professional revolutionary, Giuseppe Garibaldi. Garibaldi was born in Nice in 1807, at a time when that city too had been annexed by imperial France. Nice was a frontier city, and at that time severely divided between its French- and Italian-speaking populations. From an early age, Garibaldi identified with the latter, all unknowing that his own actions would one day lead to the ruin of his own people. He became a sailor, and in 1833 at the Russian port of Tagnarog joined a secret society—*La Giovine Italia,* headed by Giuseppe Mazzini—dedicated to driving the Austrians out of Italy and establishing a secular, united, Italian republic. From that time on, he was the sworn enemy, not only of Austria and the governments of the peninsula (at the time including Sardinia), but of the Church and any government, Italian or foreign, that supported it. In November 1833, he went to Geneva, met Mazzini, and was initiated into the *Carbonari*—the supersecret revolutionary elite, violation of whose oaths was punishable by death. In February of the next year he joined an abortive revolt against the then-conservative Sardinian government, was sentenced to death, and fled Europe.

From that time on, Garibaldi became a sort of revolutionary-at-large. Landing in Brazil in 1835, he acquired a mistress (who would become the mother of his four children); four years later he joined a band of gauchos revolting against the Brazilian empire. Although this campaign lasted until 1845 and was the second bloodiest civil war in Brazil's history, it accomplished little; still, it did give Garibaldi his trademark bit of menswear—the red shirt worn by Brazilian gauchos of the time. It was Garibaldi's embrace of this garment that led eventually to red being adopted as the color of revolution.

But he did not wait around for the defeat of his cause; in 1842 he and his mistress moved on to Montevideo, Uruguay, to fight on the liberal side of the civil war that broke out. There he raised an Italian Legion, which flew a black flag in mourning for captive Italy and whose soldiers wore the red shirts. He was a commander of liberal-held Montevideo and its navy, and contributed mightily to his side's victory. When the revolution broke out in Naples in 1848, he led 60 members of this legion back to their European homeland.

Garibaldi took command of the army of the Roman Republic that had usurped control of the Papal States and shared its defeat in 1849. Hotly pursued by French, Austrian, Spanish, and Neapolitan troops, he led the remainder of his forces on a long march toward Venice, besieged by the Austrians. He and his men were forced to seek refuge in the independent republic of San Marino. From 1849 to 1854 Garibaldi was in exile, visiting places as disparate as New York, England, and Peru. He returned to live on a small island near Sardinia in 1854, and five years later at Cavour's request raised a body of volunteers to fight the Austrians in the war of 1859. Thus began a long and fairly tortured relationship for the old revolutionary, as he seesawed back and forth between his original republican ideals and the pragmatic need to cooperate with the House of Savoy. In the immediate, he contributed mightily to his new ally's victory over Austria. Although he felt betrayed by the Sardinians when his native city was given to France as part of the price for their cooperation in the war (his dislike of Cavour stems from this time), he later invaded Naples with the connivance of Sardinia and certain well-placed Neapolitan military and civil leaders. His takeover of the southern kingdom (Naples and southern Italy along with Sicily constituted the kingdom of the Two Sicilies) was the beginning of long guerrilla warfare by peasants loyal to the deposed Bourbon

King Francis II—a conflict whose memory has been revived in recent years by those seeking autonomy or even independence for Southern Italy. Despite his dislike of Cavour, Garibaldi turned over his conquests to Victor Emmanuel II. The unification of the southern, central, and northwest regions of Italy also completely undermined the strategic position of the Papal States.

Garibaldi then turned his attention to overthrowing the Pope— whose opponents divided into the National Party, who took their orders from the Italian (as the Sardinian cabinet renamed itself and their lands) government of Victor Emmanuel, and the party of Action, who looked to Garibaldi for direction. Victor Emmanuel's regime would alternately imprison, release, fund, or restrain Garibaldi and his followers as their policies led them. Despite this ongoing manipulation, Garibaldi felt a continuing loyalty to Victor Emmanuel, reserving his scorn for the king's ministers— depending on how they were treating him at the moment. The ministers, however, employed Garibaldi as a useful threat: while retaining him as a handy tool, they would insist that they simply wished to occupy the Papal States in order to protect them from the excesses Garibaldi would undoubtedly wreak if he managed to attack the territories of the Holy See. No one can deny the old agitator's sincerity or his devotion to his cause; his judgment is much more open to question.

Victor Emmanuel II was an interesting character, indeed. His father, Charles Albert, had been king before him, but when Victor Emmanuel was born in 1820, he was not heir to the throne. In that year, Victor Emmanuel I had been restored to his throne for six years. His actual successor was his brother, Charles Felix; Charles Albert was merely prince of Carignano, head of a junior branch of the royal family that had separated from the main line of the

House of Savoy in the seventeenth century. Although his father
had fought for the king against the French when they invaded in
1792, he stayed behind—as did the Cavours—and served the new
rulers.

Born in 1798, Charles Albert had been educated at Napoleon's
insistence in Geneva, with results not too dissimilar to those
attending Cavour's time there; Napoleon made him an army
officer. When his distant cousin was restored to the Sardinian
throne, Charles Albert was sent back to Turin to be educated in
sounder principles; he was also married to a pious Habsburg archduchess, daughter of the grand duke of Tuscany, in hopes that
his wife would further alienate him from liberal principles and at
least educate their children soundly. But when a revolution broke
out against Victor Emmanuel I in 1821, Charles Albert sided with
revolutionaries, declared himself regent, and granted a constitution.
The new king, Charles Felix, was a doughtier soldier than the rebels supposed and quickly triumphed. Charles Albert switched sides
but remained under suspicion although he was officially declared
heir in 1824. He succeeded his older cousin in 1831; 17 years later
he joined the various revolutionary governments in declaring war
on Austria. Defeated, he was forced to abdicate and was succeeded
by his son.

All of this background left a heavy mark on Victor Emmanuel II.
Heir to one of the most traditional thrones in Europe, he was nevertheless wedded to the revolution. Keen on uniting Italy under his
own rule, he had grave doubts about his right to do so. Achieving
this goal involved committing what a believing Catholic could only
consider to be numerous acts of sacrilege; yet he could never bring
himself to jettison his mother's faith entirely. He married, as had
his father, a Habsburg archduchess; but his queen died in 1855 and

so was unable to exercise a restraining influence. In an eerie way, the passions contending within this king's own heart mirrored the internal divisions of the Italian people as a whole. It is said that one major job of a constitutional monarch is to represent his people. In a strange way, Victor Emmanuel II did just that. Lord Clarendon, the British foreign secretary who insured Sardinia a place at the peace table after the Crimean War, perhaps a tad unkindly said, "There is universal agreement that Vittorio Emanuele is an imbecile; he is a dishonest man who tells lies to everyone; at this rate he will end up losing his crown and ruining both Italy and his dynasty." Pius IX and his advisors might be forgiven for sharing this view, just or not.

But the Holy See was not without foreign allies. Principal of these was Franz Josef, the emperor of Austria. Ascending the throne at just 19 in 1848, when his uncle had been forced to abdicate and his dynasty was tottering, the new emperor, with the help of able generals and advisors, and Russian intervention, suppressed the revolutions in Austria and Hungary, and turned his attention to Italy. His redoubtable commander there, Field Marshal Radetzky, with the help of timely interventions by France and Spain, was able to put down the various revolts and defeat Charles Albert of Sardinia, with the results we have just seen. When the year 1849 ended, Franz Josef faced the dual task of keeping Austria paramount among both the German and Italian states. In the latter case, his work was made easier by the fact that he was himself king in Lombardy and Venetia; Habsburg cousins sat on the thrones of Tuscany and Modena, and Bourbon allies on those of Parma and Naples. He had also inherited from his forebears, the Holy Roman emperors, the duty of defending the Papal States—albeit a privilege disputed by the French.

What worked against him and his empire was the spirit of nationalism: Unleashed by the French Revolution and temporarily released once more in 1848, it was not merely a question of Pan-Germanism and Pan-Italianism that might be harnessed in Germany and Italy. His was a severely multinational empire, comprising not merely Germans and Magyars, but Czechs, Slovenes, Croats, Ruthenians, Poles, Slovaks, Serbs, Romanians, and others. The dilemma of keeping these disparate peoples in united loyalty to his dynasty was one that would plague him from his accession until his death in 1916. It also led him into numerous reversals of policy. The suppression of the Hungarian Revolution of 1848 was accomplished with the aid of the various non-Magyar (mostly Slavic) groups in Hungary, as well as with the tsar's army. But fear of antagonizing Sardinia's British and French allies led him to declare neutrality in the Crimean War, thus making an enemy of Russia. Franz Josef's defeat by Prussia in 1866 would force him to seek an alliance with the defeated Magyars, leading to Hungary's reestablishment as a separate kingdom the following year. Part of his deal with them allowed the Magyars to rule their nationalities as they pleased—the very peoples who had fought so hard for the Habsburgs in 1848. Needless to say, they were not pleased.

Yet, by and large, Franz Josef would be successful in his maneuvering. The strong traditions of his house and his fidelity to Catholicism were advantages that would be hard to understand today. In time—especially as tragedies claimed the life of his brother, son, and empress—his unswerving devotion to duty and ascetic lifestyle would, for perhaps the majority of his subjects, excuse most of his faults. As the years passed, he became the Old Emperor: steady, unyielding, the very incarnation of honor and devotion.

But this process had not yet occurred by 1859. He was still young, impetuous, and very much in love with his empress, the famous Elizabeth—who at the time was still in love with him. He had defeated the revolutionaries of 1848 and survived in fine style. At this point, Franz Josef was still convinced that he did, after all, know best—for himself, his subjects, and his allies. It was a conviction that would soon be severely tested.

Another ally of Pius IX was not a king—or rather, not a ruling one. Henry V, the count de Chambord, was the grandson of Charles X, king of France, who had been deposed in 1830 and had abdicated in Henry's favor. Unfortunately for the Bourbons, Henry's cousin, Louis Philippe, managed to have himself made king by the revolutionaries and would be deposed himself in 1848—setting off the wave of unrest that bedeviled Europe in that fateful year. Young Henry was taken by his grandfather to exile in Frohsdorf, Austria, where a miniature French court-in-exile grew up.

But the Legitimist royalists in France (to be distinguished from the more liberal Orleanist partisans of Louis Philippe and his descendants) continued to recognize Henry as their rightful sovereign. They were very numerous, particularly in such regions as Brittany and the Vendée that had revolted against the French Revolution and suffered heavily for it. Many of the oldest names (and wealthiest people) in France bound themselves to him, and in the ranks of Henry's supporters were found many of the most militant Catholics in France. For them, his word was law.

As with his host, Franz Josef, Henry's family traditions and personal conviction convinced him of the necessity of preserving the temporal power of the Church. He considered it his duty as "Oldest Son of the Church," to support Pius IX in any way he could, within his straitened abilities. Henry refused to see the blood of Frenchmen shed for his own sake, and so never directed the kind of revolt on the part of his supporters that he knew would end in a horrific civil war. But the defense of the Holy See was another matter, and as long as it was threatened, he would be one of its most outspoken defenders. It was no coincidence, therefore, that a majority of French recruits for the Pontifical Zouaves were Legitimists.

Among these friends and foes of the Papal States, however, there was one man who was key to the situation: the nephew of the great Napoleon, Prince Louis Napoleon Bonaparte—after the coup of 1852, Napoleon III, emperor of France.

Napoleon III shared his uncle's great dilemma. On the one hand, he wanted to be a legitimate sovereign and successor to Charlemagne. Both Bonapartes surrounded themselves with elaborate court etiquette and attempted to play the traditional role of protector of the Church. But at the same time, they also regarded themselves as incarnations of the "correct" principles of the French Revolution, of liberty and progress.

In the younger Napoleon's case, this dichotomy started at an early age. His father, Louis Bonaparte, had been made king of Holland by his brother, Napoleon I; but when they quarreled, Louis was deposed and his kingdom directly annexed to France—puppets ought not to have minds of their own.

After a tumultuous childhood, the young Louis Napoleon found himself in Italy during the revolutionary year of 1831; there he joined a revolt against Pope Gregory XVI, seeing action against the papal troops. It was also widely believed (though subsequently denied) that the young Bonaparte was initiated into the *Carbonari* at that time. Whether or not that was true, he was elected president of France after the revolution of 1848, at which time (despite his own opposition to the move) his predecessor in the presidency had dispatched troops to Rome. Louis Napoleon thus found himself presiding over the French intervention that restored Pius IX to Rome the following year.

Even then, though, his cross-purposes were apparent: In September 1849, he wrote to a prominent French officer in Italy, "My dear Ney, the French Republic did not send an army to Rome to stifle Italian liberty there, but on the contrary to direct it by protecting it against its own excesses.... I sum up in this sense the conditions of the restoration of the temporal power of the Pope—a general amnesty, secularization of the administration, adoption of the *Code Napoleon,* and a Liberal Government."[5] His deeper motive, of course, was—whether it would be under Sardinia or the Pope—the return of Italy to the client status it had endured under his uncle.

But fortunately for Pius IX, the new president did not force the issue; he had other matters to attend to, namely, setting the stage for his assuming his uncle's authority and title as emperor of the French. To do this, he would need the support (or at least nonresistance) of the country's Catholics. By permitting the Pope to function in freedom, he secured this support and so in 1852 was able to launch the coup that made him Napoleon III and sent Lamoricière into exile. Garibaldi and many of Napoleon's erstwhile Italian colleagues denounced the move. Cavour did not; he knew with whom he was dealing and so committed himself to the would-be conqueror's Crimean adventure, trusting that he would be able to rely on the revolutionary side of Napoleon's character as well as his desire for French-speaking Sardinian real estate.

But Pius had three cards to play in maintaining Napoleon's allegiance. The first was the new emperor's need for Catholic support;

the second was his empress, Eugenie, a pious Spanish noblewoman.
And the third was Napoleon's quest for legitimacy. One major source
of this was in an area that Pius had unquestioned control over—the
liturgy.

The Holy Roman Emperor, as the temporal protector of the
Pope and civil leader of Christendom, had particular prayers offered
for him throughout the Latin Catholic world: He was mentioned
in the canon of the Mass, in the prayers for Good Friday and Holy
Saturday, and in a special proper Mass. After Francis II, the last
Holy Roman Emperor, abdicated at Napoleon's insistence in 1806,
these ceased to be offered, save in the Habsburg dominions (Francis II
had transformed himself into Francis I, emperor of Austria).

When Napoleon III assumed the crown, he adopted as many
of the trappings of monarchy as he could, and these included
the specifically religious ones. He claimed the right to defend
the Catholics of the Ottoman Empire (and especially those holy
places in Palestine under Catholic jurisdiction; Russia attended to
the Orthodox shrines there). The emperor was a friend to French
religious orders and reintroduced such things as the Catholic military chaplaincy and masses for the opening of parliament. There
can be no doubt that he was personally religious. So it was that
he petitioned to Holy See to have all of the imperial prayers in
the missal offered on his own behalf. With the 1857 bull *Imperii
Galliarum,* Pius IX conceded these indisputable signs of imperial
authenticity to Napoleon.

Moreover, as an individual, even Napoleon's opponents praised
him. Emile Zola wrote, "At bottom a kind man haunted by generous
dreams, incapable of a bad action, most sincere in the unshakable
conviction which carried him through the events of his life, and
which was that of a man predestined to a part." What both sides

concerned in what came to be called the "Roman Question" (that is, whether the papal state of Rome would be unified with the rest of the Italian states and who would govern its populace, the temporal authority of the Pope or the Italian government) wondered was whether the emperor's kindness and his personal conviction would work for or against them. As they would find out, the answer was both.

CHAPTER II

The Crusaders Arrive

We come from the blue shores of England,
From the mountains of Scotia we come,
From the green, faithful island of Erin,—
Far, far, from our wild northern home.
Place Saint Andrew's red cross in your bonnets,
Saint Patrick's green shamrock display;—
Love God, O my soul, love Him only,
And then with light heart go thy way.

—*Song of the English Zouaves*

*C*avour's engineering of Italy's entrance into the Crimean War paid off at the 1856 Congress of Paris, where the British and French more or less pledged themselves to lend their support—moral support if nothing else—to the unification of Italy, including especially the Papal States, under Sardinia. Upon his return to Turin, Cavour harangued the parliament, attacking the papal government for its incompetence and for being a theocracy. He then secured a quiet alliance with Garibaldi and other heretofore republican revolutionaries. Finally, he secretly offered Napoleon III Nice and Savoy should France declare war on Austria and successfully conquer Lombardy (which would then be transferred to Sardinia). Unbeknown to the Pope, the dukes of Parma and Modena, the grand duke of Tuscany, and the king of Naples (to say nothing of the thousands loyal to them), all was set in motion to bring their world tumbling down around them.

Cavour's secret treaty with Napoleon III required that Austria declare war on Sardinia if France was to come into the war. To accomplish this, Cavour did his best to annoy the Austrians by staging military maneuvers close to their border. Vienna rose to the bait, offering an ultimatum to the Sardinians on April 23, 1859, demanding their disarmament. A delighted Cavour refused, and the emperor declared war on April 29. Sardinia had 70,000 troops to devote to the affair and Napoleon sent 130,000. The Austrians boasted 220,000 in or near their Italian possessions. The transportation of the French army was the first large-scale use of railways for military transportation, showing yet again that the new inventions that would crown the nineteenth and twentieth centuries need not be used merely to improve daily life. The Austrians were pushed steadily back, defeated at Magenta, lost their regional capital of Milan, and were soundly defeated again at Solferino on June 24; in the meantime, the papal legates in Romagna, dukes of Modena and Parma, and the grand duke of Tuscany were overthrown by Sardinian-funded revolutionary committees; the presence of Sardinian—and in Tuscany, French—troops sealed the issue.

The Papal States were of course immediately affected by these events. The Austrians still had garrisons at Ancona and Bologna, and agreed at Pius IX's request not to withdraw them without notifying him. The French and local troops in Tuscany, in the meantime, commanded by the emperor's cousin, Prince Napoleon, were ready to enter the Romagna using the Austrian presence as a pretext. The French fleet in the Adriatic fired a shot at Ancona and landed a party between Ancona and Bologna, which was then withdrawn. When, on June 11, the news came to Bologna of the defeat at Magenta, the Austrians withdrew, giving the Cardinal Vicar only a few hours notice. There were no papal soldiers in the city, and the revolutionary committee seized power, expelling the cardinal and tearing down the papal arms.

Prince Napoleon and his Tuscan cohorts then sent another column to the papal frontier at Umbria, to revolutionize that key province of the Papal States. A revolt was attempted at Foligno; but as the townspeople had no interest in the cause, the revolutionaries surrendered without a shot being fired. But Perugia, the capital of the province, was closer to the frontier, and Tuscan volunteers soon thronged the city, joining hands with the revolutionaries already there. On June 14 they rose up, disarmed the few papal carabinieri, and raised the tricolor over Perugia.

Immediately, the revolutionaries began preparing for a fight. Their appeal to the French at Florence was denied, but Prince Napoleon did allow 800 hundred more Tuscans to cross the frontier to join them. As the leaders of the revolt feared, the Holy See could not allow Perugia to remain in their hands, and on June 17, Colonel Antonio Schmid was dispatched with about 2,000 men to suppress the revolt. His advance guard was made up of some 100 carabinieri, followed by a main force comprising a large section of the First Foreign Regiment (the Swiss), Roman volunteers, Pontifical Custom House guards, a few engineers, and a Roman artillery section—something in the neighborhood of 1,400 troops. The rear guard featured 400 Roman regular infantry.

After two days' march, Schmid reached Foligno, where he learned that some 5,000 Tuscans were ensconced at Perugia and more were expected presently. Reasoning that delay would simply make a hard job impossible, the papal commander resolved to attack as soon as possible. He then led his men on a forced march overnight to Santa Maria degli Angeli, ten miles from Perugia, outside Assisi. On June 20, while his men had their confessions heard by the Franciscans stationed at the basilica, he sent an emissary, a popular Perugian judge named Luigi Lattanzi, to convince the Perugia's defenders to surrender. He presented the Pope's offer of peace terms to the rebel leaders, but as they were all Tuscans and not Perugians (and therefore they had the safe haven of Tuscany to flee to, should they be defeated), they refused. Upon Lattanzi's return, Schmid had no alternative but to attack.

In the mythology of Italian unification, the battle of Perugia has been interpreted as a massacre in which Swiss mercenaries fell like wolves upon defenseless and unwarned Perugians. But in fact, Schmid's column was as much Italian as foreign, and his opponents were far more Tuscan than Perugian; they had been preparing to defend the city, and they had refused peace terms. They had thought that French sponsorship would prevent the Holy See from reacting and that all Umbria would rise. They were mistaken on both counts.

Schmid, still hoping for a peaceful outcome, ordered his troops not to fire unless attacked. He resolved to enter Perugia through the Porta Romana; this would mean a march through the village of San Giovanni, at which point the road went over the river via a stone bridge. Although the village seemed deserted, a shot rang out from a single house, killing a Roman soldier. The papal soldiers entered the house and shot the one man found bearing a rifle. The advance continued to the city, where the Porta Romana was strongly barricaded. The monastery of San Pietro, about 800 yards in front of the gate, had been fortified as well and garrisoned by rebels. A volley rang out from the windows and roof of the monastery; the papal troops broke their way into the entrance. A few of the defenders were killed, more fled, and a number were taken prisoner. Schmid then set up a field hospital for both papal and rebel wounded in the monastery and turned his attention to attacking the town.

The colonel divided his forces into three parts: a thousand men, a howitzer, and a 9-pounder he kept at the monastery for the assault on the gate; the remainder he divided into two columns to launch feints at other sides of the wall to draw off the defenders' attention. After firing shots at the gate and throwing grenades over it, the main body attacked the Porta Romana. Their rather shoddy axes breaking in the attempt to demolish the doors, the papal forces threw up ladders, clambered up and over, and tore the tricolor down in the process. The gate taken, they faced the barricade set up immediately in front of them. From this barrier, from surrounding houses, and from a nearby hotel, the Tuscans kept up a steady rain of fire. A few women joined in, throwing rocks and other items from the roofs (two women were killed by gunfire). After successfully storming the barricade, the attackers turned their attention to the hotel from which furniture and gunfire were coming. The papal soldiers broke in, encountered an armed group in the lobby, and another melee ensued, in the course of which the innkeeper and two of his servants were bayoneted. Searching the hotel, the papal soldiers discovered an American named Perkins and his family, who had come to watch the pontifical soldiers defeated (one thinks of the picnickers who two years later would watch the American Civil War Battle of the First Manassas outside Washington). A guard was posted outside their door for their protection. In short order, rebels were routed out of a few other houses. Some looting occurred, but the papal officers forced their men to return most of their booty. Most of the defenders then fled to the Tuscan border, leaving behind 70 dead, 100 wounded, and 120 prisoners, compared to the total of 90 papal troops killed and wounded.[1]

Such was the "Massacre of Perugia," so remembered in no small part due to the wild tales recounted by Perkins to various newspapermen. In fact, there were no atrocities, no wholesale slaughter of innocents; even had there been, Perkins would not have been able to see them from the safety of his room. But regardless of the propaganda value this action would encounter, it had a deeper significance: It was the first major papal battle of the war. Schmid was promoted to general upon his return to Rome.

France's Catholics were annoyed with their emperor, the Prussians were threatening to enter the war, and both emperors (who had not commanded large-scale armies before) were disgusted by the carnage. The result was the Armistice of Villafranca, negotiated without the Sardinians, which was signed on July 12. This pact required that most of Lombardy be ceded to France, who immediately retroceded it to Sardinia; that Parma, Modena, Tuscany, and Romagna be returned to their former rulers; and that the Italian States be joined in a loose confederation under the nominal presidency of the Pope. Given the French garrison in Rome, Napoleon believed that this would allow him to rule Italy by proxy.

At first, Cavour and his cohorts were outraged: The Austrians still held Venetia and the powerful circle of cities of east Lombardy called the Quadrilateral. But their anger cooled, and in order to appear to abide by the treaty, the Sardinian commissioners in the conquered capital gave up their posts to hand-picked local governments on August 1. Five days later, the representatives of France, Austria, and Sardinia gathered in Zurich to draft a final treaty.

In the meantime, Napoleon III began exerting his influence to pressure Pius IX to accept Sardinian annexation of Romagna, which the Pope steadfastly refused to do. Instead, on October 1 the Holy See broke off diplomatic relations with Sardinia and ordered Victor Emmanuel's ambassador to leave Rome. The following day, British Foreign Secretary Lord John Russell, speaking on behalf of Lord Palmerston and his cabinet, officially pledged Great Britain to Sardinia's cause at a speech in Aberdeen. Talk of a European congress to discuss the matter was scuttled when the Pontiff refused to participate unless guarantee of the Papal States in their entirety was stipulated. On December 31, Napoleon III wrote an official letter to the Pope, asking him to cede Romagna to Sardinia, "for the good of the Church."

On January 19, 1860, Pius IX replied to Napoleon (and many others) with an encyclical in which he set forth his reasons for retaining Romagna and every inch of the Papal States. After speaking of the emperor's letter, he declared:

> ...We could in no way assent to his counsel. We said that "it offers insuperable difficulties, in consideration of Our dignity and that of the Holy See and Our sacred character and the rights of the same Holy See, which pertain not to the succession of any royal family but to all Catholics." Likewise We professed "what is not Ours cannot be given up by Us....We could not abdicate the provinces in Emilia without violating solemn oaths by which We are bound, without exciting quarrels and disturbances in the rest of Our provinces, without committing injustice to all Catholics, and without, finally, weakening the rights not only of the Princes of Italy but of all Princes of the whole Christian world who could not watch with indifference the introduction of most destructive principles."[2]

On March 29, without naming any individuals, Pius IX published a bull excommunicating all who had a part in the seizure of Romagna. The Papal States would resist. But where to find the men?

Conscription was out of the question, associated as it was the hated Napoleonic rule. A fresh call must go out for volunteers for "Swords around the Cross." Recruiting and finance committees were swiftly organized in dioceses throughout the Catholic world, starting with Belgium and France. Reaction was swift: A number of legitimist French officers, such as the Marquis de Pimodan, Athanase de Charette (descendant of the hero of the Vendée), Chevigné, and Bourbon-Chalus, joined General Lamoricière. The renowned bloodlines of many of the young French officers led one observer to remark that the papal officers' roster "resembled a guest-list from a party of

Louis XIV." But it was not only the French nobility who sent its sons, the great Roman families did so as well. Present also were the brother of the king of Naples (at that moment losing his realm to treason and Garibaldi) and the future Carlist claimant to the throne of Spain. Nor was it solely the aristocracy that contributed:

> Gallant men from various countries—France, Belgium, Holland, Austria, many parts of Italy—offered their services to defend the Holy See against revolutionary violence. The noblest families of France sent to Rome representatives of their valour and devotion. Fathers themselves presented their sons as their most precious offering; husbands quitted peaceful and happy homes for the hardships of the camp and the perils of the field; bridegrooms tore themselves from their brides ere the orange blossom had faded in the wedding chaplet; mere boys left for the new Crusade with the tears and benedictions of widowed mothers, whom faith alone could sustain under so great a sacrifice. The Catholic heart was stirred to its depths; and though Governments pursued towards the Pope a policy tortuous or dishonest, or openly or secretly hostile, the Catholic sentiment was everywhere true and loyal.[3]

Certainly, Lamoricière felt this way. On April 8, Easter Sunday, he issued a proclamation to both the volunteers who had arrived and to those who were pondering the call:

> At the sound of the grand voice which lately apprised the world from the Vatican of the dangers threatening the patrimony of St. Peter, Catholics were moved, and their emotion soon spread to every part of the earth. This is because Christianity is not merely the religion of the civilized world, but the animating principle of civilization; it is because the Papacy is the keystone of the arch of Christianity, and all Christian nations seem, in these days, to be conscious of those great verities which are our faith. The revolution to-day threatens Europe as Islamism did of old, and now, as then, the cause of the Pope is that of civilization and liberty throughout the world. Soldiers, have confidence, and believe

that God will raise our courage to the level of the great cause whose defence He has entrusted to our arms.

Lamoricière was also mindful of the forces he had commanded in Algeria; he had hardly reached Rome before writing to a friend, "I hope soon to have a Regiment of Zouaves in the Pontifical Army."

As chief of staff, Lamoricière chose the Marquis de Pimodan. Born in 1822, Pimodan was from his upbringing a fervent partisan of Henry V. Upon graduating from St. Cyr military academy two decades later, he refused to take the oath to Louis Philippe required of all officers. With the approval of his exiled king, he joined the Austrian army, as did many another young legitimist of the nobility. Pimodan saw service in the wars of 1848 and 1849, and rose to the rank of colonel, but to advance further, he would have had to accept Austrian citizenship. This he refused to do, and he returned to France. He took no part in political life, confining himself to writing and managing his country estate.

But when news arrived of the loss of Romagna, the marquis remarked to a friend, "If the Pope wishes to do anything to regain his States and defend what he has left, I am at his service." In January of 1860, he visited the papal nuncio in Paris and offered his services. April 4 saw him arrive in Rome, and he met with Lamoricière the next day. On April 16 Pimodan was appointed colonel in the pontifical service and chief of staff.[4]

Of the 15,000 men who first answered the call, perhaps the most renowned of the French was Baron Athanase-Charles-Marie Charette de la Contrie. Charette was perhaps fated to adventure from the start. His great-uncle was the famous General Charette, one of the leaders of the Vendée's Royal Catholic Army, who was shot by the revolutionaries after his capture in 1796. His mother was the illegitimate-but-ennobled daughter of the Duke de Berry, eldest son of Charles X. At Charette's birth on September 3, 1832, his assassinated grandfather's duchess, having attempted a failed rising against Louis Philippe, was in hiding; his own father was a fugitive from the police. Charette's arrival in the midst of this affair was kept secret, and he was brought to a distant town and his birth registered there.

With such a background, the young Charette could not serve in the army of the usurper, although strongly called to the family profession. In 1846, therefore, he entered the Sardinian Royal Military Academy; he left two years later, however, due to Sardinia's support of the revolutions throughout Italy. In 1852, Charette accepted a sub-lieutenancy in an Austrian regiment offered by Duke Francis V of Modena, whose brother-in-law, the Count de Chambord (who was the only French King whom Charette recognized and his half-uncle as well). When it became apparent, however, in 1859, that France would soon declare war on Austria, he left the service of the Habsburgs too. Charette's deep sense of loyalty would not allow him to serve an illegitimate government, but neither would it permit him to fight against the land of his birth.

His two brothers faced the same dilemma, and all three were anxious to fight the Italian revolutionaries. In May of 1860, Charette's brothers volunteered to serve in the army of their distant cousin, the king of Naples, against Garibaldi. But he went to Rome and entered the service of the Pope. Lamoricière appointed him captain of the first company of Franco-Belgian Volunteers. It was the beginning of a long and valiant career.[5]

Another descendant of the leaders of the Vendée to join the pontifical colors was Henri de Cathelineau, who had led a band of French and Belgians who called themselves Crusaders. Not only was his grandfather one of the top leaders in the Vendée, his father had been shot in the course of the same uprising in 1832 that sent Charette's family into hiding. Leading men to Rome was in complete accord with his beliefs and traditions; so far as he and his men were concerned, the Crusades, the Vendée, and this current struggle were all episodes in the same age-long war.[6]

Leopold Louis Joubert, a native of Saint Herblon, just north of the Vendée, left school at the age of 18 in July 1860; little did he know when he set off that his road as a papal soldier would lead him through Rome to the depths of Africa. It would not, alas, be so long a road for his fellow youth, of whom there were a great many in the first rush of volunteers.

Georges, Marquis d'Heliand was 18 when he graduated from the Jesuit College of Saint Francois Xavier in Vannes, Brittany (no fewer than 27 alumni of this school signed up) in June of 1860. By July—after, at his mother's insistence, taking a retreat to consider his future—he resolved to go to Rome. Born of a family that had produced Crusaders and many noble knights of France, Heliand was all too aware that if he died, his line might die with him. But, as he wrote his mother,

> It seems to me that, since you are willing to make the sacrifice, God will grant me the courage necessary to undertake this campaign. I will feel much in parting you: yes, certainly, the separation will be very painful on both sides; but if it be the will of God, as I believe it is, He will give us strength to bear the trial. I know there are a thousand chances to one that we may never meet on this side of the grave again. If I die, I hope the sufferings which I shall have endured will shorten my purgatory; and even if I return on crutches—and I don't know what says to me that I shall be maimed somehow—I shall then have nothing but gain. You often told me that you preferred my salvation to everything; it seems to me that this is not a bad means of attaining it.

Prophetic words, as it turned out. At any rate, accompanied by his cousin and best friend, he set off for the Eternal City.[7]

After the events of Castelfidardo, 150 recruits joined the Pontifical Zouaves from the ranks of the Jesuit College's graduates. So many, indeed, that Pius IX wrote of the place, "Ah! Of all the colleges of France, it is that which is most dear to me, because NONE HAVE GIVEN ME AS MANY DEFENDERS!" It is perhaps a mark of how hidden the memory of the Zouaves has become, that one will find no mention of them in the school's current website (although the "Old Boys" site does mention them).

Of the many more we could chronicle, one of the French contingent stands out: Joseph Guerin, a native of Sainte Pazanne. The year 1860 found him studying for the priesthood at the Grande Seminaire of Nantes; he came of a humble family of comfortable tradesmen. But prayer and reflection led him to believe that his true vocation was to fight, and perhaps die, for the Pope. Many of his friends could not believe that he, renowned for his humorous nature, was embarking on such a serious (and hopeless, humanly speaking) struggle. He responded to one of these, "Well, yes; I am wrong, it is true; but I err with the martyrs who went and offered themselves to the executioners. You are right, if you like, but I prefer being in the wrong with them. Blood is necessary to appease the anger of God; I give mine."

Leaving Nantes for Rome on the train, he met Count Arthur de Chalus, a young nobleman of that city who was renowned for both his piety (he often led the processions in his parish church and would never miss a Mass), and his gardener who had volunteered to go with him. The aristocrat, the servant, and the commoner became firm friends, and at the dock in Marseilles met Heliand and his cousin. Despite their extremely varied backgrounds and status, the five were united by devotion, youth, and love of jokes. It was quite a pleasant time they had together. The one resentment they felt was toward Napoleon, who had forbidden the French recruits to wear uniforms until they left their homeland (much to their annoyance, foreigners were not so restricted). Were it not for their conviction that they were headed to certain death, the friends appeared to observers on the train and steamer to be on holiday.[8]

Upon their arrival in Rome, the little band was received by Pius IX, who gave them Communion himself. Of this experience, Chalus wrote home to his aunt, "Oh ! if all those who speak against the Pope had the happiness of seeing and hearing him, in spite of their wickedness they would soon change their language." It was an impression that would be made by Pius IX on all of his defenders when at last they met him.

But the first wave of French and Belgians were joined by Irish as well, in great part because of the work of Count Charles MacDonnell. Although of a noble Irish clan, he was forced to sell his indebted estate in County Wicklow and join the Austrian service in 1845. A contemporary gives this view of him, "If ever chivalrous devotion to a fallen cause was personified it was in this loyal and brave-hearted gentleman"[9]—which was borne out in 1860, when the count returned to Ireland to organize a committee charged with recruiting his countrymen for Pius IX. Some 1,800 answered the call despite the Palmerston government's threat to prosecute them or strip away their citizenship (threats, very tellingly, never made against the British subjects who joined Garibaldi).[10]

In April of 1860, the count approached Myles O'Reilly, of Knockabbey Castle in County Louth, to command the Irish contingent. Born in 1825 to one of the few Catholic gentry families that had managed to survive the debacle of the Boyne, O'Reilly had been confirmed in Rome in 1837, was educated at Ushaw College, and became one of the first Catholic graduates of the University of London in 1843. The years 1845 to 1847 saw him acquiring his law degree in Rome at the *Sapienza,* as the university there was called. Returning to his homeland in 1853, he settled down on his ancestral estate to function as deputy lieutenant of the county, magistrate, and grand juror. O'Reilly also helped found the Catholic University of Dublin and was also appointed captain of the Louth Rifles, a local militia unit. In 1859 he married a relative of Lord Stafford, one of the most prominent Catholic noblemen in England. Newly wed, comfortable in his circumstances and position, O'Reilly had every reason to stay at home—the more so because his wife was expecting. But instead, after a momentary hesitation, he volunteered his life in a venture he knew to be risky.

He obtained permission to bring his wife, and the couple made their way to Rome arriving on June 27. After an audience with the Pope, Major O'Reilly immediately began the task of training the over 1,000 Irish who had already arrived. Twelve-hour days were his lot and that of his men; training them, issuing regulations, answering correspondence, and trying to improve their living conditions and weed out undesirables were a daunting task. Nevertheless, the young squire from County Louth set about it with a will.

It was quite an unusual company that joined St. Patrick's battalion, Major O'Reilly commanding. Myles Walter Keogh, born on March 25, 1840, at Orchard House, Leighlinbridge, County Carlow, came of a staunchly Catholic family; his uncle was executed for his part in the 1798 rising, and his mother was a gentrywoman, a daughter of the Blanchfields of Rathgarvan, near Clifden in County Kilkenny. Although his aunt willed him Clifden Castle, he chose to answer Pius's call; for him the road would lead eventually to the

Little Bighorn. John Joseph Coppinger came of a prominent Cork City family. Although at age 33 he had joined the Warwickshire Militia as an ensign in 1857 after moving to England, three years later he joined St. Patrick's battalion. In deference to his experience and skill, he was appointed captain in charge of the Second Company. John Gleason of Tipperary, Joseph O'Keefe of Dublin, and John Howlin of County Wexford also answered the call—the latter being among the first 20 in Rome. He would later find fame as a religious brother in Australia, where all his above-named comrades would enter the Union army. Patrick Buckley of Casteltownshend, County Cork, was studying law at Louvain University, yet interrupted his studies to join a group of Irish volunteers at Ostend; in later years he would be knighted by Queen Victoria and serve as a supreme court justice in New Zealand. But for all of them, their first steps led to Rome. For many, the Papal States would be as far as their paths would go.

The Austrian emperor, despite his defeat by the French, was not pleased with the idea of leaving Pius IX to face the Sardinians on his own. But neither were his ministers keen on the idea of fighting the French again so soon after their epic defeat. While sovereign and ministers quarreled over how much support Austria could or should give the Papal States, one thing was agreed: Serving officers and soldiers as well as civilians would be permitted to join the pontifical army. Among these too were some remarkable men.

Jan Chosciak Popiel was an ethnic Pole from a Galician gentry family (his province had fallen to Austria in the first partition of Poland). Although sympathetic to the anti-Habsburg Polish rebels of 1848, as a 20-year-old he joined the Austrian army in 1856 as an officer of engineers. After witnessing the defeat at Solferino in 1859, he joined the papal army in the summer of 1860, attached to the fortress artillery at Ancona.[11] An Austrian teenager who joined the forces was the improbably named Friedrich Paul Hubert Maria Walpurg Reichsgraf Wolff-Metternich zur Gracht, Freiherr auf Vinsebeck. The young Reichsgraf (imperial count, a title given as a reward to his Hessian family) at age 18 graduated from his high school and became an officer cadet in the papal army. Before he was ever commissioned, he would see combat and be decorated for bravery—a start to a career that would see him fight for Maximilian in Mexico, for Austria against Prussia, and off into sundry other adventures.[12] Gustav Count Chorinski was another Austrian officer who had witnessed defeat at the hands of Napoleon III and brought personal problems with him as well. Before combat broke out in 1859, he had defied his parents and married a Protestant girl without their permission. His pregnant bride accompanied him to the war but delivered a stillborn girl. After Villafranca, his countess converted and he was reconciled with his parents. But his parents changed their minds, and Chorinski joined the papal army in part to win their approval for the marriage. His bride also went to the Papal States to be near whatever might befall him.[13]

To be sure, several fine officers in the two regiments of foreign infantry greeted Lamoricière on his arrival. Among these were General Schmid, whom we have met; Colonel Raphael de Courten, of the Second Regiment; and Colonel Eugene Allet. There was also General Hermann Kanzler, a native of Baden, who had been a soldier of the Popes since 1822. At some risk to his own life he had deserted the now-revolutionized army, to take refuge with his sovereign at Gaeta in 1849. Since then he had held a number of positions in the papal military.

The spring and summer of 1860 were an exciting time to be in Rome, with fresh recruits arriving on a daily basis, new units being devised, old ones reorganized. As Pimodan wrote, "It is like a camp of Schiller's *Wallenstein*. All languages are spoken. I have chatted with a good many Germans, Poles, Hungarians, and even with Swedes, who serve under the name of Switzers in the foreign regiments." One is inevitably reminded of medieval chronicles, or of the scene in Tolkien's *Lord of the Rings* when the last small contingents arrive to defend embattled Minas Tirith against the forces of Mordor—and, indeed, that was much the frame of mind that dominated the Pope's paladins. As each detachment of new recruits were received, they were conducted to the piazza in front of the great basilica of St. John Lateran, and there swore the following oath: "I swear to Almighty God to be obedient and faithful to my Sovereign, the Roman Pontiff, Our very Holy Father Pope Pius IX, and to his legitimate successors. I swear to serve with honor and fidelity and to sacrifice my life for the defense of his august and sacred person, for the maintenance of his sovereignty and for the maintenance of his rights." It was an oath that many would obey to the letter, and that most of the survivors would try, in their own ways, to apply to the rest of their lives.

With the infusion of fresh troops, Lamoricière redistributed the 4,000 Swiss soldiers, organized in three battalions about 5,000 Austrian light infantrymen, organized St. Patrick's battalion from an eventual total of 3,000 Irish volunteers, and formed the French volunteers into a squadron of guides and a half-battalion of infantry. The latter also received the Belgians, hence the unit's initial name—"the Franco-Belgian Volunteers." Cathelineau's Crusaders were added to already existing Franco-Belgian units. Nor did Lamoricière neglect the existing native units. Altogether, he had at his command about 25,000 men under arms.

Nonetheless, he was faced with several seemingly impossible tasks. For one thing, the strategic situation was rapidly deteriorating: Not only was the Sardinian frontier extremely long and basically indefensible (the enemy having incorporated Tuscany), but the Garibaldians were pushing the king and his men ever further north. Should Naples fall to them completely, the Papal States would be completely surrounded. As we have seen, Romagna, the northernmost province of the Pope's domain, had already fallen to the invader. From its southern border, down along the Adriatic, Marche rolled down along the Adriatic to the Neapolitan border. Umbria, "the green heart of Italy," with its cities of Assisi and Perugia, constituted the center of the Papal dominion. Then Latium, Lazio, or, as it then was called, the "Patrimony of St. Peter," surrounded Rome. All three of the remaining provinces bordered occupied Tuscany, while the Kingdom of Naples stretched away south on the other side. The Pontifical dominions thus lay athwart the Sardinian road of advance.

The possibility of being threatened on both sides thus had to be accounted for, and garrisons must remain in mountain fortress towns such as Spoleto; not only had the frontier to be covered, but civil unrest inspired by exiles and outsiders had to be guarded against. This ensured a further drain on already vastly outnumbered forces. Moreover, Lamoricière's troops, despite a few months of rigorous training, had not for the most part the experience of the Sardinian army. Worse still, fortified by ruinous taxation and conscription, the Sardinians had 150,000 to employ against the papal forces—to say nothing of the added troops Garibaldi would throw into the fray once Naples was subjugated. Moreover, although a French garrison protected Rome and its environs (and its commander was sincerely dedicated to Pius IX's welfare—and expected to join in the fray, once it occurred, on the papal side), Napoleon III was playing a double game, whose ultimate end was to unite Italy under the House of Savoy, with himself pulling the new kingdom's strings. Farther afield, Palmerston's London cabinet was openly allied to the revolutionaries. The only hope of foreign intervention on the papal side was Austria—and we have seen that, despite the volunteers, Austria might well let events take their course.

As that summer of 1860 wound to its close, events were moving. While papal detachments were occupying old hill-citadels and fortresses, and the spies of Cavour and Garibaldi were organizing for action in Rome and the Pope's other cities, volunteers continued to arrive. Having succeeded so well with his revolt in no small part due to the treason of highly placed individuals in the Neapolitan government, Garibaldi's forces pushed ever northward. Meanwhile, Sardinia, all the while assuring Cardinal Antonelli, the Pope's secretary of state, of its pacific intentions and its love and respect for Pius IX, was preparing to invade.

In Paris and London, diplomatic dispatches and reports went back and forth between foreign ministries and agents in the field. Surely, Pius IX would yield in the face of overwhelming force, both military and diplomatic? But what the Pontiff and his general had that Cavour, Napoleon III, and Palmerston had not—and could not—bargain on, was the unshakeable conviction that they could not do other than resist, and that their immortal souls depended upon their doing so regardless of the outcome. This certainty was shared by the greater part of their army.

The opponents the papal forces faced far outnumbered them. The 70,000-man Fifth Army under General Fanti was designated for the war by Victor Emmanuel. Plentifully supplied with modern rifles and rifled artillery, the Sardinian army also numbered many seasoned veterans and officers whose experience in the Crimea and in the recent Franco-Austrian war gave it a preparation for combat sadly lacking in most of the papal troops. The armies of Tuscany,

Parma, and Modena had been merged with the Sardinian, and the Sardinian fleet was ordered to leave Neapolitan waters and assist the army. Thanks to Sardinian railroads, mobilization was swift. In a word, Victor Emmanuel's forces were as prepared for a nineteenth-century version of the blitzkrieg as any force of the time could be.

If Sardinia, despite all of Cavour's assurances, should invade, blows would decide whether fervor and devotion could stand at all against sheer power. In the event, the answer to this question would surprise both sides. It would show the ever more modern nineteenth century that might was not all.

CHAPTER III

Baptism of Fire

When can their glory fade?
O the wild charge they made!
All the world wonder'd.
Honour the charge they made!
Honour the Light Brigade,
Noble six hundred!

—*Alfred Lord Tennyson,*
"The Charge of the Light Brigade"

For all of the activity, both military and political, on either side of the Sardinian-Papal frontier, on the diplomatic front all was quiet. Officially, relations between Turin and Rome seemed cordial, at the very least. That the nineteenth century witnessed the birth of modernity was evident in Cavour's public speeches, which would have looked at home in the pages of *1984*. The wily Prime Minister would continually speak of his country's desire for the peace, and the warlike intentions of the Papal government, all the while preparing for a quick and decisive military blow. Cavour touchingly invoked the wishes of "the People of Italy," while insuring that the majority would be intimidated in his arranged plebiscites. The Sardinian government was very concerned with the security of the Papal States—or at least those provinces not yet snatched from the Pope's rule. Victor Emmanuel's chief minister assured papal secretary of state Antonelli that the only reason for Sardinian intervention in the Pope's territories would be if they were threatened by revolutionaries.

Although the Holy See was only too aware that Sardinian ships, money, men, and arms were at that moment assisting Garibaldi in conquering Naples, the Pope was less than reassured. Indeed, in May, when Garibaldi began his attack on Naples, he had sent a trusted lieutenant, Zambianchi (known as the "priest slaughterer" for his ordering the massacre of clergy at San Callisto during the 1848 Roman Republic) to start the revolution in the Papal States. On May 11, he crossed the Tuscan frontier near Latera with 60 Redshirts and 300 Tuscans. He quickly took the town as the prefect fled with the police. But despite the appeals during previous weeks to rise "for Italy and Victor Emmanuel," the locals would have nothing to do with him. After pillaging the place, Zambianchi moved his band on to the more defensible town of Grotte. But the next day the freshly promoted General Pimodan arrived with 60 papal troops and chased him back over the border.

Nor were Napoleon III's statements via his ambassador that Cavour could be trusted very helpful; given his role in backing Sardinia's conquest of the duchies, the French emperor was more than a little suspect. The fact that his troops were currently guarding Rome and Latium, however, precluded any rough words in response by the papal government. Truly, it was a frustrating time for Pius IX and Antonelli.

One individual who did take Napoleon's assurances literally was his commander at Rome, General Goyon. So convinced was he of his sovereign's sincerity (and so eager to fight alongside Lamoricière) that he returned to France to expedite the dispatch of the extra soldiers he had asked for. Much to his surprise and annoyance, the general was sent back with clear orders not to interfere with actions outside the area already occupied. In any case, he would not return before the outbreak of hostilities.

On August 31, Cavour wrote to Admiral Carlo Persano, who commanded the Sardinian fleet supporting Garibaldi. He informed the admiral that an insurrection would break out in the Papal States between the September 8 and 12; and regardless of how it played out, General Enrico Cialdini, commanding the 4th Corps' 60,000 men, would attack Ancona. The following day General Noue, standing in for Goyon in command of the French at Rome, proclaimed that he would defend the territory under French protection—thus making it clear to Sardinia that the Marches and Umbria were theirs for the taking.

As duly planned, "insurrection" broke out on September 8. On that day, groups of armed men crossed the former Tuscan frontier, tore down the papal arms in a few places, and skirmished with the police. Although the locals did not join them and the whole affair was a flash-in-the-pan, the Turin newspapers announced that a major revolution had broken out in the Papal States, and the story was picked up by journals all over Europe. Cavour sent an ultimatum to Lamoricière, declaring that Sardinia would invade if the insurrection was suppressed or if the papal army were not immediately evacuated from the affected regions. Reporting the incident to Merode, Lamoricière wrote "...it would have been more frank to declare war against us...notwithstanding the numerical superiority on the side of Piedmont, we should not forget that there are times when, in order to defend the outraged honor of the government they serve, officers and soldiers must neither count the numbers of an enemy nor give a thought to their lives."

Brave words, to be sure, and these sentiments were shared by the rank-and-file. Although Lamoricière had 15,000 men trained and ready at his disposal (with 10,000 more as yet untrained recruits), he had first to properly garrison Rome and Ancona. He further placed detachments of about 500 each in the fortress towns of Viterbo, Orvieto, Spoleto, Perugia, and Pesaro. This left a field force of less than 10,000, of whom only three companies of sharpshooters had rifles—the rest made do with muskets. St. Patrick's battalion had not been issued knapsacks and—thanks to a lack of a sufficient number of their regulation green uniforms—many had to wear clothes too small for them.

Lamoricière was at first a bit over-sanguine; he did not realize that he would have to deal with more than Garibaldian "riffraff." He also believed that the Austrians and perhaps—despite all evidence to the contrary—the French might well come to his aid. But Lamoricière soon became aware of the reality of his position when the Sardinians not only massed on the frontier, but intelligence reported the arrival of a siege train near Ravenna.

Due to a mishap at sea that delayed Victor Emmanuel's emissary, the official ultimatum to Antonelli (mirroring that presented to Lamoricière) came a day later than intended. But Cavour was not perturbed. Before his demands were even handed over to Antonelli, the wily minister declared that Pius IX spurned "just demands of his master the King of Piedmont." The only possible response to this papal insolence was war. The invasion was ordered, the Catholic states protested (although France did so in a muted manner), and Prussia and Russia recalled their ambassadors. All for naught—the Sardinians crossed the frontier and the invasion was on.

A total of 70,000 Sardinians entered the country, with the immediate goal of besieging Ancona—assisted in this effort by Persano's fleet. One column headed directly to Ancona, another set out to seize Umbria, and the third attempted to secure the hill towns in the Apennines in order to link the other two. Lamoricière's response was to concentrate what forces he could in Ancona and hold out until France, Austria, or Spain came to Pius's aid. Admittedly, it was not much of a plan. But under the circumstances there was little else to do.

On September 11, Cialdini's Sardinians reached Pesaro, the first stop on the way to Ancona. In the center of the town, the garrison under Colonel Count Giovanni Battista Zappi numbered about 500 men. Quartered in the old Rocca Constanza, a square fortress built in the center of town by Constanzo Sforza in 1473, Zappi and his men were vastly outnumbered and outgunned. But they refused to surrender and held out against heavy bombardment for 22 hours. With ammunition exhausted and the Rocca in ruins around him, Zappi at last conceded, having delayed the enemy almost a day.

Meanwhile, the Swiss General de Courten, who was commanding at Ancona, sent out two 1,200-man columns, one headed by the old veteran staff officer Colonel Hermann Kanzler. Their mission was to reconnoiter the Sardinian advance and, if possible, to delay it. On the September 13 Kanzler's column found that an enemy division numbering 20,000 had occupied Senigallia, the Pope's hometown. They then began their withdrawal toward Ancona.

But the Sardinian division pursued them, and at 1 in the afternoon caught up with Kanzler's men near the village of San Angelo. The papal troops turned and fought, repelling several charges by the Sardinian lancers. Kanzler employed his few old cannon well, and his infantry kept up a withering fire. At 5 P.M., the Sardinians withdrew. Kanzler lost 150 men (including a couple of Polish volunteers whose graves are still shown to visitors in the San Angelo churchyard), but skillfully withdrew his men through 45 miles of back roads. They reached Ancona at midnight to the cheers of the garrison. It was a small but glorious fray and surely deserves to be better known. Today at the battle site there is a small commemorative stone, a truncated column placed a century after the event. Its terse inscription reads: "On these hills hundred years ago, Italian and papal forces fought hard on the eve of Castelfidardo, Senigallia 13 September 1860."

While these skirmishes were going on in the Marches, the invasion of Umbria was proceeding. Orvieto boasted the fortress dell'Albornoz, built by the doughty Cardinal Albornoz when he reunited the city to the Papal States in the fourteenth century. There was also a papal palace that had served as a refuge for Clement VII after the 1527 sack of Rome. With such fortifications and the strong memories of papal battles past, one might have expected a strong resistance to the invaders. But upon the arrival of the Garibaldians, the garrison withdrew speedily, retreating all the way to Viterbo.

Holed up in Orvieto, the revolutionaries had little to fear from the small forces of General Schmid, still based in Perugia. Schmid's pursuit column had consisted of Swiss and Italians, and a company of the St. Patrick's battalion—145 strong, one of whom was young John Howlin. To this small group were added the 400 of the garrison. On the morning of the September 14, General Fanti and 23,000 Sardinians arrived, surrounded the city, and began their assault. For three hours the papal forces repelled them, but some of the less well-trained Italians and Swiss began to waver. Thus, when Fanti offered a cease-fire to negotiate and care for the wounded, Schmid accepted. Instead of withdrawing from the suburbs as they had agreed, however, the Sardinians built barricades in the streets and brought up cannon. When the truce ended, Schmid decided to surrender on the proviso that the officers would keep their swords and be allowed to return home. The Irish protested and 16 of them cut their way through the Sardinian lines to freedom. This was just as well for them because the Sardinians again broke their word: The officers' swords were taken and their owners imprisoned. Howlin was one of the Irish sent off to captivity but he never forgot his short period of service. When in later years he led the Patrician Brothers (a teaching order in Ireland, Australia, India, the United States, Kenya, and Papua New Guinea), he included in their habit a green sash, in memory of his bold companions of the St. Patrick's battalion; it is worn to this day.

More of Howlin's brethren were holding Spoleto, Fanti's next target. In advance Fanti sent a division commanded by General Brignone, consisting of 8,000 men and 24 cannon. They arrived at Spoleto on September 17. Facing them in the city was Major O'Reilly with a total of 589 men—two companies of St. Patrick's battalion, comprising about 300; 116 Swiss and Austrians from the Second Infantry; 23 Franco-Belgians; and 150 Italians of various formations. These the major had quartered in the citadel, having been informed in a letter from Merode the previous day that, although there could be no help from Rome, he was to resist as long as he could.

O'Reilly placed his Irish, under the command of Captain Coppinger, at the gate and in a breach in the wall that had been plugged with a barricade. Using their ability as sharpshooters, the Franco-Belgians were positioned with a view over the gate. The spot on the wall was given to the Swiss and Austrians, while, in deference to their inexperience, the Italians were held in reserve. A single aged cannon comprised the whole of the citadel's artillery.

Under a flag of truce, a Sardinian officer approached the gate at six in the morning on September 17, and pointed out the overwhelming odds. The intrepid Irish major refused to surrender, and two hours later found his forces under attack. Four Sardinian batteries were set up only 600 yards from the gate and walls. They then began a horrific fusillade, under cover of which the Sardinian forces, the Bersaglieri (an elite unite of sharpshooters), attempted to take the heights nearby. Once ensconced there, they could lay down a withering line of fire within the citadel. O'Reilly's men stayed under cover and in three hours managed to kill four horses and 30 artillerymen, and wound many more. At the end of this time, a Sardinian officer under a white flag accompanied by the archbishop of Spoleto approached the gate. They both called upon O'Reilly to surrender, to which he replied that it was his duty to hold out as long as he could.

The firing resumed, and by three that afternoon large sections of the wall and the gate itself had holes in it. Brignone ordered an assault and led it himself. He accompanied two companies of Bersaglieri in the front of the attack, backed up by two battalions of grenadiers. "Notwithstanding two discharges of grapeshot from our one cannon, they came up bravely to the gate, and tried with axes to break it down. But it was strongly propped on the inside, and our men drove the enemy back with musket-shots and bayonet-thrusts through the holes in the broken gate," wrote O'Reilly, describing the event.

The Sardinians were repelled. They returned to a steady artillery fire upon the gate and its surroundings; twice buildings near the powder magazine caught fire from the shells. Putting these out was as dangerous as transporting food, water, or ammunition, because the Bersaglieri on the heights were now able to fire at any moving object in the citadel. By nightfall, O'Reilly was faced with a difficult decision. His men were exhausted, nearly out of ammunition, and manning breached walls. Although he did not doubt that they could hold off another attack, the enemy's command of the heights combined with the other factors meant that eventually the citadel would fall. At eight that night he sought and was granted an honorable surrender. He and his men were allowed to march out with the honors of war and make their way to pontifical lines. Suffering casualties of three dead and twelve wounded, they had inflicted on their foes one hundred dead and three times that number wounded. With the fall of Spoleto, Brignone was free to occupy the rest of Umbria, which he proceeded to do.

Fortunately for the papal forces, Lamoricière had managed, through forced marches, to extract his field army from the collapse of Umbria en route to Ancona. Departing from Spoleto—which prior to its siege had been his field headquarters—they reached Macerata on September 15. He was well aware that the Sardinian juggernaut was rolling south from Pesaro; to succeed, he and his second-in-command, Pimodan, needed to lead their forces through Loreto and on to Ancona. There they should be able to hold out until Austria or some other country came to their aid.

As far as the landward side was concerned, Lamoricière's confidence was partly warranted. Over the summer, Lamoricière had worked hard to get Ancona into shape for a siege. The old walls were repaired, and a fortified line, bristling with bastions, connected these with the height of Monte Gardetta, itself newly fortified. In accordance with then-current military practice, four detached forts were built in front of the main lines. Altogether, it was a formidable defensive system, formidable enough to make up to a great degree for the poor armaments contained within. The cannon were a hodgepodge of different times and places— Lamoricière himself declared his cannon were drawn from every country in Europe. But they were all smooth-bore, lacking the rifling of more modern, and so more lethal, guns. Similarly, the infantry had muskets, whose rounds would not spin as they flew, resulting in less damage when they reached their targets. Nevertheless, especially when reinforced with the 5,000 men of the field army, Ancona would be a hard nut to crack by any besieging army on the land.

Facing the sea, however, it was a bit different. Despite being a tremendous port (second, in the Papal States, only to Civitavecchia), famed for its *brodetto*—a sort of local bouillabaisse—Ancona's maritime defenses were not nearly as impressive as its cuisine. An enormous chain had been stretched across the harbor mouth. This was at one time a leading feature of the seaward defense of fortified cities—Constantinople's fall in 1453 was due in no small part to the Turks finally getting round and then breaking the chain set out by the Byzantines. Rejecting further modernity, however, Ancona would be the last city in European history to protect itself this way. Six small gunboats armed with one 18-pounder gun apiece, were set in defense of the chain, as were the small forts of the Lazaretto (once a customs post and quarantine site), the mole, and the somewhat stronger fort of the Cappucini. In total, these positions boasted 49 smooth-bore cannon. Fortunately for his peace of mind, Lamoricière did not know that Admiral Persano had been ordered by Cavour (in the same letter in which he told the admiral of the planned spontaneous rising) to bring his fleet from Naples to Ancona. Under Persano's command were six frigates and seven smaller craft, together bearing 400 guns. Not only was the Pontiff's harbor outgunned, if Austria were to intervene it would undergo a naval battle immediately.

When Persano arrived off Ancona on September 16, however, he feared that there might already be Austrian or other foreign ships in the harbor. He therefore sent into the harbor one of his frigates flying the British flag. The British consul in Ancona boarded the ship, where he no doubt discovered the true nationality of the vessel during the half hour he stayed there. But in keeping with Prime Minister Palmerston's instructions, he kept this knowledge to himself when he returned ashore—in a sense, therefore, acting as a spy.

Armed with the knowledge that Ancona was free of foreign shipping, Persano kept his fleet outside the harbor and in his own ship steamed northward along the coast. A boat he passed informed him that the Sardinian army was in possession of Senigallia, so the admiral landed there and journeyed via carriage to Cialdini's headquarters. The general had already proceeded southwest of Ancona, and his 23,000 troops had taken up their positions on the north bank of the River Musone, in the hills of Castelfidardo.

In those days, a single road ran from Macerata to Recanati, then to Loreto (with its famous shrine of the *Santa Casa* or Holy House), along the south bank of the Musone through the town of Castelfidardo, and on to the coast and Ancona. Cialdini was well aware that the papal army had to pass this way if it were to reach its goal. The two invading officers discussed the situation; intelligence had reached the general that Lamoricière and his men had reached Loreto. Expecting their assault the next day, he asked Persano to begin shelling Ancona to prevent any divisions from the city coming to Lamoricière's aid. Persano agreed and returned to his flagship to swiftly rejoin his fleet.

Cialdini was well informed. By a forced march from Macerata, Lamoricière and his 2,300 men and five cannon arrived at the approaches to Loreto on the evening of September 16. From their position, they could see the campfires of the enemy and easily guess how badly they were outnumbered. That very afternoon, a squadron of Sardinian dragoons had occupied the town, and the enemy's flag was flying over it. The Holy House of Loreto—held to be the house in Nazareth in which Jesus, Mary, and Joseph had lived, and in which the archangel Gabriel had delivered his great announcement to the Virgin—is one of the holiest shrines in Christendom (and at that time one of the best known: Pius IX had been healed of his mysterious youthful disease there). To see it in the hands of their foes was more than the papal troops could stand. The pontifical cavalry swept into Loreto and soon drove off the Sardinians. Lamoricière settled his brigade in the great square before the shrine with its large dome and awaited the expected arrival, the next day, of General Pimodan, with 2,700 more troops. Once these troops came together, the attempt to break through to Ancona would be made.

In the meantime, the onset of night permitted the dispatch of a small reconnaissance party to assess the situation along the Ancona road. Four men were sent: the Hungarian staff officer, Captain Pallfy; Mizael Mesre de Pas of the Guides (who had been the first French volunteer to arrive in Rome); and two gendarmes. They discovered an artillery battery placed across the road, intended to discourage any nighttime assault. They were no more than 30 yards away when a cannon unleashed its grapeshot against them. A gendarme was hit, and Mesre de Pas's horse killed; he himself was wounded mortally. His companions helped him back to Loreto.

The following day, Lamoricière readied his men for combat. The military chaplains heard the confessions of all the soldiers, who on the mornings of both September 17 and 18 received Holy Communion; a large number were more or less unknowingly receiving their last rites. Pimodan's brigade duly arrived without incident on the evening of September 17, and the Sardinian lines were spied out. After Mass the next day, the assault would begin.

Loreto sits up on a hill, as does Castelfidardo. At that time, the road descended from the Holy House and its encasing basilica, ran down to a ford over the Musone, and then curved up a slope toward Castelfidardo. This rise was dotted with clumps of wood, and two farmsteads, each composed of a main house, outbuildings, and various enclosures. They were named after the families who owned them—the Crocetti and the Cascini. The former was a name that would be remembered so long as any remembered the papal volunteers.

Sardinian Bersaglieri were deployed in the woods, each farm boasted a large detachment, and on the higher slopes were batteries of rifled cannon and massive numbers of Infantry. Altogether, it was a daunting site as Pimodan's brigade set out at 8:30 A.M., flying at its head the same banners that had flown over Don John of Austria's fleet at Lepanto and that for centuries had reposed in Loreto's basilica. A half hour later, Lamoricière and his men set off after them.

Pimodan led his men toward the ford. In the vanguard were the Franco-Belgians commanded by Colonel Louis de Becdelièvre and Captain Charette, and the Swiss Rifles, advancing despite the fire of the Bersaglieri. Becdelièvre had served in the French Army from 1849 to 1858 and had been awarded the Legion of Honor for his valor in the Crimean War. They were followed by a Roman infantry detachment, and D'Arcy's 4th Company of St. Patrick's battalion, in whose ranks was young Patrick Buckley. The Irish had the additional burden of dragging two cannon through the ford and up the hill. Obviously, the only way to secure their goal was a quick assault; Pimodan ordered his brigade to fix bayonets. But frightened by the withering gunfire from the Sardinians, the young Roman militia took cover behind the reeds at the water's edge and opened fire, heedless of friend or foe. Despite this unexpected excitement to their rear, the Franco-Belgians charged and took Crocetti while Pimodan's staff restored order among the Romans.

Having secured Crocetti, the Franco-Belgians, Swiss, and carabinieri assaulted Cascini. But the Sardinian artillery and infantry rained down on them a hail of shot and shell. Falling back upon Crocetti, the papal troops found themselves hotly pursued by Sardinians charging down the slopes; they turned round and attacked with bayonets—the Sardinian charge faltered and broke, with the defenders fleeing back the way they had come under cover of fire.

Returned to the relative safety of Crocetti, Pimodan's men were now once again under assault. The general himself was hit by a bullet that broke his jaw. Not bothering to dismount, he tied up his wound and cried to his men, "*Courage, mes enfants!* God is with us!" Lamoricière threw his men into the fray in support, but as his Swiss infantry and Italian chasseurs came in contact with the fusillade, they broke and ran, followed by a battery of artillery; the latter cut their horses loose, abandoning their cannon. What remained of Lamoricière's brigade continued and reached Pimodan's force.

Pimodan was hit by another bullet, and another, and a fourth that entered his chest. He fell from his horse, once more crying "God is with us!" He was then placed on a stretcher and taken back toward Loreto. When Lamoricière heard the new of Pimodan's fall, he was trying to rally the fugitives. He sent two officers after the deserters and he rode toward Crocetti. Having already sent Major Fuchman's little band of Austrian sharpshooters to reinforce the embattled farm, he was out of men. On his way to the farm, he encountered Pimodan and his party, with whom he shook hands and exchanged a few words. The veteran of Algeria then rode on through the rush of bullets to the farm.

Arriving there almost at noon, he found Becdelièvre in command with his Franco-Belgians, Fuchman's Austrians, D'Arcy's Irish, and Swiss carabinieri on the left flank, and Roman chasseurs on the right. Enemy artillery had destroyed the roofs of the farmstead's buildings, and the battalions of the Sardinian division were slowly advancing down the slope, covered by their sharpshooters and closing in on all sides. The Franco-Belgians had lost 190 men; only 90 were still able to fight.

Pulling together his remaining effective troops and some of the Irish and Swiss, Becdelièvre launched a counterattack that halted the onslaught. Fuchman and his Austrians used this as a springboard for an assault, but they were driven back by overwhelming fire. At length, Lamoricière ordered a retreat from Crocetti. What was left of the papal army withdrew in good order, covered by Fuchman's sharpshooters, driving off an attack by Sardinian lancers who attempted to cut off their retreat. Of the 5,000 who had marched out from Loreto, only 2,000 returned.

The Sardinians, meanwhile, poured into Crocetti, but as they approached the main house, they were shocked to receive a volley of musketry. A few of the Franco-Belgians who had been posted to the house (and who were also tending the wounded in an adjoining shed) had not heard the order to retreat. Wave after wave of Sardinians assaulted the house and were driven back by gunfire. Cialdini ordered the artillery brought up and began shelling the hapless structure. The house caught fire, and then the makeshift field hospital was endangered by the flames. At that point, the desperate little band of papal troops surrendered. So angered were the Sardinians by this resistance that they would have slaughtered all the survivors had not a Sardinian officer, captured by Charette earlier in the day, intervened to save them. The enemy then set up their positions on the banks of the river.

Meanwhile, Lamoricière was faced with a dilemma. It was obvious that his remaining men would not be able to cut their way through to Ancona. Nevertheless, he himself was needed to command the fortress if it was to hold out long enough for Austria to come to the Holy See's aid. Apart from the intense personal danger involved in attempting to get through to the beleaguered city, such a bold action would mean leaving his men to their fate. The general decided that the risk was worth it. Gathering 50 cavalry and 300 hundred infantry as an escort, he set off for the coast.

Loreto was now cut off, Recanati having been occupied by the Sardinians. The papal forces were exhausted. Their dead had been shot or bayoneted repeatedly, as had many of the wounded, including almost all the remaining Franco-Belgians; Patrick Buckley, for example, had been wounded twice, as had Charette. The basilica became a hospital for the many wounded. Early on the morning of September 19, a little more than 24 hours after the papal army had set out, the commanding officers held a council of war. In addition to the senior remaining staff officer, Colonel Guttenhoven, there were Becdelièvre, D'Arcy, Fuchman, Bourbon de Chalus of the Guides, and several others. A dispute broke out: the French, Belgian, Austrian, and Irish officers, together commanding a thousand men, wanted to fight for the besieged town to the last man. But the Swiss and Italians would not. They agreed to surrender, and Guttenhoven rode to Cialdini's headquarters to ask for the following terms: "1. The soldiers shall be free and shall be restored to their homes. 2. Military honors will be given to the papal troops; the soldiers will lay down their arms; the officers will retain their swords. 3. The evacuation of Loreto will take place in twenty-four hours." These terms were accepted.

Late in the afternoon, the survivors began the march to Recanati, where the actual surrender was to take place. Arriving after nightfall, they were greeted by a Sardinian division in formation on either side outside Recanati's gate. Torches were set up, and the victors presented arms to honor their foes as they passed by. At the gate, the column was met by General Leotardi and his staff, mounted on horseback. As the defeated army marched in, they deposited their muskets and other weapons in a large pile, while, as agreed, the officers retained their swords. During the two days they waited in that city before their dispersal, the papal troops were well treated, and the officers invited to dine with their Sardinian peers. Their gallantry was thus recognized by those who had actually fought them: This treatment stands in shocking contradiction to the accounts of many journalists, politicians, and Sardinian staff officers at the time, and historians since. It *was* rather an embarrassment that so few had fought so well against such odds.[1]

The Sardinian high command refused the numerous requests of the families of the dead who wished to repatriate their bodies; instead ordering that the dead should all be interred in a trench, where they remain today. Nor were the prisoners treated very well after they left Recanati. The Italians were abused and ridiculed as they returned to their homes. The French were imprisoned in the citadel of Turin until released half-starved and sent over the

French frontier (Napoleon III was not terribly concerned, given the large number who were legitimists). The Irish were imprisoned in a dungeon in Genoa in truly miserable conditions and finally placed on a ship bound for their homeland. In a time when abuse of a British subject's property (let alone his person) often enough led to the Royal Navy's bombarding innumerable foreign harbors, Palmerston seemed singularly uninterested in the fate of these Irish, many of whom had served under the queen's colors in Crimea and India.

As for the wounded left in the basilica at Loreto, given the state of medicine at the time, many were doomed to lingering deaths. Reading the letters they sent to their homes is sobering but inspiring. Among the letters extant, was one from Paul de Parcevaux, a young Breton, renowned among his friends for both piety and joviality. He was one of the first Frenchmen to answer Pius's call and had served under Pimodan at Grotte. Mortally wounded, he wrote to his mother from his sickbed:

> My wound is serious, but as I find myself much better to-day [and] I hope to recover. As for the rest, when going out to battle, I asked God that I might do my duty and die well, and now, since my wound, I fear death no more than I feared the shots on the 18th. In Brittany I should have very little chance of dying under such easy conditions to gain heaven. If I die here I hope to die joyfully. If there are cries of pain in the church that is our hospital, there is laughter too.... Were it the will of God to call me to Himself my last thought would be of you.

He died on October 14 at Loreto. Given the vast amount of such documentary material, it is not surprising that there grew up among Catholics at the time a sort of unofficial cult of "the Martyrs of Castelfidardo."[2]

While all this was going on, the besiegers of Ancona were not idle. As ordered, at 11 A.M. on the September 18, Persano began bombarding the city—preventing any thought of a sortie toward Castelfidardo. The forts were little damaged, but a civilian in the street was wounded and a woman and two children killed. Persano left several of his ships to keep up the bombardment and sailed toward Senigallia.

Lamoricière and a party of 50 horsemen were spotted and joyfully welcomed to the city; the infantry that had accompanied him had stayed behind to hold back a column of Bersaglieri who were in hot pursuit. After successfully evading Sardinian patrols and using back roads through small villages, the general arrived to the booming of the Sardinian naval guns and shouts of *"Viva Lamoricière!"* Meeting with his close friend Count de Quatrebarbes, the Governor of Ancona and all available officers, Lamoricière revealed the utter defeat of the papal arms at Castelfidardo and called for a war council at 7 A.M. the next day. He then went to sleep in an armchair. The shelling had stopped at last.

When the officers met the next morning, Lamoricière was informed of the state of Ancona's defenses; and then toured the city himself. Since the Sardinian army had not yet arrived, the general sent out foraging detachments, who returned with many cattle. Three blockade runners evaded the Sardinian fleet: a ship from Trieste with flour; and two fishing boats bringing a few soldiers who had escaped Castelfidardo. Throughout the siege, local fishermen would be of immense help, working behind the lines against the invaders.

Apart from a bombardment in the early hours of September 20, which did little damage save to kill a mother and child as they slept in their house, the next few days were relatively quiet. But on

September 22, the Sardinian army of 50,000 men arrived and took up positions around the city. General Fanti in supreme command directed the troops in front of Monte Gardetto while Cialdini was given the zone before the citadel itself. The navy with its 400 guns was given two locations—near Monte Gardetto, where their guns could support Cialdini, and by the harbor mouth. At midnight the fleet opened fire, and the next morning Cialdini's and Fanti's cannon joined the attack—the shelling would go on continuously for the next eight days. September 23 was a Sunday, and many of the shells hit churches packed for morning Mass. As Count O'Clery, a Papal Zouave at a later date, rather caustically observed, "It had been the fashion at Turin to call Ferdinand of Naples '*Bomba*,' because his ships once opened fire on a rebel Sicilian town. Victor Emmanuel might fairly have claimed the title after the exploits of his fleet before Ancona in 1860, Gaeta in 1861, and Palermo in 1866, and of his army at Rome in 1870." But, of course, history is indeed written by the victors.

Despite their relatively primitive weaponry, the papal forts returned the fire and managed to damage a Sardinian frigate. On September 25, an attempt to cut the chain and allow the Sardinian fleet access to the harbor was repelled. All this time the shelling could be heard in the Austrian port of Trieste, and the emperor made an attempt to enter the war—going so far as to sign an order to his fleet to break the blockade and relieve Ancona. But his ministers refused to cooperate and he was forced to desist. Lamoricière could not know it but his last chance at outside aid was gone.

As they had throughout the campaign, the four companies of the St. Patrick's battalion fought well and audaciously, cheering the Pope and singing Irish war songs whenever the rifle fire burst about them. Myles Keogh, Joseph O'Keefe, and Daniel Keily all received their own baptisms of fire in this manner; the results would be seen in their bravery in the American Civil War, and, for Keogh, in the Indian Wars thereafter.

The morning of September 26 saw Fanti's men assaulting the two little land-side forts of Pulito and Monte Pelago. At the former post, the garrison was able to spike the guns before evacuating the fort. At the latter, Jan Chosciak Popiel's Austrian gunners were able to drag their cannon with them, thanks to a sortie made by two of the Irish companies, who made off with 15 Sardinian prisoners. Lamoricière buoyed morale by pointing out that occupation of the forts would at last place the Sardinians in range of the garrison's smooth-bore cannon.

This rise in spirits was doubled later in the day when the Sardinians stormed the lunette (a sort of two- or three sided fort whose rear was open to interior supply) of San Stefano, which lay near the front of the citadel. The Irish troops held their fire as the Sardinians advanced up the slope of the lunette; they then let fly a lethal storm of musket and cannon fire. The Sardinians broke, leaving behind 700 dead and wounded casualties.

But if September 26 ended on a happy note, the next day did not. The Sardinians attempted the same tactic against San Stefano the next morning. Not only were they again repelled, but this time the Irish charged them with fixed bayonets as they withdrew: retreat became rout. But Cialdini's troops at the same time were attacking the built-up area between the citadel and the sea toward the fortress's main gate, the Porta Pia. Then Persano's guns opened fire, and the papal troops were forced to withdraw to the citadel. Worse still, the naval guns had ignited the Lazaretto. The garrison withdrew, and later in the day the Sardinians were able to occupy the fort thanks to naval gunfire. Only the onset of night ended the combat around Ancona.

At sunrise, Cialdini attacked the Austrian-manned Porta Pia, commanded by Swiss-born Colonel Wilhelm de Gady. Anxious to avenge their country's defeat the year before, with musket and bayonet the Austrians threw back five Sardinian assaults before Cialdini gave up and ordered his men back. Persano lent him two guns and crews from a ship to man them, and with these and his own cannon, Cialdini made ready to batter down the gate. In the meantime, however, the smooth-bore artillery of the papal gunners drove the Sardinians out of the ruins of the Lazaretto. The Sardinian army was defeated, and the fortifications held.

But the navy was still to be heard from. So far, the chain still held and kept the Sardinian fleet out of the harbor; the papal troops had steadfastly repelled every attack upon it. But Persano realized the fort on the mole was the key to breaking the chain. About noon, six 50-gun frigates were sent in close to the harbor's mouth and ordered to concentrate their fire on the fort. Its two batteries surrounding the lighthouse boasted a mere twelve smooth-bores, and a garrison of 150 gunners commanded by the Austrian Lieutenant Westminthal. The frigates fired their 150 rifled guns into the fort and were answered by the 12 papal cannon. Piece by piece, the little fort and its detachment began to show the strain. Chunks fell out of the walls, cannon were silenced, their crews slaughtered. At last, there were only three left, still keeping up a brave fusillade against the foe, with the less gravely wounded acting as ammunition carriers. A frigate drew up close to the crumbling fort and launched 25 shells apiece at each of the remaining guns, destroying one of them. Westminthal himself was working one of the last until he too was killed. Then, at 4:40 P.M., an enormous explosion occurred as a shell hit the magazine under the lighthouse, and the mole was blown to bits. The chain across the harbor mouth, attached to one of the mole's walls, went with it.

The harbor was now open to the Sardinian ships. Realizing that further resistance was futile, Lamoricière sent an officer in a boat flying a white flag into the harbor. The officer explained that the general wanted to surrender to Persano as it was the navy that had defeated them. The admiral's response was that the negotiation of surrender terms lay with Fanti, as commander in chief and offered to take the emissary to him. The papal officer returned to Ancona for orders. In the meantime, all firing had stopped, and the white flag flew over the citadel.

It was Lamoricière's belief that use of the flag and cease fire would, in accordance with the rules of war of the day, end the carnage until terms were agreed upon. But at nine that night the land batteries opened up again on the entire city—whose garrison did not respond. For twelve hours the murderous rain continued. Enraged and disgusted, Persano demanded the return of the naval guns and sailors he had lent Cialdini to bombard the Porta Pia. This was refused. When he sent a second demand, the sailors were returned but Cialdini kept the guns. The firing would not stop until nine in the morning of September 29. The surrender terms were those given at Loreto.

Jan Chosciak Popiel, upon his release by the Sardinians, returned to Rome and was awarded the Cross of St. Gregory by the Pope. He returned home to Galicia to settle down on his estate, but when Russian Poland erupted in revolution in 1863, he joined the fight. After the tsar's army crushed the Poles, he went back to Galicia, entering Austrian politics as a conservative. Fritz Graf Wolff-Metternich, having been seriously wounded at the Porta Pia, also returned to

Rome and received the Cross of St. Gregory as well. He joined an Austrian Ulan (Lancer) regiment, then went with Maximilian to Mexico, where he fought Juarez's men. In 1866, he returned to the Austrian service, to fight in the Austro-Prussian war. That debacle concluded, he joined the household of exiled Grand Duke Adolf of Nassau, whose country was swallowed up by Prussia as a result of its alliance with Austria. When the grand duke inherited Luxembourg in 1890, Fritz went with him, and acted as head of government. At his patron's retirement in 1902, Fritz at last returned to his ancestral estates in Germany, where he made a fortune selling mineral water from the springs there. Count Chorinski also served with distinction at Ancona; after his release, he took his long-suffering wife to Heidelberg, finding the peace of that old university town far more pleasant than shot and shell or wrangling with his parents.

For the Irish who survived, a far different fate awaited. Keogh, Keily, O'Keefe, and the remaining Irish joined their countrymen in the prison in Genoa. But while most of their comrades returned to Ireland, they and 42 others went back to Rome where the St. Patrick's battalion was being re-formed as a company.

Patrick Buckley returned to Cork, but in 1862 emigrated to Australia, and three years later to New Zealand. He became an attorney; not only was he a zealous defender of the Catholic community in his new home, but he was several times a cabinet minister and finally a Supreme Court justice. In the end, he was knighted by Queen Victoria.

There was, even then an at least one American prisoner of the Sardinians: Louis Loistman, a native of Philadelphia, whom the American consul at Trieste worked to release. Apparently he succeeded because Loistman went on to serve and was wounded in the Civil War.

What of the most illustrious of the prisoners, Lamoricière himself? Persano kept him aboard his flagship and then found a steamer to return him to France. He retained his title of papal commander, but he was never to see Italy again—an exile in his native country. On September 10, 1865, he was found dead in bed. On the table next to him were a crucifix, a military book, and an open copy of *The Imitation of Christ*.

CHAPTER IV

The Watchful Peace

And when it is close
To the moment to die,
Without fear and reproach,
The Zouaves will see it coming.

—*Chant des Zouaves Pontificaux*

The aftermath of Castelfidardo was somber for the Pope and his supporters. In the conquered provinces of the Marches and Umbria, a guerrilla war against the invaders broke out, not unlike the one they had faced in the fallen kingdom of Naples. While the latter conflict has begun to receive a great deal more interest from Italian historians in recent years, the insurgency in the Papal States deserves to be better known. Called the *Brigantaggio* ("Brigandage") by the government of Victor Emmanuel, it tied up large numbers of Sardinian (or, in token of the proclamation of the kingdom of Italy, Italian) troops. The partisans of the defeated governments were treated with great cruelty when captured by the occupiers. Of course, as in the American Civil War, merciless civil conflict did indeed give rise to real banditry.

Although not strictly within the bounds of our tale, it would be well to remember these papal irregulars, whose spirit was so similar to that of the Zouaves. The most famous of these was Giovanni Piccioni, a native of Acquasanta del Terme in the ever loyal province of Ascoli Piceno in the Marches. Piccioni first achieved notoriety when he led a group of his neighbors in ambushing a republican rear guard at Teramo. After papal authority was restored, Piccioni was instrumental in ferreting out local officials who had collaborated with the revolutionary regime. He would also take part in the defence of Civitella del Tronto, the last fortress in the Kingdom of the Two Sicilies that resisted the Sardinian invasion.

When the papal forces were defeated at Castefidardo and Ancona, Piccioni, his sons, and a number of other volunteers took to the hills of Ascoli, from which they emerged at intervals to harass and ambush the invaders and their local allies. Helped by the mountainous terrain in which they operated and a steady stream of information from the peasantry and the priests, the *Volontari Pontifici* held down many times their numbers in Italian troops, scourging the "long-coats," as Piccioni nicknamed them, at every turn. Hiding weaponry and booty in the trunks of trees, sleeping with their weapons under the skies, he was regarded by the locals as their own Robin Hood or Zorro.

Until 1863 Piccioni and the Italian general Pinelli dueled through the area (in the course of which, Pinelli burned and pillaged such towns as Paggese). But the Italians had ever more fresh men and weaponry, while the *Volontari* numbers declined with every pitched battle and their weapons were whatever they could find. At last, the survivors gave up the struggle and remained hidden in the mountains. Finally, in 1867, Piccioni resolved to go to Rome to offer his service to the Pope. But he was betrayed at the train station of San Benedetto del Tronto, and seized by Italian police. Sentenced to 17 years in prison, he died in the grim fortress of Fort Malatesta in Ascoli Piceno in 1872.

It was quite different for the captured foreign troops after Castelfidardo. When the 1,100 Irish were released from their Genoese prison, they were released from papal service and put on a steamer for home. A general order in their honor, issued by the pro-minister of arms, Merode, on October 6, offered official praise:

> At the moment in which, in consequence of the present sad state of affairs, the brave soldiers of the Battalion of St. Patrick, who had hastened hither for the defence of the States of the Holy Church, are

about to leave the Pontifical army, the undersigned Minister of Arms experiences the liveliest satisfaction in being able to express to those soldiers his entire satisfaction, and in bestowing on them the highest praise for their conduct. Nothing more could be expected from them. The Battalion of St. Patrick at Spoleto, at Perugia, at Castel-Fidardo, and in Ancona, has shown the power of faith united to the sentiment of honour, in the treacherous and unequal contest, in which a small number of brave soldiers resisted to the last an entire army of sacrilegious invaders. May this recollection never perish from their hearts! God, who defends His Church, will bless what they have done. It is not Irishmen who require to be reminded, that we must suffer and persevere in the good fight.[1]

When the ship finally arrived at Cork harbor and discharged its weary passengers, they were greeted as conquering heroes by the leading men of the city and the county. The people of Cork cheered them as they marched through the streets, and they were treated to a victory dinner. A public subscription had produced money and clothes for them all, and they returned to their homes satisfied that they had done their duty in a worthy cause.

About 65 of the surviving Irish returned to Rome to form the Company of St. Patrick. But garrison and ceremonial duty was not much to the liking of men who had seen action at Spoleto, Castelfidardo, or Ancona. Too few to be deployed in the field, they grew restive. In the meantime, civil war broke out in the United States, and the federal government was looking for recruits wherever they could find them. At the request of Secretary of State William Seward, John Hughes, Catholic bishop of New York, successfully attempted to enlist these Irishmen for the American army. John Coppinger took a leave of absence from the papal army, traveled to New York, and was commissioned a captain in the U.S. Army. In March of 1862, Myles Keogh, Daniel Keily, and Joseph O'Keeffe also sailed to Manhattan. There, the trio were likewise made captains and appointed to the staff of Brigadier James Shields, commander of the Union forces in the Shenandoah Valley. Keily would die of yellow fever in Louisiana, and his comrades would go on to highly decorated careers before and after Appomattox. The Irishmen who remained in Rome joined the main body of the Zouaves.

For the surviving Franco-Belgians who remained in papal service, the time after Castelfidardo was one of intense mourning and veneration of their fallen comrades. So many great men had been lost! Pimodan, of course; Georges, Count d'Heliand; Arthur de Chalus; Alfred de Nanteuil; Alfred du Beaudiez; the 17-year-old Georges Miyonnet; the ever-jolly Joseph Guerin; and on and on.

Arthur de Chalus's gardener survived the battle and returned to Rome to rejoin the army. He was told by a well-wisher that he would be happier if he returned to Brittany. His response was, "M. le Count was happier than I, and he has gone. I have only my person, and I willingly give it. My one desire is to see the Holy Father, and receive Holy Communion from his hands, get his blessing, and then die for him; I hope then to reach heaven." Nor was he alone in his sentiments; others as well as their surviving comrades began to honor the dead of Castelfidardo as martyrs.

In the primitive medical atmosphere of the time, many of those wounded at Castelfidardo took weeks to die in nearby makeshift hospitals. Chalus and Guerin (who had been wounded in the chest) were laid in neighboring beds in the monastery of San Domenico Osumo; as long as Chalus hung on, Guerin wrote letters for him, in deference to the count's shattered hand. On October 19, after his friend died, Guerin was transferred to another hospital and continued to write cheering and inspiring letters to his own friends and family and those of his dead and dying comrades. When at last he himself succumbed on October 30, the attending physician wrote a detailed account of the death of the young man and sent it to his bishop in Nantes. Guerin was embalmed and placed in a triple coffin of fir, lead, and oak for shipment home.

Meanwhile, a Mass was said in his and Chalus's memory at the former's home town of Saint Pazanne, with 80 priests and an enormous number of laity in attendance; in the estimation of the locals, Guerin was a saint. Soon, pilgrims began converging on his grave in the cemetery of the Barberie, on the road to Rennes, inundating it with prayer requests and letters. By April 1861, 400 to 500 people were visiting the grave every Sunday, to the great consternation of the Sulpician priests. Miraculous healings and the like began to occur among the pilgrims: At Mouzillon, for example, it was reported that a young shepherdess was healed by the application of a strand of Guerin's hair.

The religious authorities were cautious, but began to concede that—perhaps—these events were indeed miraculous and might be a sign of heavenly support for the cause in which Guerin laid down his life. In January 1862, Archbishop Jaquement of Nantes, replied to the bishop of Blois who had asked about Guerin:

> Many graces and surprising healings have been obtained through his intercession, I do not say by miraculous healings. . . . In fact, no canonical investigation has been made, and I have only spontaneous stories of eyewitnesses, confirmed by the acclamation of entire populations. These stories, in their naiveté and simplicity, we are to make our consolation in the midst of our grief. I have not yet decided if there is here some exemption to the laws of nature. However, I admire quietly in a large number of cases, the amazing coincidence of prayer and simple touch of a relic from the young Zouave with instant cures, or occurring at the end of a novena.

Several times, Pope Pius IX spoke of Guerin, "Although we can not yet bear any judgment, we understand that these occurrences must enhance the reputation of a very pious young man, and we would not be surprised if among this number of elite men who have fallen in battle, the departed encounters a God who would have thanked him by giving special graces." Nor was Guerin the only one of his fallen comrades who received a sort of popular canonization. A whole cult of the Martyrs of Castelfidardo arose and commemorating them became an annual event among the Zouaves.

Despite the fact of defeat, stories such as Guerin's led to many more recruits for the Pope's forces, echoing the sentiments of the men who had set out at the first call. One factor for many of the legitimist French was the support of the man they considered their rightful king, Henry V, in his Austrian exile. A letter he wrote to his kinsman Charette on October 3, 1860, was quickly published throughout France and Europe and brought many who supported him as king to fight for the Pope. To the Zouaves, and those who thought like them, King and Country, Church, Pope, and God were all indissolubly linked—to fight for the one was to fight for the rest.

One of the newest crop of recruits was Henri Le Chauff de Kerguenec, who arrived in Rome in January of 1861. Having been at school with several of the dead of Castelfidardo, he had wanted to go with them. But his father had insisted that he finish his second year law examination, and, reluctantly, he watched as his friends marched off. In a letter to a friend written shortly after he arrived, Kerguenec wrote, "my second law examination [at Paris] . . . made me miss Castelfidardo where gloriously fell several of my college friends . . . since Castelfidardo I could not sleep in peace: the shades of George d'Héliand, of Hyacinthe de Lanascol,

Joseph Guerin, Rogatien Picou did not cease passing and passing by again in front of me!"

If the might of the Sardinian army, the rapidity of its victory, and the deadly efficiency of its weaponry were intended to cow either Pius IX or his followers, it failed miserably. Instead, papal recruiters redoubled their efforts, many of the prisoners returned to Rome as soon as they could, and Merode was very pleased indeed with the influx of volunteers. Nevertheless, the pontifical army needed urgently to reorganize. The need that had called them from their homes remained, and the French army that protected Rome and its environs from the Italians might be withdrawn at any time the whim of Napoleon III demanded it. Although Lamoricière in his French exile remained nominal commander of the Franco-Belgians, Major Count de Becdelièvre was in effective command of the 300 or so survivors; Pius IX promoted him to lieutenant colonel on October 6, 1860. Sufficient new recruits had arrived by that time to permit their organization into a battalion of six companies.

Despite the defeat of his army and the death of so many of his men, the Pope was not brought down; he celebrated Mass on Christmas Eve in the Sistine Chapel, giving Communion to 200 Franco-Belgians. On January 1, 1861, the name of the Pope's forces was officially changed to Pontifical Zouaves, and a new uniform was assigned that would serve the Zouaves for the remainder of their history. Gray-blue in color, the uniform comprised a short jacket with red crosses on either side and an open collar, large baggy breeches with a wide red belt, and a small kepi with square visor. Officers wore black crosses on their jackets. St. Peter's tiara and the crossed keys were engraved on the copper buttons. The officers wore boots, and the soldiers yellow puttees. The first to wear this costume were Captain Charette (now second in command) and First

Corporal Moncuit. Although a number of members of the curia were somewhat dismayed by the Muslim-looking get-up (it was, after all, modeled on the dress of Algerian tribesmen), it pleased Pius IX.

Almost immediately the Zouaves were called to battle. Near the boundary of Umbria is a hamlet called Passo Corese, close to the town of Fara in Sabina; it is an important junction on the roads between Terni and Rieti. A band of 58 Italian irregulars had seized the place, unaware that the pontifical army was renewed. At night, the Zouaves attacked; two of their opponents were killed, six wounded, and the rest captured and brought back to Rome.

This initial victory was overshadowed by the strategic and temperamental differences that now arose between Becdelièvre and Merode, the pro-minister of arms. The former resigned on March 21, 1861, and returned to France with a few officers who refused to serve under anyone else. This left Merode the task of finding a replacement. Charette was the obvious choice. But his close connection with Henry V (who continued to urge his supporters in France to volunteer for the papal army) made his appointment impossible; after all, Pius was still dependent upon Napoleon III's garrison. So the old Swiss officer, Colonel Allet—whose loyalty and bravery were proven, and yet who was not a political liability—was appointed to replace him. Charette, in his turn, called upon the men who were so devoted to him to support their new commander. With cheers of *"Vive Charette!"* they did so. Allet had, after all, fought well at Castelfidardo. Another veteran of that fight was returned to them. The bullet-riddled flag that the Franco-Belgians had flown at Castelfidardo was blessed at St. Peter's by the Pope and given to them as their regimental banner. Charette was promoted to major.

Recruiting for the Zouaves and the other papal units went on. The native units included not only men of the current and lost provinces of the Papal States, but from the occupied duchies and Naples, and even from the old kingdom of Sardinia. As for the Zouaves, they became ever more multinational. In addition to the French, Belgians, Irish, Austrians, Germans, and Swiss who formed the bulk of the foreigners at Castelfidardo, English, Poles, Spaniards, Hungarians, Swedes, and Russians swelled the ranks, as did Americans, Latin Americans, and a scattering of Asians and Africans. As far as the French were concerned, some 37 percent came from the west of France, those regions that had suffered the most in the revolution.

An especially large number of recruits came from the Netherlands—3,000 in all, from 1862 to 1870—who were immediately stripped of their Netherlands citizenship upon swearing the oath. Even so, a number of Protestant Dutchmen had to be diplomatically turned away because one had to be a Catholic to join. The Dutch went first to Amsterdam, the assembly point, and then to the West Brabant town of Oudenbosch. The pastor of the town, Father Hellemons, who was called the *zouavenpastoor*, let many of the recruits shelter in Pensionaat Saint Louis before they departed by train to Marseilles.

Although their numbers dropped to 300 in 1863, the Zouaves expanded to 700 three years later and increased to two battalions in December of 1866. A number of remarkable men had joined the ranks by that time. The Montreal paper *L'Ordre* declared in its issue of February 13, 1861, that the name of the first French-Canadian to "enlist as a Zouave in the papal troops" was Benjamin Testard de Montigny, "Montreal lawyer, former student of Université Laval." In November of 1861, an Irish-born Canadian teacher named Hugh Murray signed up; he would prove one of the most determined of the Zouaves. These two would be the beginning of a wave of Canadian volunteers that would crest in 1868.

Pay was not substantial, and neither were rations: a half penny a day, and soup, bread, and coffee. All social classes were represented, but nobility and peasantry predominated. Unlike so many armies of the time, social rank had nothing to do with military rank: All who entered the corps started as privates, whether they were ex-factory workers or younger sons of royal dynasties. Treatment was rigidly egalitarian, and promotion was strictly on the basis of seniority and aptitude. Since the senior officers and NCOs were primarily survivors of Castelfidardo, and most of them were French, that was the language of command.

It was never expected that the papal army would be able to resist a full-scale Italian invasion unaided. The Holy See would have had to spend ten times its entire treasury to build up such a force; as it was, Merode had to scramble to find what funds he could to provide even minimal weaponry, uniforms, and equipment. The one place where class distinctions did arise was the expectation that wealthy soldiers would pay for all of their own kit—including their firearms.

Recruits tended to be young; there were a fair number of 16- and 17-year-olds fresh from secondary school. But one new Zouave, a Monsieur de Coislin, was 65 at the time he joined the corps. Many joined not only to protect the independence of Pius IX and the Church, but also, in a sense, to even old scores. If a Frenchman could not fight for Henry V, or a Spaniard for the Carlists, or a Pole for his country's independence, he could still fight for the common father and sovereign of them all.

Not surprisingly, the Zouaves' religious life was intense. Not only did recruits have to be Catholic, they also had to produce a letter of recommendation from their pastor. Their chaplain was Monsignor Jules Daniel from Nantes, assisted by two Belgian monsignors, Sacré and Wœlmont (who spoke both French and Dutch). Josef Maria

Muller, a Swiss who joined the Swiss carabinieri in 1866, wrote of the Zouaves (by way of contrast with his own unit):

> The Zouaves were Christian soldiers and all who belonged to them were glad and content, and fulfilled their professional duties with eagerness and good will; they were particularly however characterised by their deep religiosity. One could meet Zouaves on his free time more often in a church than in a tavern. And if they looked for recreation, then they went into a coffee house and played games with one another. The Zouaves were truly Christian soldiers, serving from love for the Most Holy Father and for the support of his throne in Rome, and had not left their homelands to escape some trouble.

As a result, Zouaves on duty in Rome were extensively used in papal religious ceremonies, playing major roles in processions and Masses on Christmas, Easter, Corpus Christi, and the other feast days of the Christian year. When the Pope would appear on the balcony of his palace to bless the city and the world, a line of Zouaves inevitably appeared under it. Pius IX's opinion of his multinational defenders is well summed up in a speech he gave to their officers on Christmas Day 1865:

> It customary that on holy Christmas Day we bless a sword [the custom whose origin we saw in chapter I]. It must be sent to the prince who has best served the Church, and who must make use of it for the cause of justice.
>
> In the midst of many great armed nations, of so many drawn swords, I look and I see: I see that this sword of justice I must keep for myself. It is I who must gird it, and it is into your hands that I entrust it.
>
> Be proud, go with your head raised before God, full of confidence among men, because it is you, you only, who carry the sword for justice and the truth, the dignity and the freedom of mankind. You are thus armed against those unhappy men who have bloodied their hands

with the profit of unjust causes, supports of iniquity, enemies of God whom they madly hope to fight, oppressors of His Church and her ministers....

I dare to say that you will present yourselves safely at the court of the Supreme Judge, in front of whom they will also have to appear who carry the sword for injustice and the oppressor.

I thus approve with happiness the expression of your fidelity. Receive in return my blessing, which confirms you in all these finer feelings; that it strengthens you in danger and accompanies you all your life.[2]

For all their religiosity, the Zouaves were also much in demand in Rome's social life. One happy event that drew their ranks together with those outside was a marriage that united several old causes—the marriage of Charette on July 17, 1862, with Antoinette de FitzJames, daughter of Jacques, Duke de FitzJames and a direct descendant of the Duke of Berwick, illegitimate son of England's James II.

On August 3, 1862, Victor Emmanuel, in an oblique slap at Garibaldi, declared in a proclamation that the Italians should not attempt to seize Rome under anyone's direction but his. "When that hour comes, the voice of your King will be heard amongst you. Every call to arms, which is not his, is a call to revolt and civil war." On August 4, the Italian minister of war, General Pettiti, repeated: "They call upon you to join them in a mad enterprise; but in your name I renounce it." On that day, a detachment of Italian troops crossed the former Neapolitan frontier near Ceprano. The closest papal post was commanded by Lieutenant Victor Mousty, a former law clerk and native of Saint Hubert in the Belgian Ardennes. Although his little company numbered only 16, they threw back the invaders over the border. Moreover, the French commander in Rome, General Montebello, wired his subordinate in charge of the French garrison at Velletri ordering him to reinforce Mousty's Zouaves and to assist them in repelling any further incursion. This was taken by Victor Emmanuel to mean that, for the moment, Napoleon III was serious about sustaining the Pope's power over Lazio. The Italians thereafter regarded the border scrupulously—for the moment.

The larger goal of Victor Emmanuel and his ministers was to prevail upon Napoleon III to withdraw his forces from Italy. On the one hand, the mercurial emperor would no doubt have wished to withdraw; but this would inevitably increase support for Henry V among his country's Catholics—whose support he still needed. On the other hand, a practical excuse for a withdrawal presented itself with the French intervention in Mexico.

Mexico had spent the later part of the 1850s in the "War of the Reform," a bloody civil war between anticlerical liberals and pro-Catholic conservatives. Monarchist as well as religious, the conservatives had in 1859 offered the crown of Mexico to the younger brother of the Austrian emperor, Archduke Maximilian. At the time, he refused. But not only had the triumphant Mexican liberals under their president, Benito Juarez, proved as oppressive to the Church and his enemies as feared, in 1861 he had suspended all payments on the country's enormous foreign debt. Seeing an opportunity to establish a French protectorate in North America (and strengthened in his resolve by the fact that the Civil War gave the United States, Juarez's patron, other things to worry about), Napoleon came up with a plan. On October 31, 1861, France, Spain, and Great Britain signed a treaty that bound them to occupy Veracruz and force the Mexican government to pay its bills.

By January of 1862, the allies had seized that port and Campeche. But the Spanish and British soon realized that Napoleon intended to conquer the entire country and withdrew their forces. The French went on to conquer most of the country; their Mexican allies renewed their invitation to Maximilian and this time he accepted. He entered his new capital with his Belgian empress on April 10, 1864, accompanied by Austrian and Belgian volunteers, as well as a scattering of other nationalities. Indeed, the Mexican imperial forces were often compared to the papal Zouaves—not merely because of their multinational make-up, but because for many the struggle against Juarez's anticlericals was seen as a crusade. Although Pius IX recognized the new government and blessed its endeavors, he was not pleased with Maximilian's refusal to undo Juarez's laws against the Church, nor with his refusal to allow Zouaves to recruit Mexicans (a refusal that did not prevent a certain number from joining up anyway).

In any case, the enormous investment of French army men and materiel gave Napoleon III a reason to lessen French military commitments elsewhere, for reasons he believed he could justify to his subjects. On September 15, 1864, he signed a secret convention with Victor Emmanuel in which he promised to withdraw the French forces from Rome within two years; in return for this the Italian king promised to respect the independence of the remaining Papal State and not oppose the existence and expansion of the pontifical army. Contemporary witnesses maintained that Napoleon was all too aware of Victor Emmanuel's casual view of solemn oaths and treaties; Garibaldi and his men were always present in case civil unrest requiring Italian intervention was required.[3]

Early the following year, the agreement was made public and Pius IX officially informed. Lamoricière was mortified by this betrayal, and was preparing to return to lead the papal army when he died When the news of his death reached Rome, Kanzler was made commander of the pontifical army in name as well as fact. In response, more volunteers poured in. The Zouaves swiftly rose to 1,500 men: December of 1865 saw two more companies added to the regiment, as well as a depot company. There were about 5,000 indigenous and Swiss troops, and with the dragoons, chasseurs, and the various guard units, the army once more reached a total of 10,000. But this time, if their equipment was not the best, they were at least well trained and battle-ready, Another change of leadership occurred in October 1865: having more frequently crossed swords with Antonelli, Merode resigned; he would spend the rest of his life helping the poor of Rome. To his title of commander in chief, Kanzler added that of pro-minister of arms.

The announcement of the French prompted brigands and would-be revolutionaries alike to become more active in the interior, convinced that without their French protectors, the papal forces would be ineffective. Throughout the spring and summer of 1866, unrest grew, especially in the province of Frosinone. The Volscian hills became extremely unsafe. Zouave detachments were sent to Sezze, Piperno, Prossedi, and various other towns in the region.

Things came to a head on November 22. About 60 or so brigands had handily defeated three detachments of Swiss carabinieri who tried to take their stronghold on Monte Lupino; it was decided to throw the nearest formation of Zouaves against the entrenched foe. Unfortunately, this formation numbered a mere 27 men plus Captain Adeodatus Dufournel and Lieutenant Coüessin. For four hours the outnumbered Zouaves blazed away until at last their enemies took flight. To better fight the brigands, when not in Rome, the Zouaves were deployed to towns like Tivoli and Monte Rotondo east of Rome, Anagni and Velletri to the south, and Viterbo, Bagnorea (now Bagnoregio), and Montefiascone to the north.

During this same period, the end of the American Civil War would affect the Holy See and the Zouaves in particular. The defeat of the South would drive irreconcilable Confederates far away from their conquered homeland. Some sought service under Emperor Maximilian; others established colonies in then-slaveholding Brazil (where their descendants live today); a few would serve the Ottoman sultan or the khedive of Egypt. But a few, remembering Pius IX's attitude toward the Confederacy, came to Rome. Among these was Henry Van Ness Bentivoglio Middleton, Count Bentivoglio.

The son of a former American ambassador to Spain and his second wife (the only child of the last Count Bentivoglio), Middleton was born in Charleston and educated in Paris and at the Citadel. During the Civil War he served in the Confederate Army at Charleston and in Virginia; Middleton returned to Rome and, after a short stint as a private, was made a captain in the Pope's military.

The correct supposition of Middleton and other former Confederates that they would be well received at Rome stemmed, in great part, from Pius's recognition of the Confederacy and his correspondence with President Jefferson Davis. After the war, when Davis was kept prisoner in Fort Monroe, Virginia, the Pope sent him a crown of thorns he had made with his own hands, and an engraving of himself with the inscription in Latin: "Come to me all you who labor, and are heavy-burdened." This sympathy for the Southern cause on the part of the Pope and other foreign Catholics was due in part to the higher status of Catholics in the South than in the North. Although the latter region had far more Catholics in its population, most were poor immigrants. In the South, by way of contrast, although there were far fewer Catholics, they had much higher social status. There were Catholic cabinet secretaries in Richmond, which would have been unthinkable in Washington. Beyond that, many foreign aristocrats saw the Southern planters as their equivalents in a way that they could never see the bankers and industrialists who dominated the North. Indeed, just as men like Marx and Mazzini saw, perhaps wrongly, their cause in Lincoln's, so too did many Europeans see—perhaps just as wrongly—their own fight against industrialization and centralization in the Southern struggle to retain slavery. For a Pope who was seeing many of his allies' lands eaten up by Sardinia and Prussia, a region fighting to gain independence from a centralizing state could not help but strike a chord. Even so, thanks in great part to New York's Archbishop Hughes, relations between Washington and Rome remained fairly cordial, and Lincoln returned the California missions to the Church.

Nevertheless, it was this perceived friendliness for the South on the part of Pius and the Church that led to one of the most bizarre chapters in the annals of the Zouaves. It began with the assassination of President Lincoln by John Wilkes Booth on April 14, 1865. This event gave rise to as many conspiracy theories as did that of John F. Kennedy. Booth used a preexisting plot by Confederate Secret Service agents to kidnap Lincoln (in order to effect the release of Davis and other Confederates) as a springboard to murder. One of his partners in the abduction scheme was a Maryland ex-seminarian named John Surratt; their plan took shape in a Maryland tavern run by Surratt's mother, Mary.

Surratt, during the war, had run messages between Richmond and the Confederate agents working in Canada, then a British colony. (Just as Napoleon saw an opportunity with Mexico in its Civil War, so that conflict eased Britain's fears for Canada.) When Booth murdered the president, Surratt fled north of the border and was hidden by various Confederate sympathizers and priests he had come to know during the war. The hanging of his mother (who almost certainly knew nothing of the plot) proved to him that he would not find justice before an American court. Friends helped Surratt flee to Liverpool, England, where after his arrival on September 25, 1865, one of his traveling companions alerted the American consul in Liverpool as to Suratt's identity. The Department of State in Washington, when consulted, instructed the consul to do nothing—a fact that Lincoln conspiracy theorists have seized on.

Surratt, in the meantime, moved on to London, Paris, and finally Rome, where in April of 1866, he enlisted in the Pontifical Zouaves under the name of John Watson. He was posted to the town of Sezze, where he met an old acquaintance, a French-Canadian named Henri de Ste. Marie. Although Surratt begged him to keep his identity a secret, when Ste. Marie went to Rome on leave, he stopped by the American legation on April 21, and reported Surratt's presence to the envoy, Rufus King. King in his turn notified Washington, and this time the State Department ordered their representative to act. The envoy approached Cardinal Antonelli with a request for Surratt-Watson's arrest and delivery to American authorities. There was, however, no extradition treaty between the United States and the Holy See (a fact that had allowed many revolutionaries from the Papal States to seek refuge in New York). But given the severity of the case, Pius agreed to surrender the fraudulent Zouave.

Allet ordered Watson's arrest, which occurred without difficulty on November 7 at Veroli, where he was on leave. Imprisoned that evening in the city's jail, he was moved at 4:00 A.M. the next morning. Conducted by six Zouaves, he was led out of the prison gate near a hundred foot drop into a ravine. Suddenly, Surratt ran and leaped into the ravine. The guard party fired their weapons over the edge and chased after him, soon joined by 50 more Zouaves, but the prisoner had made his escape.

Surratt fled over the border to Naples. The Italian authorities were quite happy to help a deserter evade papal justice and allowed him to board a ship bound for Alexandria, Egypt. Once he arrived there, still wearing his Zouave uniform, however, he was arrested by the American consul, who put him aboard a U.S. warship the next month. He stood trial, but a mistrial was declared, and he was eventually released.

This event has lived on, however, in the minds and hearts of historical mystery lovers. For those who see the Holy See, or the British Crown, or the American government, or all three allied together, as being at the center of all the world's troubles, the Surratt case is often invoked, even today. For the Zouaves, however, it was simply an unpleasant episode of losing a prisoner.

But more serious problems were facing the Holy See. The Italian government having increased its armed forces and its bureaucracy in its conquered territories, and facing an insurgency in some of them, required even more money than a ruinous taxation could extract from its subjects. The continual cry of Cavour and his disciples had been "a free Church in a free State," and often did the governing circles, first in Turin, and then Florence where the capital was moved, claim that their opposition to the papacy was purely political. Were the Pope's temporal power to be given up, then Church and state would flourish in a new partnership.

Reality was brought home in the spring of 1866, when a far-reaching law was passed by the Italian parliament that called for the exile and imprisonment of bishops deemed disloyal to the new order, keeping dioceses vacant, and preventing the communication of bishops with Rome; forbidding publication of papal encyclicals; suppressing chapters of canons and seizing their property; closing seminaries and subjecting clerics to conscription; demanding civil marriage for all, secularizing education, and closing Catholic schools; removing religious emblems from government offices, and forbidding the religious processions so loved by the Italians; and abolishing all monasteries and religious orders, giving their property to the government. Perhaps the most important requirement of this law was this last. There were many religious houses in the country: such beloved abbeys as Monte Cassino and Farfa were either emptied of their monks and transformed into barracks, public offices, or simply sold, or else the religious stayed on as unpaid caretakers on government property. The huge windfall thus realized was quickly spent; but this measure, combined with the impending withdrawal of the French, strengthened Pius's determination never to come to an accord with the government and naturally raised the number of recruits for the pontifical army, both from Italy and abroad.

In the meantime, Otto von Bismarck's Prussia was preparing to go to war with Austria, in order to eject the Habsburgs forever from the affairs of Germany. Given that only a few of the smaller north German states would ally with him, the Iron Chancellor looked to Italy for an ally to draw off the Austrian strength; he promised Victor Emmanuel Venetia if he would march at Prussia's side. The Seven Weeks War featured a speedy crushing of Austria and her allies by the Prussian army. Hanover, Hesse-Kassel, Nassau, and the free city of Frankfurt (heretofore capital of the loose German Confederation) paid for their support of the Habsburgs with annexation; Austria's south German allies were allowed continued existence, but only by subordinating their foreign policy to Prussia's.

The Italian front did not go so well. Although the ever-present Garibaldi did manage to conquer southern Tyrol, on July 20 the Italian fleet was decisively defeated by the Austrians at the Battle of Lissa in the Adriatic. What was left of Persano's fleet limped back into Ancona. The Sisters of Charity, who had been expelled under the law of 1866 were urgently called back to the port to nurse the wounded sailors. But when their charges had recovered, their convent was seized, and they were once more expelled.

But in the end, this victory did not matter. Bismarck insisted that Franz Josef cede Venetia to Italy. Unable to bring himself to deal directly with Victor Emmanuel, the Austrian Emperor surrendered the province to Napoleon III, who passed it on to Italy in turn as he had with Lombardy.

Antipapal opinion throughout Europe rejoiced; surely Italy's occupation of Venetia heralded the rapid seizure of Rome as well! But these voices failed to reckon with the indomitable spirit of the Pope and his defenders. Napoleon, on the other hand, began to worry about the results of his actions since the Italy he had helped create, so far from being a French puppet state, had become an ally of Prussia. He permitted the formation of the Legion of Antibes or Legione Romana: French Catholic soldiers, primarily from Alsace and the southeast of France, who were to serve the Pope for five years. In August of 1866, this group had 1,000 men under the command of Colonel d'Argy. They entered Rome on September 22. Their uniforms and equipment were basically French issue with pontifical buttons and badges; their officers retained their French commissions.

December of 1866 saw the withdrawal of the French from Rome; on December 8, while they were evacuating, Pius invited the bishops of the world to join him the next year for the anniversary of the martyrdoms of Saints Peter and Paul. On the eve of the departure of the last of the French, the Pope addressed the officers: "Go, my children; leave with my blessing, my love. If you see the emperor, say to him that I pray each day for him. It is said that his health is not very good, I pray for his health. It is said that his heart is not quiet, I pray for his heart. The French nation is Christian, its chief must be Christian too. Do not believe that you leave me alone; the good God remains with me."

But it was not only God who would remain with the Pontiff. In addition to the Legion of Antibes, ever more recruits were flocking to the pontifical banners: to accommodate them, a second battalion was created in the month the French left. In January of 1867, the Zouaves became a regiment of four battalions. As the events of the New Year would show, Pius IX would need every man.

CHAPTER V

Garibaldi's Last Throw

To die in arms! 'Twas all our hope,
There, round the shrines of Rome;
Our souls to God, our names bequeathed
Through all the years to come,
A memory of reproach and shame
To recreant Christendom.

—*Katherine Mary Stone, "Our Flag"*

$\mathcal{A}$lthough the Pontifical Zouaves were now a full regiment, and the papal army was far better organized and equipped than it had been at Castelfidardo, the Pope's men were still no match for the Italian army. Italy's government, now based in Florence, was fully committed to Cavour's policies, despite his death six years earlier. While the rump Papal State was now stripped of its French garrison, the lack of real internal opposition to the Holy See promised a prolonged period of tranquility. This was a situation that Cavour's disciple, Prime Minister Rattazi, was resolved to change. The National (as opposed to the Garibaldian Revolutionary) Committee at Rome was reorganized and more carefully subordinated to Florence. A strategy was being hatched that would resort to the old game of having Garibaldi and his men initiate fighting, and then insert the Italian army to restore order. This plan had worked well in 1859 and 1860 in the kingdom of Naples and the Papal States.

During the summer, the irrepressible Garibaldi began promising his followers that they soon would "drive the Papal mercenaries from Rome with the butt-ends of their guns." Rattazzi was, for his part, doing his best to set the stage as well. For starters, he declared that the French government had itself broken the September Convention, whereby Napoleon III had withdrawn his forces from Rome in return for Italian guarantees to respect the remaining papal territories. Many of the men of the Legion of Antibes were by no means so pious as their Zouave comrades in arms. There were reports of desertions and even that some of the men had been in touch with Garibaldi's Revolutionary Committee in Rome. Napoleon III dispatched a general to look into the accusations.

Unlike the Zouaves, the legion's officers had French commissions and its soldiers, serving the Pope for five years only, did not relinquish their French citizenship as had the French Zouaves, this inquiry was a legal undertaking. But Rattazzi declared that the proceeding violated the convention, and so justified whatever support Victor Emmanuel's government might give Garibaldi. That support was not slow in coming. With government funds, Revolutionary Committees were set up alongside the National ones all over the peninsula. With the connivance of the royal administration, volunteers were recruited for the attack, and weapons purchased and stockpiled. In true Cavouresque fashion, if an assault succeeded, the royal army would march into Rome to "safeguard" the Pope; if not, the government would declare how horrified it was and place Garibaldi (if he survived) under loose house arrest, in order to stash him away for the next attempt.

Pius IX, however, was quite serene in the face of all this plotting. In the summer of 1867, nearly 121,000 pilgrims (a number that included 500 bishops and 20,000 priests) converged on Rome to celebrate the anniversary of the martyrdom of St. Peter. At that time, Pius announced the convening of an Ecumenical Council for October of 1869. In the midst of all the jubilation, a disaster struck that was beyond the control of the Pope, the king, and even Garibaldi.

Albano is a beautiful lakeside town southeast of Rome, in the midst of the Alban Hills. Its location and elevation have ensured its position as a summer vacation spot. Then as now, anyone who can flee Rome during August does. A continuing testimony to this is the large number of lovely villas dotting Albano and its surroundings. But as is often the case in resort towns, the year-round residents had a great deal of contempt for the summer people. For economic reasons, many of the populace also displayed envy and hatred toward the aristocracy and higher clergy who summered with them. As a result, Albano had been fertile ground for Garibaldian propaganda.

In the less-than-sanitary nineteenth century, this annual retreat was not merely a matter of convenience but of health. In hot weather the as-yet-undrained marshes of the countryside around Rome were a constant breeding ground of malaria and other maladies. Today it is said that "no one of consequence stays in Rome in August." In 1867 going to the Alban Hills was both a social activity and often enough an act of physical survival.

But in August of 1867, the unthinkable happened: Cholera hit Albano itself. It must be remembered that back then, cholera ranked alongside malaria and yellow fever as one of the chief scourges of cities in warmer areas. It was a relatively new disease, having first emerged about 1830 from Bengal, after which it came to Europe, killing thousands as it progressed. Worse still, there was no known prevention or cure for it: One caught it or not; one survived it or not.

Its eruption in Albano was a nightmare. Wealthy visitors left or canceled their stays on hearing the news. Civil government collapsed as the mayor and city council fled. Bodies piled up in the streets or rotted in houses. The sick were left to care for themselves and recover if they could. This neglect doomed many who might have recovered otherwise. The archbishop, Cardinal Altieri, was the only public figure who stayed, as did the vacationing (and exiled) royal family of Naples, who took their places beside the Sisters of Charity caring for the sick. Albano was a town waiting to die.

Pius IX ordered in the 6th Company of the 2nd Battalion of the Zouaves. Upon their arrival, the Pope's soldiers immediately began their work. Some were assigned to dig graves in the cemetery, where, the first night, ninety corpses were brought to them. The remainder spent their time finding and nursing the sick—feeding them, caring for them, and seeing that the dying received the sacraments. In the stifling heat, with the odor of death and excrement all round, it must have seemed like a chamber of hell. Cardinal Altieri, the Queen Mother of Naples, and her youngest son, Don Gennaro, caught the disease and died, as did two Dutch Zouaves. One of these, Henri Peters, spent his final hours clutching and kissing a crucifix, his last words being "I know that Heaven is before me when all this is past."

After having claimed so many lives, the epidemic cleared up all at once, and by August 20 the Zouaves were ready to leave. What no one involved realized, however, was that in fighting the cholera so well, they had in reality struck the first victorious blow in the campaign of 1867. So far as the people of Albano and the surrounding towns—a month before so sympathetic to Garibaldi and his aims—were concerned, the Zouaves were heroes, if not living saints. The sight of such poorly paid men, for the most part unconnected by ties of language or nationality to the people for whom they had risked their lives, tending the sick and interring the dead, had the effect of reconciling a large portion of the people of Lazio to the Zouaves and the Pope whom they served.

Another development of that spring and summer was the entrance into the Zouaves of a number of English-speaking recruits. Perhaps typical of the Americans was Paul Edmond Beckwith, born in St. Louis in 1848. His father was of an old New England family who had fought in the American Revolution, while his mother was a descendant of the French founder of the Missouri city. Another enlistee was young Charles Tracey. He had distinguished himself as a member of his school's cadet company; after graduation he visited the Holy Land, where young Charles resolved to serve the Pope. He went to Rome the following year and enlisted in the Zouaves; later on he would become a distinguished congressman from his native state.

Another English-speaker and close friend of Tracey's in the unit was another teenager, Patrick Keyes O'Clery, son of a Catholic landholder in Ireland. The two friends arrived in time to face Garibaldi; but unknown to them, they would have to act as guerrilla fighters before their careers in the Zouaves were ended.

England, too, contributed recruits that summer. The Collingridge brothers, Alfred (who had been studying for the Sulpician priesthood in Rome), Arthur, and George came from an old Catholic family in Godington, Oxfordshire. Alfred, the oldest, had been born in 1847, and George in 1841. Despite the family's deep English roots, their father sold the manor in 1853 and emigrated to France with his family. Alfred quit his clerical studies in 1866, and joined the Zouaves. Soon after Arthur left Paris to serve with his brother. George remained at home in Paris, but events would soon inspire him to follow his older brothers' footsteps.

The youngest of the Zouaves at that time was Julian Watts-Russell. Although of English descent, Watts-Russell's father had moved his family to Florence because of his wife's ill health. Julian and his older brother, Wilfred, were educated in England but enlisted in the Austrian army in early 1867; after three months they went to Rome and joined the Zouaves.

When enough English-speaking men had joined the unit, they formed a billiards club. Although Julian entered fully into the unit's social life and was zealous in his military training, he was renowned for his piety—which, in that company, was not looked down upon. A frequent guest at the English College (where priests for his homeland had been trained in exile since the time of Queen Elizabeth), Julian attended Mass every day, the rosary each night, and confession weekly. One day, while loading his rifle, he said to a fellow soldier that the bullets he was putting in the weapon would be a beautiful gift for Garibaldi. "Yes," the friend replied, "but perhaps you'll get another in exchange."

"This would be better," responded Julian, "because in that case I have the hope to go straight to Heaven."

While these English-speakers and their fellow citizens made the Zouaves ever more cosmopolitan, the enemy had not been idle. The headquarters of the antipapal irregulars was fixed at Terni. The Italian government gave its volunteers weapons, ammunition, money and free railroad passes; even so, the Rattazzi cabinet denied any part in the activity. On September 21, 1867, the government declared that the ministry opposed any attack on the Papal States. But Rattazzi's word meant as much as Cavour's, as the succeeding cabinet showed the following year when they published proof of their predecessors' part in setting up Garibaldi's army.

At the same time the government was issuing the pious declaration described above, they were also busy assisting Garibaldi with his planning. It was agreed that he and his sons, Menotti and Ricotti, proceeding from their base at Terni, would invade the papal territory from the north. Meanwhile, another of Garibaldi's lieutenants, Nicotera, was ordered to invade the provinces of Frosinone and Velletri from the south. Both columns would head for Rome, where a carefully organized popular uprising was planned. Should papal resistance prove too great, the Italian army would follow to restore order and guarantee a plebiscite leading to annexation—all to safeguard the Pope, of course.

Thinking that his troops would be welcomed by the Pope's subjects with a revolution, and that the outnumbered Zouaves would pose little threat (he derided them constantly as "foreign cowards" and mercenaries), in September of 1867, Garibaldi began launching raids against the remaining papal territory. Estimates of his available forces range from 100,000 to 10,000, but all sources agree it was no less than the latter figure. The old revolutionary, although ostensibly acting on his own, was permitted by the Sardinian authorities to range freely around the borders of the papal territory, north, east, and south. He could strike anywhere he wished, concentrating his forces as he pleased.

By contrast, the papal forces, although at the time numbering about 13,000 on paper, had about 8,000 men who were ready to bear arms. Of these, the Zouaves numbered 2,237. Not only was the pontifical army smaller than its adversary's formations, there was no way for General Kanzler to know where the blow would fall—or, if the boasts of incipient insurrections on the part of locals, so loudly proclaimed by the liberal press in Italy and across Europe and eagerly expected by Garibaldi, were true. The result was that the Zouaves and other units of the papal army were strung out in various garrisons in order to watch all the borders and maintain internal security.

When Garibaldi began his campaign, his triumph seemed inevitable. But he and his supporters in Turin, across Europe, and in America reckoned without the mettle of the Zouaves and their comrades in arms. In September, the Garibaldians began raiding across the frontier and engaging the papal forces in numerous small encounters. The plan was for Garibaldi to enter the Papal State on September 23, but a French consul found out and notified the Tuileries palace. Napoleon III demanded that Garibaldi be arrested. The Italians complied, catching the old revolutionary on his way south. He was incarcerated in the old fortress of Alessandria in the north, but a few days later was released to his own home on an island near Sardinia.

Nevertheless, on September 28, the first large column of Garibaldi's Redshirts crossed the papal frontier. They attacked and drove off a small detachment of gendarmes from the town of Grotte San Stefano in the eastern portion of the province of Viterbo. On October 1, they moved on toward Ronciglione but were attacked by a group of Italian papal infantry.

On September 29, another band of 300 Garibaldians attacked the 27 gendarmes at Acquapendente. For three hours the papal police held out in their barracks. At length, out of ammunition, they surrendered and were made prisoners. The Garibaldians quickly passed on to Montefiascone, where another small detachment of Italian pontifical forces dispersed them after a short scuffle. Through the first few days of October, other such bands were defeated by small Zouave units in such towns as Bolsena, Canino, Ischia, and Monte Landro. In all of these engagements, the locals welcomed the papal troops and acted as scouts for them. The Garibaldians were seen as foreigners, and the memory of Albano was fresh.

So far, these were mere skirmishes. It was at Bagnorea (now Bagnoregio) that the first pitched battle of the campaign took place. Famous as the home of Saint Bonaventure, in 1867 the town boasted a population of 3,000 people. Colonel Azzanesi, the Roman officer in command of the province of Viterbo, had at his command two companies of gendarmes, a battalion of papal Italian infantry, two companies of the Zouaves, an artillery section, and some dragoons. On October 1, another Garibaldian band seized the town, profaned its churches, and seized the town treasury. With some remnants of the bands that had been dispersed in the passed few days, Menotti Garibaldi soon had 500 men guarding the town.

Having arrived near Bagnorea on the October 3, Azzanesi sent out a reconnaissance column comprising 40 line infantry, 20 Zouaves, and 4 gendarmes, under a line officer, Captain Gentili; the senior Zouave was Lieutenant Guerin (a cousin of the martyr of Castelfidardo). Although ordered simply to spy out the Garibaldian positions, Gentili decided on his own initiative to attack. It was a disaster, and 24 of the papal troops fell into the hands of the defenders. The Zouaves covered the retreat of the remainder.

But Azzanesi decided to mount a proper assault and reinforced his troops in the neighborhood with several more companies totaling 460 men and two guns. Three companies of Zouaves under Captain le Gonidec, using only bayonets, swept the Garibaldians from the convent of San Francesco just outside town, while four companies of line infantry took the barricades around the front gate of the town. The artillery succeeded in blasting open the gate and the papal troops rushed in. But the Garibaldians had fled, leaving 96 dead and wounded and 110 prisoners behind. Six of the Zouaves were wounded; one of them, the Dutch Zouave Nicholas Heykamp, was shot in the chest and died in the town hospital two days later. He was the first papal soldier to die in the campaign of 1867. Once again, the Zouaves were hailed as liberators by the townspeople.

Meanwhile, news came to the newly promoted Colonel Charette that the towns of Monte Rotondo and Nerola had both been occupied by Garibaldians commanded by the old revolutionary's son, Menotti.

Charette led a column of Zouaves and gendarmes toward the towns, arriving in the neighborhood on October 8; the papal soldiers were greeted by the townspeople with cries of "Long Live Pius IX!" Nerola is also on high ground, and from the town Charette could see that the Garibaldians had withdrawn to the slopes of Monte Carpignano, whose summit ran through the border. On the following day he led his troops against them. But they withdrew behind the frontier, just out of rifle range. To their rear were two companies of Italian troops, supposedly present to protect the border, but obviously ready to join the Garibaldians should Charette take the bait and fire on the fugitive invaders. Despite his notorious temper, the Zouave commander did not fall into the trap. He withdrew.

Unaware that the Garibaldians were heading toward Monte Libretti, Charette set off for Monte Rotondo the morning of October 13, where he found Lieutenant Guillemin with 95 Zouaves. He ordered the lieutenant to leave 15 men to garrison Monte Rotondo and to take the rest to link up, if possible, with Veaux and proceed to Monte Libretti. If the place was unoccupied, Guillemin was to garrison it; if not, he must act as circumstances demanded. Charette then rode to Monte Maggiore, arriving before noon, where he found Lieutenant Ringard, with sixty men of the Legion of Antibes, about to set off toward Monte Libretti on a scouting expedition. Charette approved his plan, informing him that he should link up with Guillemin and Veaux, should the latter have arrived.

By early evening, Guillemin and his 80 Zouaves found themselves at the approach to Monte Libretti; they had met neither Veaux nor Ringard. Passing a small hill, they were fired on by a makeshift Garibaldian outpost, whose men then retreated to the town. Now he knew that Monte Libretti was occupied, but by how many? The sun was setting and the redoubtable Guillemin was forced to make a decision. If he waited for the promised reinforcements, there would be no hope of retaking the town before the next day. Already, the other Garibaldian sentries were falling back to the town. He divided his men into two sections: His friend Quelen was to lead one section in an attack on the suburb to the left; he himself would lead the other through the vineyards to assault the town itself. Guillemin gave the order, "fix bayonets!" His primarily Flemish command roared back, *"Vive Pie Neuf!"*

Guillemin's sections rushed through the vineyards, down a long street, and into the open square in front of the gate. Fired on in front and from both sides, the Zouaves fought their way through the square. Guillemin himself was hit by a ball; as he fell, he shouted *"Vive Pie Neuf!"* Even as his men lifted him up, he was shot again in the head and died instantly. This survivor of Castelfidardo, whose men had named him the Guardian Angel, had fallen, but the loss of their captain did not dampen their enthusiasm. Bach, the Bavarian sergeant-major, took command, and the advance continued toward a body of Garibaldians drawn up in front of the main gate. The Zouaves closed in on their foes with the bayonets and fierce hand-to-hand fighting ensued.

The tall, athletic Dutchman Pieter Janzsoon de Jong killed sixteen Garibaldians with the butt end of his rifle before succumbing to mortal wounds and falling upon the bodies of his enemies. Alfred Collingridge, backed up against a wall, killed two of the enemy before collapsing from four bayonet wounds. So it went, as the Zouaves fought on despite receiving numerous bayonet thrusts. After a quarter of an hour, Quelen's section arrived and attacked the Garibaldians on the left flank. He himself immediately received a ball, but he continued the assault. The bugler's right arm was shattered, but the young man took his bugle in his left hand and continued to sound the charge.

The Garibaldians fled inside the town but were unable to entirely close the gate. Night had fallen and the Zouaves continued the assault. Three times they managed to get inside, but everyone who did so was shot or bayoneted; Quelen himself fell with nine balls in his body. With both officers dead, and an apparently large Garibaldian force inside the city (it turned out later that there were at least 1,100), the 40 surviving Zouaves decided to withdraw. Separated from the main group by darkness, Bach and a few others occupied a house on the square. The Garibaldians were unsuccessful at flushing them out and instead began barricading the gate. In the end, the survivors escaped through the back door, eventually finding their way to the main body of survivors at Monte Maggiore. But the Garibaldians, sure that they had encountered the vanguard of a huge army, withdrew to Nerola under cover of night with their own and the Zouaves' wounded, including Collingridge.

The next day, Charette occupied the town with a strong body of Zouaves, the Legion of Antibes, and gendarmes. Menotti Garibaldi was at Nerola with three thousand men, and there were other Garibaldian bands at large in the province. But there was no general rising, and the locals were uniformly uncooperative toward the invaders.

Charette resolved to do something about Nerola. The town lies high on a mountain, clustered around a medieval castle (today a five-star hotel). Setting out from Monte Libretti on September 18, the Zouave commander divided his force in two. His Zouaves and artillery were to proceed along the main path to the town; the legionnaires of Antibes, gendarmes, and carabinieri would advance to the right along a mountain path. When they arrived, they found that Menotti had evacuated the town, leaving a small garrison in the castle. The younger Garibaldi did not realize that Charette's men had cannon with them. He wanted the castle to hold out, and then, while the papal troops were busy with the siege, intended to fall on them from the rear. This miscalculation would cost him.

By midmorning the legionnaires attacked and seized the outposts. The castle was now surrounded, and the papal artillery opened fire while the infantry shot at the defenders with their rifles. The Garibaldians fired back, killing 16 papal soldiers and Charette's horse while he sat upon it. Still there was no sign of Menotti and his men, and the Garibaldians threatened to mutiny if their commander did not surrender. Soon the white flag flew over the castle and the 135 defenders surrendered. With them were the papal wounded and prisoners from Monte Libretti.

The chaplain of the Zouaves, Father Daniel, visited the wounded. With him were Alfred Collingridge's brother, George, several other English Zouaves, and Katherine Stone, an Englishwoman who had been serving as a volunteer nurse with the papal army.

At first Collingridge was unconscious. When he came to and saw who was around him, he declared that "The Lord has given me the favor I asked—to die for the Holy Father. Oh, yes, may God accept my death and my blood for the triumph of Holy Church and for the conversion of England!" He then mentioned that the Garibaldians had taken his rosary. Mrs. Stone gave him hers; Father Daniel heard his confession and gave him the last rites. He began to weaken, and a few hours later declared, "My Jesus! My dear Jesus! I offer to you my life for the Roman Church, the Pope, and my parents...Jesus, Mary, Joseph!...Tell my parents, my brothers, and my sisters that I love them." Father Daniel sent a message to George Collingridge, who was on guard duty in the compound, to come quickly, but Alfred died in the priest's arms before his brother arrived.

Charette, in the meantime, had decided to pursue Menotti, but word arrived from General Kanzler that Charette's men were

required in Rome, where there was fear of attack. On the morning of
October 19, the little army made a forced march to Monte Rotondo
and from there took a train back to the eternal city.

Skirmishes were continuing elsewhere, however. At Farnese,
on the Tuscan frontier, a band of Garibaldians were attacked by a
company of Zouaves. Before heading into the fray, the detachment's
second-in-command, Lieutenant Emmanuel Dufournel, said to his
men, "My friends, let us go to our deaths, in the name of the Father,
and of the Son, and of the Holy Ghost." The Zouaves prevailed but
Dufournel was mortally wounded.

Minor as these skirmishes and little battles might seem, they had
an enormous effect on the government in Florence. Two things were
apparent: first, that there would be no popular uprising; second, that
neither in leadership nor in personnel were the Garibaldians on their
own any match for the pontifical forces, outnumbered though the
latter were. One thing was lacking: Garibaldi himself.

Rattazzi and his colleagues resolved—regardless of whatever
temporary annoyance might afflict Napoleon III—to put Garibaldi
in command. What escaped the prime minister's attention was that
the mercurial emperor was himself under pressure by the Catholics
of France. Newspapers, deputies in parliament, leading laity and
clergy—all demanded that the emperor, dependent upon them
politically, act to defend the Papal States. None believed Rattazzi's
assurances, and so at last, on October 18, Napoleon ordered the troops
assembled at Toulon to embark for the voyage to Civitavecchia. But
once in the open sea, they were recalled. This happened twice until
events in Rome forced his hand.

Garibaldi, in the meantime, had been allowed to escape his
island. He arrived in Florence on October 21. The following day the
Roman insurrection was supposed to begin. The old rebel set off for

1. Henri de Cathelineau, descendant of the hero of the Vendee, Jacques Cathelineau. He led volunteers to Rome in 1860, and in the Franco-Prussian War. (Collection JD, www.military-photos.com)

2. The Charette Brothers: *(from l. to r.)* Alain, a Second Lieutenant in the Zouaves; Ferdinand, a private; Athanase, rose to command them in France and acted as head until his death in 1911; and Louis, a Papal Dragoon. (Collection JD, www.military-photos.com)

3. Colonel Joseph Allet, Swiss-born volunteer who joined the Papal Army in 1832 and served at Castelfidardo; he became commander of the Zouaves in 1861 and served at Mentana; and, unable to join the French Army by Swiss law, he tearfully parted from his men in 1870. (Collection JD, www. military-photos.com)

4. Louis de Becdelievre: served at Castelfidardo, and was named commander of the Zouaves after the battle. Quit in 1861 after conflicts with de Merode. (Collection JD, www.military-photos.com)

5. Colonel Joseph Allet (Collection JD, www.military-photos.com)

Camp de Rocca di Papa (août 1868)

Officiers de Zouaves

6. Zouave officers at their field camp, Rocca di Papa, August of 1868 (Collection JD, www.military-photos.com)

7. Captain de Veaux, Captain of the Zouaves. He distinguished himself at Mentana where he was killed. (Collection JD, www.military-photos.com)

8. Hypolyte de Moncuit de Boiscuille: first corporal of the Franco-Belgian Sharpshooters; Captain at Castelfidaro, where he lost an arm; commanded a company at Mentana; commanded the second battalion of Volontaires de l'Ouest at Loigny, where he was killed. (Collection JD, www.military-photos.com)

9. The charge of the Zouaves at Mentana (Zouaven Museum)

10. The last stand of Pieter de Jong at Monte Libretto (Zouaven Museum)

Terni to assume command. Unfortunately for his cause, there had been no sign of popular unrest during the preceding weeks.

In the meantime, Garibaldians had been infiltrating the Eternal City. On the morning of October 22, they struck. At 7 P.M., a bomb went off in the Piazza di Colonna, a detachment of about five hundred rebels attacked the Porta S. Paolo, and about a dozen other places—including the Capitol—were menaced. In each case, however, the rebels were swiftly dispersed by the Zouaves and other papal forces. Then, a huge explosion illuminated the night sky.

A number of Garibaldians had dug a tunnel under the Zouave barracks at the Palazzo Serristori, not far from St. Peter's, at what is today the corner of via della Concilizione and via dei Cavalieri del S. Sepolcro. While the blast destroyed a wing of the building and 37 Zouaves were killed—including a Spanish drummer boy who had hiked all the way from his country to Rome, been refused admission to the regiment by General Kanzler, and at last been accepted as a musician when he protested the length of his journey—most of the building and the unit were unhurt. As a result, when the Garibaldians responsible attacked the building, they were met by a volley from the unexpectedly alive (and very angry) Zouaves. The noise was intended to serve as a signal to the population for general all-out revolt, but the opposite occurred. Romans began to converge on the barracks to dig out the survivors and the dead.

The following day, however, another band of revolutionaries led by the brothers Cairoli occupied the Villa Glori. They were swiftly overcome by the papal forces. Although a small occurrence in the course of events, this skirmish has become a legendary battle in the mythology of the Italian revolution. So too has the affair in Trastevere at noon the following day, when a group of revolutionaries holed up in their leader's house. This time it was given to the

Zouaves to smoke out the enemy. They stormed the house and took its occupants prisoner after a fierce, though short, battle. Here as in all their other combats on these two days, the Zouaves showed a mercy toward their captives that might not be expected, given the explosion at their barracks.

By end of the month, therefore, it was obvious that mere rebellion would not unseat Pius IX; Garibaldi would need to resort to more conventional warfare. The French Catholics and the Empress Eugenie finally prevailed upon Napoleon III to send his troops. At long last, the French forces set off from Toulon. Victor Emmanuel issued a proclamation denouncing the events of the past few days and claiming that his government had not been involved.

Garibaldi was undaunted, however. Had the revolt in Rome gone as expected, he would have attacked the gate of the city on October 23. As it was, he decided to gamble on a single major assault. He concentrated his forces—about ten thousand all told—for an attack on Monte Rotondo, which was the only city other than Civitavecchia where Kanzler had left a garrison when he gathered his forces in Rome three days earlier.

In 1867, Monte Rotondo was a small mountaintop town dominated by a fortified palace, surrounded by a medieval wall with three gates and no bastions, and further encircled by a more recent suburb. The palace was just inside the Porta Ducale. Captain Costes of the Legion of Antibes was in command, with two companies of his own unit, a company of carabinieri, a handful of gendarmes and dragoons, and an artillery section with one howitzer and a rifled gun—about 323 men in all. Kanzler had ordered him to resist if attacked by Garibaldians. If the Royal Italian army appeared, he was to fall back on Rome.

On Saturday, October 26, six thousand of Garibaldi's best began their attack on Monte Rotondo. They burned down one of the gates and surged into the town. Costes's men holed up in the palace, and held out for just over a full day, fighting literally for every foot of space. Before noon on the following day, when they had been pushed up to the third floor and the building set aflame, Costes realized that the time had come to surrender. After spiking his guns and ordering most of the rifles broken, he did so. Garibaldi had lost five hundred men and two crucial days in which Kanzler finished his preparations for the defense of Rome.

Garibaldi and his men set out for the Eternal City on the October 28. Although they soon reached the outskirts and skirmished with papal troops, they were too late. On October 29, the French army arrived at Civitavecchia, and a day later they reached Rome. Garibaldi pulled back and changed his strategy. He withdrew his troops to Monte Rotondo, hoping that the French would follow and be drawn into conflict with the Royal Army. This might well bring about a war that Napoleon III would not want to pursue. But here, too the great revolutionary miscalculated.

On November 2, Kanzler convinced the French general that destroying Garibaldi's force before either his other troops or the Royal Army linked up with him, far from risking war with Italy, would remove any danger. With Garibaldi out of the way, the Italian government would either have to withdraw from its new conquests or be shown before the eyes of the world to be utterly dishonest.

All over Europe and Latin America, November 3 is the feast of Saint Hubert, the patron saint of hunters. In 1867 as today, Protestant and Catholic churches in regions given over to the chase featured members of the hunting fraternity accompanying divine worship with hunting horns, with the blessing of the hounds immediately afterward. But this November 3, General Kanzler resolved to mount a greater hunt. He gave the order to pursue the Garibaldians and ordered the newly arrived French troops as well as the Papal Zouaves, the Legion of Antibes, the Swiss carabinieri, and the papal dragoons into the field.

It was a dark and gloomy morning, pouring rain, when this little army of some five thousand men filed out of the Porta Pia in a colorful parade, Pius IX's Swiss General Rafael de Courten's papal troops leading and the French contingent bringing up the rear. At the head were the Papal Zouaves with gray and red-trimmed uniforms. The Swiss carabinieri wore their dark blue coatees, yellow-trimmed kepis, and light blue trousers. The Legion of Antibes wore the clothing of the French line, blue coats and red pants. Mounted on their horses, the pontifical dragoons wore their combed Italian helmet, with green coatees faced with red. Behind them all were the blue-and-red-clad French. The rain let up and the sun shone as the army made its way along the Via Nomentana. After a brief halt for food and rest, the soldiers of the Pope were in high spirits; they would meet the invaders at the town of Mentana.

Famous since classical times as a suburban retreat some twenty kilometers away from Rome, Mentana had known its share of history, thanks to its position on one of the major routes to the capital city. The battle that engulfed the town on November 3, 1867, would fix Mentana forever in the Italian imagination.

The area around Mentana is rather hilly, with the town built around the castle at the top of a steep elevation. This promontory is dotted with bushes, rather than high trees. In addition to this stronghold, a wall surrounded Mentana itself. Although delayed by the need to issue shoes to his men, Garibaldi occupied the town with between four and ten thousand troops. The continuing flow of desertions made a proper count difficult. Yet there is no disagreement about their organization: thirteen battalions, a hundred-man squadron of mounted guides, and a single battery of four guns made up the complement of Redshirts. Those who had uniforms were clad in red kepis (with light blue bands) and red short jackets (hence the name "Redshirts"), with gray or light blue trousers, and white leggings. But this was an idealized uniform—many wore brimmed hats in place of the kepi, or even civilian dress. They ranged wildly in experience—some were veterans of Garibaldi's earlier adventures while others were green recruits, still others were Piedmontese soldiers lent secretly by Victor Emmanuel to stiffen the newcomers. Whatever discrepancies there may be in records of their numbers, the Redshirts had the advantage in terms of the terrain.

General Kanzler's forces pursued them hotly, however. The 3,000-man papal contingent, commanded by General Rafael de Courten was in the vanguard, lugging their percussion rifles. The French column of roughly 2,000, commanded by General Baron de Polhés brought up the rear. Although the French were under strength, their line battalions were equipped with the new rapid-repeating *chassepot* rifle.

Kanzler's troops arrived at the approaches to Mentana in the early afternoon of November 3. Just a few miles from the village, he sent three companies of the Zouaves around the Redshirts' right flank, up the valley of the Tiber to cut the road between Mentana and Monte Rotondo. With the dragoons at the front, the remaining papal soldiers marched on the Via Nomentana, with the French following a mile or so behind.

Almost immediately, the main column saw action. They punched through Garibaldi's three forward battalions, positioned as they were on both sides of the road, in the woods, on the heights of Monte Guarneri, and in dug-in positions within the Santucci Vineyard.

Shortly after noon, the papal scouts encountered the first Garibaldian outposts. Four companies of Zouaves, led by Captains d'Albiousse, Thomalé, le Gonidec, and Alain de Charette (brother of the colonel), moved in light skirmishing order, and quickly cleared the Redshirts out of the woods. Then Colonel de Charette himself arrived. He led the Zouaves in a furious bayonet charge, driving the Garibaldians from their positions. At last they reached the walled and fortified Santucci Vineyard. The 1st and 4th companies of the Legion of Antibes along with the carabinieri soon arrived to act as reserves.

The Santucci vineyard, with its wall and strongly built house, was a formidable obstacle. The Redshirts laid down a furious wall of fire, and the Zouave assault faltered. The balls flew like flies and opened holes in the papal ranks. But Charette rode up and shouted, "Advance, Zouaves, or I will be killed without you!" Then, carrying on the point of his sword the red bonnet of a Garibaldian officer whom he had just killed, he charged the enemy.

The Zouaves stormed the compound and fought a quick, furious skirmish with the Redshirts. Colonel de Charette's horse was shot from under him, while Captain de Veaux died from a bullet that drove into his heart the cross of valor he had won at Castelfidardo. The surviving foes fled, leaving house and vineyard to the Zouaves.

The next Redshirt-held obstacle on the road was an unused monastic building called Il Conventino. Kanzler placed six of his guns there to cover his men from the enemy artillery fire coming from the castle. He then sent a company of Zouaves to flush the Redshirts out of Il Conventino, with five companies of Swiss carabinieri in support. But under the command of the impetuous Colonel de Charette, the Zouaves refused to wait for any assistance and charged the enemy positions pell-mell.

By early afternoon., the Redshirts were driven from Il Conventino and their neighboring positions. The papal artillery was then set up on Monte Guarneri. But this relatively easy advance was not to last. Most of Garibaldi's troops had dug in around the walled village and the castle on the hilltop. Their artillery battery was behind the town, up on Monte San Lorenzo. In a pitched set of attacks and counterattacks on the steep slopes leading up to Mentana itself, the Redshirts halted the papal advance. They then launched an enveloping counterattack on both flanks of Courten's men.

One of Garibaldi's two flanking columns almost succeeded in capturing two companies of the Swiss carabinieri. But these fell back in good order, firing as they did so; unexpectedly more of the Swiss arrived. The tide of attack then turned as the carabinieri became the pursuers, charged the Redshirts, and, breaking their line, chased them up the road toward Monte Rotondo. The second column of Redshirts fared no better. Their intended target, the Légion of Antibes, likewise turned the tide of action and became the attackers. The Garibaldians were forced to flee before them into Mentana itself.

Unable to communicate with Garibaldi, for reasons that will shortly become clear, his commanders resolved to throw everything they had—reserves and all—into a frontal attack. Up to this point, the vastly outnumbered papal forces had done all of the fighting, to the annoyance of the French. But seeing fresh Redshirts pouring out of Mentana, Kanzler asked Baron de Polhés to deploy his men.

Meanwhile, Colonel Allet's Zouaves had been steadily advancing on the road to Monte Rotondo. Before they could reach it, however, Garibaldi and his staff fled, leaving his hapless troops to continue the struggle. Allet was a rock. All through the fray, the colonel had been quietly smoking a cigar. He then saw a Garibaldian out of the corner of his eye. Without showing any emotion, Allet watched as the Redshirt took aim at him. The Garibaldian fired and the colonel was unwounded. Turning to the Zouaves, Allet called out while laughing: "Oh! How stupid he is! He aimed, he fired, and he didn't kill me! Give me your rifle," he said to a nearby Zouave. The colonel shouldered the rifle, aimed it at the Garibaldian, fired, and the Redshirt fell dead. When the Zouaves did cut the road, the Redshirts' doom was sealed, though they were not as yet aware of it.

Just as the Zouaves were cutting off the Redshirts' line of retreat, the French had pushed through around the Redshirts' left flank. Their position in Mentana collapsed. The *chassepot* rifle, not as yet used on any battlefield, was now employed by those of the French troops who had been issued them (according to Colonel Du Picq's account, not all of Napoleon's soldiers had them). The sound of these new rifles, so different from anything ever heard before, caught the attention of both sides. In a little while, the Garibaldians all over the battlefield broke and ran.

Those of the enemy fortunate to have already fled beyond the range of the Zouaves continued their flight to Monte Rotondo. Most of the remainder withdrew into the castle, although a few secreted themselves in various houses in the town. As night fell, the Redshirts kept up an intermittent fire. One of these bullets claimed the life of young Julian Watts-Russell. His death was the subject of poems and laudatory essays alike when the news got back to England. At the same time, the Zouave bugler, the Frenchman Lolande, finally succumbed to the wound he had received in the first skirmish. All through the advance, heedless of his pain, he continued to sound the advance until the day was won.

Rather than contend with the famous Garibaldian guerrilla tactics after dark, Kanzler decided to delay the seizure of Mentana until the morning, although he kept the town closely surrounded.

He ordered his troops to sleep with their weapons and kept the area well lit with bonfires. As the officers of the Zouaves conferred about the day's events around a campfire, Charette declared: "It is as well that I had not to order the Zouaves to retire today; for if I had, they would not have obeyed me." At the break of dawn, the papal army was awakened. To reward the French for their aid the previous day, they were given the honor of marching into Mentana first. As they did so, the Redshirts remaining in the town and the castle—several hundred of a force of ten thousand—surrendered. Kanzler permitted them to return to the frontier unmolested.

Garibaldi himself had not been content with flight to Monte Rotondo; he had gone farther back to Corese. Accompanying him were five thousand survivors, at least half of his entire force. The other two Redshirt columns who had previously pulled back from Rome withdrew as well.

The Zouaves, meanwhile, guarded the recaptured city and saw to the wounded on both sides. One of the more prominent nurses was Katherine Stone, who had accompanied the Zouaves on the march from Rome. During the battle, she had ministered to the wounded, her dress riddled with bullet holes. All of the shots miraculously missed her although one had shattered the water pitcher she carried. None of this stopped her, and she gamely got another pitcher and went back to work. The following day, she continued work among the wounded of both sides. In token of her bravery, she was the only woman to whom Pius IX gave the Cross of Mentana. This medal—a Maltese cross with the papal arms in the center, and the Cross of Constantine with the words, *Hanc Victoriam* on the back—was given out to the bravest of the papal and French troops. For the rest of her life, Mrs. Stone, who swiftly returned to her customary role of society hostess, accounted it her proudest possession.

The Redshirts had fought and defeated at various times the French, the Austrians, and the entire Neapolitan army. How could they possibly have succumbed to a few mercenaries? The myth was born and promoted that it was the French and their newfangled rifles that beat Garibaldi's men. This is the line immortalized to this day at the Mentana monument. But as we have seen, while the French and their new rifles did play a crucial role, they were not the reason for the victory. It was the audacity of the Zouaves and their brethren of the Swiss carabinieri that broke the back of the Redshirts at Mentana.

CHAPTER VI

To the Porta Pia!

ROME! what a scroll of History thine has been
In the first days thy sword republican
Ruled the whole world for many an age's span:
Then of thy peoples thou wert crownèd Queen,
Till in thy streets the bearded Goth was seen;
And now upon thy walls the breezes fan
(Ah, city crowned by God, discrowned by man!)
The hated flag of red and white and green.
When was thy glory! when in search for power
Thine eagles flew to greet the double sun,
And all the nations trembled at thy rod?
Nay, but thy glory tarried for this hour,
When pilgrims kneel before the Holy One,
The prisoned shepherd of the Church of God.

—*Oscar Wilde, "Urbs Sacra Æterna"*

Three days after the memorable battle, the victorious army returned to Rome to the cheers of the populace. Their prisoners were lodged in Castel Sant'Angelo, from which they were released in groups to return to their homes. Pius IX went to visit the two hundred remaining prisoners who had been assembled in a large hall in the old fortress. Their chief foe walked among them and, smiling, declared, "You see before you the man whom your general calls the Vampire of Italy. It is against me you have taken up arms; and who am I?—a poor old man." He asked them what they needed and promised warm clothing, shoes, money, and free passage home. At this, the prisoners surged around him, cheering his name and kissing his hands. As the Pope left, he said, "I merely ask of you as Catholics to think of me in a short fervent prayer to your God."

Although papal sovereignty had survived the most recent attack, it was obvious that there would be more. If the defeat of Castelfidardo had inspired many foreigners to join the pontifical ranks, the victory at Mentana brought even more recruits. Enlistees continued to arrive from Europe and the British Isles, but the summons was heard elsewhere as well.

In the United States, many Catholic voices urged sending a group of volunteers to aid the Pope. This desire on the part of the rank and file American Catholics came with certain complications.

On the one hand, Pius IX had recognized the Confederacy during the war—the only foreign ruler to do so. The Southern bishops had loyally backed the South; the Northern bishops, on the other hand, had stridently supported the Union cause; as we saw, President Lincoln returned the California missions to the Church.

Anti-Catholicism was strong in 1860s America, and the memory of the previous decade's Know-Nothing riots, in which convents were burned and immigrant Catholics were hanged from lampposts was still fresh in the minds of America's bishops. Tarred by the Confederate brush and with a largely foreign-born flock, the prelates feared charges of dual loyalty. Nothing would, in the bishops' minds, fan that particular set of flames more hotly than recruiting American Catholic veterans for service under Pius IX. Although the bishops might wish to save the remnants of the Pope's temporal sovereignty, the United States government was very much in favor of its destruction. Moreover, however many of the Pope's veterans had fought for the Union, their opponents had manned an entire regiment in the Northern service. Made up of veterans who had fought with Garibaldi or who at least sympathized with his views, the 39th New York Volunteers, the Garibaldi Guard, had been raised in New York City, numbering no fewer than ten companies recruited from various European nationalities. Then, as now, the Catholic bishops could not afford a confrontation with the civil power.

Worse yet, the nation was still bruised by Lincoln's murder. Surratt's having found refuge among the Zouaves was used by anti-Catholics as proof of the Pope's complicity in Lincoln's murder, as was the Pontiff's regard for Jefferson Davis. In hysterical Protestant novels, "Papal Zouave" assumed for a while the sinister tone so long reserved for "Jesuit." Completely forgotten, of course, were the facts that a fellow Zouave had turned Surratt in and that the papal government had moved so swiftly to deport him.

Upsetting the applecart, as was his custom, was Catholic journalist James McMaster, editor of the *Freeman's Journal* of New York. A staunch states' rights Democrat before the war, he consistently attacked President Lincoln as an enemy of civil liberties and free speech. As a result, he was arrested and his newspaper suppressed in 1861. Upon his release in April of the following year, he was allowed to resume publishing on the condition that he would not criticize the government ever again.

Despite the corrective to his thinking provided by eleven months at Fort Lafayette, McMaster was still not one to take the easy path. The plight of Pius IX and the warning provided by the events at Mentana convinced him that something must be done. In January of 1868, he began editorializing in favor of raising an American contingent for the Papal Zouaves in response to a letter from Private Charles Carroll Tevis, a member of the Zouaves. The West Point graduate, having quit the American army in 1850, had served the French in the Crimea, rejoined the Union Army for the Civil War, and commanded a contingent of Fenian raiders attacking Canada in 1866. More letters from Tevis were published over the following months, and money and offers to serve began to pour into the office of the *Freeman's Journal*, forcing McMaster to remind his readers that while he supported the idea, he could only send the money and offers on to Rome. But the idea was gaining ground.

Meanwhile, in Mexico, the defeat of the Confederacy meant that the United States were now in a position to aid their client, Benito Juarez. Napoleon III withdrew his troops from the country in response to American pressure, leaving Maximilian to his fate. Maximilian's empress, Carlotta, who had become increasingly unstable, collapsed during an audience with Pius IX. When the imperial couple discovered that they could not have children, they adopted Prince Salvador Iturbide, grandson of the first emperor of Mexico, as their heir. When his adoptive father was executed, the prince rushed to Rome, enlisting in the pontifical dragoons. Given his status, General Kanzler offered to give him an officer's commission, but Iturbide refused and insisted on entering as a private.

In Canada, the news of Mentana rocked the country—particularly the province of Quebec. In every French-Canadian parish (and many English-speaking ones), a recruiting drive was launched in the manner of a new crusade. After establishing a central committee in Montreal, its members consulted Rome. Although the Canadians wanted to establish a separate unit of their own, the Ministry at Arms warned them that unless 600 or more recruits came, Canada's contingent would be integrated into existing units. The committee's resources were so overwhelmed that it had to declare recruiting closed.

Having survived as a culture for over a century after the English Conquest, French Canada was undergoing an interior change—its people were beginning to see themselves as a nation and as a bastion of French and Catholic culture in a continent overwhelmed by Anglo-Saxon Protestantism. One of the leading lights of this current was Mgr. Ignace Bourget, the fiery bishop of Montreal. Foremost among the cheerleaders for the new crusade, on February 18, 1868, he hosted a ceremony for the new recruits at Montreal's Notre Dame cathedral. A milestone in the history of the French Canadians, it featured the presentation of a regimental banner to the first party of 137 recruits to depart for Italy. About 15,000 people turned out for the event, which was attended by five bishops as well as political, military, and social leaders in the province. The following day the contingent set off for New York, boarded a ship for France on February 24, and arrived at Rome on March 10. The Canadians marched to the Piazza San Pietro, music playing and colors flying, to pass in review before the Pope, and then entered the basilica to pray before the tomb of the apostle.

Six more detachments set off for the Eternal City between February of 1868 and September of 1870, for a total of 507 men. Among these men were several who would play key roles in the formation of French Canada's identity—such as Ephrem Brisebois, later to find fame as an officer of the Canadian Mounted Police, Ernest Lavigne, the noted musician, and Joseph Couture, who would pioneer Canada's quarantine system. All of this activity did not go unnoticed in the United States.

Spurred by the letters and money that McMaster forwarded and by the large numbers of French Canadians who were coming to Rome, in May of 1868 Pius IX wrote to the bishops of the United States authorizing them to raise a thousand men for the papal army. To say that this authorization pleased neither the bishops nor their government is a great understatement. Nevertheless, the Pope, who throughout his reign would always have a deep fascination with the United States, planned a separate American battalion and commissioned Tevis as commanding general of the proposed unit. Tevis was then dispatched to America to recruit men and raise funds.

He had gone no farther than Paris before the news came that four American prelates were attacking his character and record in print. In the face of this opposition, he resigned his commission. Declaring to the papal war minister that he could not understand the bishops' views, he supposed that their actions were "prompted by a determination to defeat at any cost a movement in which they were unwilling to cooperate themselves, but which might have succeeded without their assistance." All further attempts to recruit Americans ended in the face of this opposition—especially as their government warned the American bishops that Congress had outlawed such recruiting. Leaving the papal service, Tevis went on to pursue a wild and varied career that would see him at various times as an officer in the Turkish, Egyptian, and Bulgarian armies, and as a British spy. But the absence of the Americans would soon be felt.

The following month, another illustrious European joined the ranks. Don Alfonso de Bourbon, brother of the Carlist claimant to the Spanish throne and best friend of Prince Salvador Iturbide, arrived in Rome. As his Mexican friend had done, Don Alfonso refused any special treatment and was enrolled in the Zouaves as a private. A number of his brother's partisans followed his example.

England, too, contributed high-born recruits: the son of Lord Herries, Walter Constable Maxwell, and his nephews, William and Oswald Vavasour. The fabulously wealthy marquis of Bute, a convert to Catholicism, became a steady drumbeater for the cause. The German aristocracy was present too. By 1868, the high nobility in Westphalia had 45 Zouaves in Rome, and every year sent 500 francs to the papal treasury for each of them.

This influx of recruits would be necessary for security, because on December 8, 1869, the First Ecumenical Council of the Vatican (Vatican I) opened. Prelates and laity from all over the world gathered in Rome for the event, and the Zouaves of various nationalities spent a good deal of time, when not on duty, with their respective bishops. For the Garibaldians and their allies across Europe, it was an infuriating display of Pius's confidence in the future, particularly because all knew that the council would define the doctrine of papal infallibility—to which the liberal governments of Europe were particularly opposed.

So offended by this doctrine were the followers of Garibaldi that they decided to attempt another revolution in the spring of 1870. But this time, they did not have the Italian government behind them. In late May, 50 revolutionaries eluded the Italian troops guarding the border and crossed into papal territory near Montalto. They fled back over the border when a company of Zouaves and a troop of pontifical dragoons approached, and were swiftly arrested by Italian troops. The fact was that so long as Napoleon III remained committed to the defense of Rome, Italy would make no move. It also showed how little Garibaldi and his men could accomplish without the aid of the Italian government.

The summer of 1870 brought ominous changes. France and Prussia began to quarrel over the succession to the Spanish throne; if the two powers went to war, the temptation for the Italian government to seize Rome outright—rather than bothering with Garibaldian proxies—would be irresistible. Nevertheless, the revolutionary cells told their members to be ready for action, a fact that the pontifical police were soon aware of. In response, General Kanzler canceled all but emergency leaves and redoubled training.

On July 18, Vatican I solemnly defined the doctrine of papal infallibility. The following day, France declared war on Prussia. The Italian government was torn in three directions: the king wished to go to the aid of France in repayment of all that the nation owed Napoleon III; a number of cabinet ministers favored Prussia because of her help with Venetia; the Garibaldians called for neutrality and a march on Rome. While the government dithered, Napoleon announced that he was withdrawing the 4,000 French troops from Rome and returning to the rules of the September Convention agreed to between France and Italy in 1864, and under which the French had previously withdrawn—only to rush back in time for Mentana.

Catholics in France and elsewhere were outraged even though the French garrison was too small to mean much for the war, and the government that Napoleon was trusting to keep the peace had shown its untrustworthiness many times since 1859. Yet the Zouaves—especially the French ones—were oddly relieved. The followers of Henry V in their ranks had always been uneasy at being allied with the man they considered a usurper. They believed that Napoleon had at last shown his true colors. General Kanzler was with the French ambassador on July 26 when the diplomat received the telegram from his government notifying him of the troop withdrawal. Upon reading the note, Kanzler exclaimed, "we shall be crushed, but we shall do our duty!"

While the French troops were being evacuated from Civitavecchia, Napoleon was meeting defeat at Wissembourg and Metz. By early August, when the last of the French left Italy, Napoleon had lost more men fighting the Prussians than were coming back from Italy.

As all this excitement was taking place, the government in Florence was waiting to see on whose side victory would fall. By mid-August, although General Bazaine and the greater part of the French army were besieged at Metz, a French recovery was not impossible. The Italians must wait until all fear of a replay of Mentana was out of the question. Fortunately for Victor Emmanuel's government, they would not have long to wait. In the meantime, although the government maintained a scrupulous observance of the status quo, once again the Garibaldians were allowed to plan, agitate, and recruit openly. At the same time Garibaldi himself was returned to his island, ten divisions of the royal army were massed on the border and the navy readied for action. Successive Sardinian and Italian governments had had a useful weapon in Garibaldi, but he and, more particularly, his revolutionary followers were also potentially a great danger to the Italian state. If Rome were in fact to be seized by the revolutionaries, could a radical Italian republic be far off? Rome must fall to the regular army if the government of Victor Emmanuel was to survive.

Despite the threatening atmosphere, Rome and the other papal domains were quiet. Garibaldi had long complained that the Pope's subjects were, in the main, too fond of their sovereign. It was neither the first nor the last time in history that so-called friends of the people planned to liberate that people, regardless of whether or not liberation was wanted. While there were occasionally a few arrests of Garibaldi's agents, even with 60,000 troops on the papal frontier, Pius's popularity was manifest. The Pontiff still appeared frequently in public and was cheered whenever he did so. Morale was high in the papal camp and never more so than among the Zouaves.

Nevertheless, as the French military situation deteriorated, the government in Florence grew bolder. Near the end of August, the Italian cabinet issued a circular letter to all the governments of Europe, in which it declared that the time had come to end the Roman Question. On the one hand, the document declared that it was time to fulfill the "legitimate aspirations" of the Italian people; on the other, that the "the independence, the freedom, and the spiritual authority of the Pope," had to be safeguarded. The greatest threat to Italy, in the cabinet's opinion, was neither its own perfidy nor the revolutionaries' violence, but—the Pontifical Zouaves! As one Zouave wrote of this remarkable message some years later, "the wolf told the story of the crimes of the lamb!" The circular ended with a list of guarantees to the Pope: in essence that he would retain control of the Eternal City and be independent in his dealings, and that neither he nor the current Papal State would be held to the restrictions on religious institutions and property in the Law of 1866, which we saw in chapter 4. Pope Pius's and his secretary of state Antonelli's response to this document, as expected, was scathing, but it was apparent that invasion was not far off.

On September 6, Pius IX held a council of cardinals to discuss strategies. Three possible avenues were looked at. The Pope might accept the Italian guarantees, try to carry on the government of the Church as well as he could, and trust to the government's honesty; he might leave Rome for Malta, Trieste, or Innsbruck, and carry on in exile; or, he might stay, make an armed protest, withdraw to the Vatican, refuse to recognize the new situation, and hope for better times. The last course was decided upon. Pius would refuse to surrender the city, would make only so much of an armed demonstration as was necessary to show the world that the Italians were guilty of aggression, and would stay in the city so long as he physically could.

Victor Emmanuel, by this stage bothered by his conscience, wrote a long letter to Pius asking him to accept the occupation peacefully. The king mentioned his conscience repeatedly in the note, but the letter was read by a Pontiff who had spent most of his reign suffering from the king's policies. Pius sent a curt refusal in reply.

Without a declaration of war, on September 11 the Italian army invaded the Papal State. Altogether, 75,000 men in five divisions under General Cadorna were earmarked for this campaign. The 2nd Division, commanded by General Bixio, was centered on Orvieto. Its mission was to march through the province of Viterbo to Civitavecchia, and together with the navy, capture the city. That goal secured, they would march on to help the rest of the army with Rome. The 4th Corps, under Cadorna himself, stretched along the Umbrian frontier, comprised three divisions whose mission was to march on Rome. Lastly, on the old Neapolitan frontier, Angioletti commanded the 9th Division: his mission was to occupy the provinces of Velletri and Frosinone en route to linking up with the others at the Eternal City.

To oppose these forces, General Kanzler had about twelve thousand men under his command. A third of these were foreign; the other two thirds were native Italian, despite the fact that there was no conscription. As in 1867, Kanzler ordered his outlying garrisons to resist only if they were assaulted by Garibaldians; save for the troops at Civitavecchia, the pontifical forces were to withdraw if the attack was mounted by royal troops. The strategy was to concentrate the papal army in Rome for a last armed demonstration—following Pius's orders, Kanzler intended a show of resistance rather than a last stand.

At five o'clock on the afternoon of September 11, Bixio's 12th Division advanced on Bagnorea. Ferrero seized the bridge of Orte, and Angioletti made for Ceprano in the south. In the face of the Bixio's onslaught, the little bands of Zouaves and gendarmes at Acquapendente, San Lorenzo, and La Capraccta retreated, but the twenty Zouaves at Bagnorea were not aware of Bixio's movements and were taken prisoner. Bixio then entered Montefiascone, finding that its garrison of two Zouave companies had already decamped to join Charette at Viterbo. When the Italians arrived there, they found only twelve people awaiting them; the rest of the townspeople stayed in their houses.

Bixio spent the night at Montefiascone from which he could menace Viterbo, already endangered by Ferrero's advance from Orte. But in the morning, rather than attack the provincial capital, Bixio's division proceeded along the south shore of Lake Bolsena and down to Monte Roman, where they blocked the road between

Viterbo and Civitavecchia. He believed that this would cut off the retreat of Charette's main body.

But Bixio reckoned without the resourcefulness of the canny Zouave. Charette held out at Viterbo until the afternoon of September 12, when Ferrero's column began to approach. Withdrawing to Vetralla, the following day he continued his retreat toward Civitavecchia. His scouts reported the presence of Bixio's men on the road. At that, Charette's men took to mountain paths, guided and given food and water by local peasants; it was, in its way, an epic march. The Zouaves arrived safely at Civitavecchia in the wee hours of the morning without once engaging the Italians, although they had passed their outposts on several occasions.

It was not until that evening that Bixio discovered that he had been outfoxed. Up until then, he kept expecting to see the Zouaves on the road and had prepared to smash them with his superior force. Realizing that his prey had escaped, Bixio went down to the sea at Porto Clemente to confer with the admiral whose ships were lying off the coast. They agreed to begin the assault on Civitavecchia the next day. Bixio moved his headquarters just outside the now-beleaguered city.

At Civitavecchia, the Spanish commander, Colonel Serra, had proclaimed a state of siege two days earlier. He had at his disposal between eight and nine hundred men, both Roman chasseurs and Zouaves. Although the landward fortifications were well built, those to the sea had no heavy guns—essential for a duel with the then-modern ironclads. But it would have been possible, with thought and cunning, to resist as had Ancona a decade before.

On September 14, an Italian ironclad appeared before the port and then sailed away for a rendezvous with Bixio. That evening, despite the hopes of Major d'Albiousse, commander of the city's

Zouaves, Charette and the Viterbo detachment, acting on General Kanzler's orders, took the train to Rome. The following morning, Italian dragoons appeared before the city and began skirmishing with Serra's mounted scouts. He ordered his men under arms and the alarm was sounded. Soon after, the Italian fleet reappeared, heading for the harbor entrance. A major port, Civitavecchia, was probably the most liberal of all the Pope's cities; the city council members were sympathetic to Victor Emmanuel, and at this point begged Serra not to resist. He reassured them, saying that resistance would be token.

By late morning, the fleet was deployed off the harbor mouth. An Italian officer arrived at one of the city gates under a flag of truce. He bore a message for Serra, in which Bixio demanded that Civitavecchia surrender within 12 hours. If this was done, the native soldiers would be incorporated into the ever-manpower-hungry royal army with their current rank, and the foreign troops would be conducted to their homes. If not, the city would be bombarded. Serra asked that the period be extended to 24 hours and sent the officer off. He returned a few hours later with the message that had Bixio refused; if Civitavecchia did not surrender within 12 hours, hostilities would commence.

In the meantime, a deputation from the city council had gone to Bixio's camp. Although the general would not see them, they were allowed to talk to one of his staff officers and assured him of their "patriotic sentiments." His response was that the bombardment of the town would be very sad, indeed, but could be prevented if they would prevail upon Serra to surrender. Returning to the city, they gathered a mob which surrounded the colonel and begged him to capitulate. He responded that he could do so only if the council of war, which he was about to attend, agreed.

Once closeted with his senior officers, Serra told them that surrender was their best option. Major d'Albiousse answered angrily that both their honor and Kanzler's orders demanded that they make at least a token resistance; to surrender without firing a shot would be a disgrace. But Serra insisted that since they would have to capitulate anyway, they might as well do so for the best terms they could get. The majority of officers agreed with the colonel; d'Albiousse refused to sign the resolution. The following day, an Italian ship sailed into the harbor and their troops marched into town. The 300 Zouaves of the garrison were taken to a fortress in Tuscany.

Angioletti crossed into papal territory on September 12. The next day the town of Anagni surrendered, followed by Valmontone and Velletri in the succeeding days. On September 17, Angioletti saw Rome from the Alban Hills. The 9th Division had linked up with Cadorna at last. As Angioletti advanced, fresh troops poured over the frontier to secure his conquests and garrison the major towns. With them came the political agents, whose goal was to find in each of these places enough allies to form "committees of government." This was a difficult task, given the views of the majority; but once the improvised committees were established, they sent "loyal addresses" to Victor Emmanuel.

Meanwhile, Cadorna and his 40,000 men of the 4th Corps were advancing. On the night of September 11, Ferrero's men crossed the bridge at Orte: the papal gendarmes fired a few shots at them and withdrew. He swiftly advanced to Viterbo, confident that Bixio would deal with Charette—a confidence that was misplaced.

Meanwhile, the 12th Division had crossed at Ponte Felice and moved on Civita Castellana. That city was, and is, dominated by the Forte Sangallo, an enormous fifteenth-century fortress. Although the last word in military architecture when it was built, it could not stand up to modern cannon and had for years been used as a prison. There was no artillery in the place, but there were 180 convicts. There was also a detachment of seventy soldiers guilty of various misdemeanors, and so unarmed; few could be trusted with weapons. Twenty-four gendarmes and Squadiglieri (militia), as well as a company of Zouaves under Captain Resimont were posted there to maintain order. When the news came of the invasion, Resimont swiftly prepared the old fortress as well as he could for the attack. His men blocked up the windows with mattresses. After going to confession, all the Zouaves received communion at Mass in the fortress chapel. At 3:30 in the morning, Resimont posted detachments to defend the approaches to the town at the Ponte Clementino and the Borghetto Road.

The vanguard of Maze de la Roche's division arrived shortly after— 3,400 men under Major-General Angelino: an infantry regiment, a bersaglieri (riflemen) battalion, two squadrons of cavalry, and an artillery battery, as well as engineers. After daybreak, Angelino sent one of his infantry battalions against the Capuchin convent that Resimont had occupied, while the riflemen were sent round via a ravine to outflank the town. A few sharpshooters whom Resimont had posted halted the Italian advance, while steady fire from the convent did the same for Angelino's infantry. But in the meantime, all of Maze de la Roche's division of ten thousand men had surrounded the town. Resimont withdrew his men into the fortress.

At nine o'clock in the morning, the Italian artillery was in place, ready to blast the fortress, and the bersaglieri had entered the town. Cadorna himself took command. The Zouaves, shouting *"Vive Pie Neuf!"* opened fire at the nearest invaders, who responded with artillery shells and rifle shot. After a half-hour of this, Cadorna ordered all his men under cover. He then brought up twelve more guns and ordered a general bombardment of Forte Sangallo. For an hour and a half this continued, while the Zouaves could do nothing, save to fire their rifles in return. Despite 240 shells landing in the fortress, only five of the garrison were slightly wounded.

A council of war was held. One of the Italian officers in the papal service said that as they could not really defend themselves, they ought to surrender. But Resimont and another Zouave officer refused; since the Zouaves were the bulk of the defenders, they prevailed. Nevertheless, as the eighteen Italian guns kept up the barrage, the ancient walls weakened, the great keep appeared to be on the verge of collapse, and the only flanking tower from which the Zouaves could fire had been wrecked.

By late morning the governor of the prison begged Resimont to think of the ruinous state of the defenses and the lives of his convicts. For their sake, Resimont agreed. The next day, the Zouaves, now prisoners of war, were sent by train to Florence. At Spoleto, where the train stopped, and again at their destination—the enemy's capital—they were cheered by papal sympathizers.

The next day, Cadorna and his army moved on to Monterosi, on the Rome-Viterbo road where they were joined by Ferrero. The following day, the whole force moved on to La Giustiniana, nine miles northwest of the Eternal City. From there, Cadorna could see the dome of St. Peter's, but he could not enter the city just yet. Bixio had just taken Civitavecchia, and Angioletti was still south of Velletri. Only when all his forces were in the neighborhood of Rome could the siege begin.

In the Eternal City itself, however, all was peaceful. There were no signs of solidarity with the invaders, and no civil unrest. Normal, indeed, except for the defensive preparations; soldiers and workmen began walling up some of the gates; engineers threw a bridge of boats across the Tiber from the Aventine to Trastevere; and artillery was mounted on some of the old walls. More and more Romans enlisted in the volunteer militia, and the entire male population of Trastevere offered to join the colors—an offer that would have been accepted, had the Pope wanted to make a last stand. But, as it was, he already had enough troops to do what he wanted. The offer was gratefully refused.

That evening, the Italian vanguard was sighted about 21 miles from the city. A company of Zouaves was sent out to the Convent of San Onofrio, out beyond the Monte Mario; their accompanying detachment of dragoons was to be sent a bit further, to La Giustiniana. Another company was dispatched to barricade the Ponte Molle on the Tiber. Cadorna would have to pass these detachments to reach Rome. Before dawn on September 14, the sixty Zouaves had reached San Onofrio, bivouacked before the church, and sent ten men into the vineyards toward La Giustiniana as an advanced post. These in turn had a sentinel a hundred yards in front of them.

It was foggy at sunrise when Cadorna's cavalry occupied La Giustiniana; the pontifical dragoons on watch withdrew toward the Ponte Molle. They sent no word to the Zouaves at San Onofrio, who expected them to retreat to their position when the Italians appeared. As a result, when Sergeant Shea, who was commanding the picket in the vineyard saw horsemen emerge from the fog, he thought they were the dragoons. He advanced to meet them with five of his men and was charged by thirty Italian horsemen. The six of their number remaining behind opened fire at the advancing foe, but realizing that they could not rescue their comrades, they retreated to San Onofrio.

The company there went into action, killed a number of the enemy, and captured one of their officers—as it happened, the son of the leader of the pro-papal opposition in the Italian parliament. Artillery appeared behind the Italian cavalry, and realizing they faced either capture or death, they marched back to Rome. Shea and his men, though surrounded, had fought on until all were too seriously wounded to continue; they were then captured. Pius released the Italian prisoner, as a gesture of gratitude to his father. The Italian cavalry returned to La Giustiniana.

By morning the sounds of battle could be heard in the city and the troops were ordered to their stations. The Roman volunteers mustered and joined the Swiss Guard at the Vatican. Later on, Charette and his men arrived from Civitavecchia, as did Azzanesi and Lauri's troops. They immediately went to their assigned locations. Although scouts reported that the foe was still far enough away, there was no doubt that Rome was in danger. Day and night soldiers, militia, and volunteer civilians worked at strengthening the city's walls. It was an impossible task. While the terrain, the Castel Sant'Angelo, and the bastioned walls of the Vatican City made defending Trastevere manageable, its fortifications, at the ripe age of two centuries, were the youngest Rome had to offer. The long wall enclosing the rest of Rome had been built by the emperors and repaired from time to time by various Popes. A section of wall that was 1,500 years old might border a stretch that was merely four hundred.

Although some of the gates, such as the Porta Pia, were modern, most of the wall was too high and often too thin to allow artillery to be mounted on it; in some places it was only three feet thick or had interior tunnels. Field artillery could easily breach these areas. In sum, a fortification intended to keep at bay fourth-century barbarians would provide little protection against a nineteenth-century army. Still, the defenders did what they could with sandbags and other material, and managed to plant 160 cannon—most of which were ancient smooth-bores—on various makeshift platforms.

Cadorna was only too aware of the strength of the defenses of Trastevere, which he earmarked for Bixio. But he wanted to attack at one of the city's weaker points. On that side, too, he would have the railway to Florence. But the nearest bridges were held by papal forces that could hold him off there at great cost. The Italian commander resolved to cross farther upriver.

Three days later, Cadorna threw a bridge over the Tiber at Castel Giubileo. The Pope went to Santa Maria in Ara Coeli about 5 P.M. This ancient building, then as now the civic church of the senate and people of Rome, houses two miraculous images— one of the Madonna attributed to St. Luke the Evangelist; and the Santo Bambino, an image of the infant Jesus much resorted to, then and now (although the original was stolen in 1994 and replaced by the current copy), by the sick of the city. Pius IX prayed before them for the welfare of the people and the city committed to him. Coming and going, he was surrounded by the acclamations of the Romans. All that night and the following day, however, Cadorna's army was crossing the Tiber. By the afternoon of Saturday, September 17, his troops were within two miles of the city. A few of his men deserted and entered the city, swearing they would not fight the Pope.

The next day was the tenth anniversary of Castelfidardo, and it was expected that Cadorna would celebrate by attacking. But he was not yet ready, even though his troops were quite visible. An Italian column got too close to the Porta Maggiore, and received some shells for its effort, while a party of Zouaves at the Porta del Popolo traded rounds with an enemy picket. But from the Janiculum Hill, papal observers watched as Angioletti's troops descended from the Alban

Hills. Cadorna fixed the morning of Tuesday, September 20 for the attack.

On September 19, Bixio arrived before Trastevere and the encirclement of Rome was complete. Three former Zouaves—the American, Charles Tracey; the Irishman, Patrick Keyes O'Clery; and the Englishman, George Kenyon—eluded the Italians and managed to make their way to the city, to the great joy of their comrades in arms. They were immediately readmitted to the service. There was skirmishing here and there: shots fired at the Porta del Popolo, when some Garibaldians made a surprise visit, for which their chief paid with his life; cannon fired at some too-close Italian regulars from the Porta San Sebastiano; and rifle shots at Tre Archi, in those days the sole breach in the wall, where the railway entered the city. In the afternoon, this sensitive spot was attacked by Italian scouts, who were quickly repelled. Scattered firing and small skirmishes occurred throughout the day.

An army of sixty thousand men, bristling with over a hundred guns of the most modern make, encircled Rome. Cadorna had chosen the section of old wall between the Porta Salaria and the Porta Pia, as well as the latter gate, for the site of the main assault; heavy siege guns were brought up for the purpose. To draw all the defenders to the ramparts and deny the papal forces the luxury of a reserve, three other minor attacks were to be made: Ferrero's division was to attack the Tre Archi; Angionelli was to attack the both Porta San Sebastiano and Porta San Giovanni. To Bixio would go the honor of attempting the walls of Trastevere and the Porta San Pancrazio. The only area not to be earmarked for assault was the Leonine Wall, behind which sheltered the Vatican Gardens.

The artillery barrage soon began over Tre Archi. Then the other batteries opened fire, and soon all the walls were under attack. Rome was filled with the clamor of shellfire and the glare of explosions. The heaviest guns were trained on the Porta Pia. At first, damage was worst at the Tre Archi, where huge chunks of wall fell down on the outwork where the papal guns were placed. By nine, the wreckage made it impossible to move the cannon, and the Zouaves simply blazed away with rifle fire. After another hour, a breach was opened in the wall, and Ferrero drew up his men in preparation for an assault.

Charette was in command at the Porta San Giovanni, where an outwork had been set up with two cannon, and three more were on the wall. Four more mountain-guns arrived, accompanied by Captain Daudier, a hero of Castelfidardo and Mentana, who took command of the artillery section. Although greatly outnumbered in cannon, so skillful was his direction of fire that five of the Italian guns were silenced, and three times the enemy gunners had to change position. After five hours the Italian guns were making little headway against either Porta San Giovanni or Porta San Sebastiano.

Bixio, on the other hand, waited an hour and a half before opening up on Trastevere. Finally, the shells began bursting around Porta San Pancrazio. This delay was perhaps inspired by the fact the conqueror of Civitavecchia did not face Zouaves or other foreign crusaders, but native Italians under Colonel Azzanesi. If Bixio thought this would make a difference in their bravery, he was sadly mistaken. The Trastevere rampart was solid, and the defenders were supported by fire from the papal batteries in the bastions of the Leonine Wall. Perhaps annoyed that he was unable to dent the defense in his assigned sector, after two hours Bixio directed his guns to shell within the city. Hospitals and convents were hit, and a few civilians killed or wounded; three shells landed near the Vatican—all to no avail.

But the main event was Cadorna's assault on the antique section of the wall between the Porta Portese and the Praetorian

Camp—pierced in two places as it is by the Porta Pia and the Porta Salaria. Colonel Allet, commanded over 1,000 Zouaves, carabinieri, line infantry and 16 guns. Facing him were Cadorna's 30,000 men and 54 cannon. The latter opened fire all along the line; but as with Daudier's guns, the skill of the papal artillerymen, seconded by the fire of Remington rifles all along the ramparts, forced the Italians to alter their positions several times. Even at 1,200 yards, the Remingtons were a threat to the enemy gunners. The bersaglieri charged with attacking the wall fell in great numbers under the withering fire of the Zouaves and their comrades.

Nevertheless, numbers told. After four hours of fighting, the earthwork in front of the Porta Pia was an utter wreck, and both of its cannon were silenced. To the left of the Porta Pia, the ancient wall was finally breaking, huge chunks falling off with each barrage. On the Pincio, two officers and several Zouaves and gunners had been killed. The Italian artillery was busy widening the breach with their fire. Cadorna readied his men for the assault, dividing them into three columns—two for the breach, the third for the Porta Pia itself. Slowly, they advanced toward their chosen targets.

Just then, a pontifical dragoon arrived with orders from General Zappi to fly the white flag, in keeping with Pope's orders that only such resistance would be mounted as to show the world that it was only through violence that Victor Emmanuel would be master of Rome—similar messengers were sent out at the same time to all the places on the walls that fighting raged.

But Major Troussures refused to accept such an order from a private and sent Lieutenant Van der Kerchove to headquarters for either written orders or verbal ones from a staff officer. In the meantime, the two companies of Zouaves kept up such a well-directed line of fire that the approaching column was stopped in its tracks. In a few minutes, Van der Kerchove returned with an order to cease fire. The Zouaves halted their fusillade, and raised a bayonet with a white handkerchief.

The two columns at the breach had not been doing well either. They had mingled ranks as they approached, and when a hundred yards from the walls laid down a heavy line of fire. But the company and a half of Zouaves at the breach broke cover, and mounting the debris of the ruined wall, commenced a killing fusillade on the Italians. Although 15 Zouaves had fallen, the enemy column began to withdraw. At this, the Zouaves shouted *"Vive Pie Neuf!"* In response, their foes rallied, shouting *"Hourra Savoia!"* and returned to the charge. Just then, a staff officer sent by Troussures from the Porta Pia arrived on the scene, bearing the white flag. The Zouaves ceased their fire, and waved the flag on the breach. This whole affair was the famous "Breach of the Porta Pia" which, like Mentana and the Villa Glori, was destined for a place in national legend—though not, perhaps, for the right reasons.

The white flag provided little protection in either place it was flown, however. In both spots the Italians rushed in firing, killing a few Zouaves who stood before them, weaponless. They tore their decorations and swords from them, and one Zouave officer was pulled off his horse. Don Alfonso de Bourbon, who had been at the Porta Pia, was able to hold on to his sword only by threatening to use it. It was much the same across the city. Despite the white flags displayed prominently over the walls, and Ferrero and Angioletti halting of their guns, Bixio's cannonade continued over Trastevere for another half hour. The Italians rushed in and rapidly occupied the city.

The Zouaves who had faced Cadorna's forces were made prisoner; their supporting troops withdrew toward the Tiber bridges, while those soldiers still manning the southern and eastern walls also retreated toward the Vatican City. Trastevere was evacuated; and all of the papal troops still at large bivouacked in the Piazza San Pietro, save the garrison of Castel Sant'Angelo. Both the Zouave prisoners and those in the Piazza San Pietro could not possibly have realized that while the story of the Papal States might have ended on September 20, 1870, that of the Papal Zouaves had not.

CHAPTER VII

Same Foe,
Different Field

God of clemency,
O God the Victor,
Save Rome and France,
In the name of the Sacred Heart!
In the name of the Sacred Heart!

—*"Cantique du Sacre Coeur"*

*a*t 9 A.M. on September 20, as the Italian cannon rained shell on the Eternal City, the diplomatic corps gathered at the Vatican. Pius IX entered the room and reminisced about the occasion 22 years before when he had presided over a similar gathering at the Quirinal. Although very sad indeed, the Pontiff showed his usual serenity under the stress. It is hard to guess what he was thinking at that moment, but doubtless he was recalling how, in his own lifetime, three Popes (including himself) had been driven out of Rome, and each time had returned. But now, come what may, he did not intend to leave.

To the diplomats he restated his case—that he had been illegitimately despoiled of his dominions by mere brute force, and that this was not entirely a political question but an attack upon Catholicism itself. Pius spoke of many matters at that conference, including the fact that the seminarians of the North American College had asked for arms to fight in his defense, a request that he refused (he had thanked them and bade them tend the wounded). After an hour or so he was informed of the breach at the Porta Pia; he first dismissed the ambassadors and then recalled them to tell of his decision to capitulate.

In a teary voice, the Pope declared, "I have just given the order to capitulate. The defense could not now be prolonged without bloodshed, and I wish to avoid that. I will not speak to you of myself. It is not for myself I weep, but for those poor children who have come to defend me as their father. You will each take care of those of your own country. There are men of all nations among them. Give a thought also, I beg of you, to the Irish, English and Canadians, who have no one here to represent their interests." After being informed by his secretary of state Antonelli that there was indeed a British representative in Rome, the Pontiff went on, "I recommend them all to you, in order that you may preserve them from the ill treatment which others of them suffered some years ago. I release my soldiers from the oath of fidelity to me, in order to leave them at liberty. As for the terms of the capitulation, you must see General Kanzler; it is with him you must come to an understanding on that matter."[1]

The ambassadors then went to see Cadorna at his headquarters. The general had already figured out what they wanted and told the ambassadors that the Zouaves and the Legion of Antibes were free to leave, and praised their valor. The Eternal City would not be occupied, and the papal army would receive the honors of war.

The night of September 20 saw the Piazza San Pietro turned into a campground, complete with fires. The mingled papal troops sat about comparing notes, sharing fears and hopes, and one and all affirming their love of Pius and the cause. The following day, just before noon, they once again gathered into ranks by their proper units. Colonel Allet called out, *"Mes Enfants! Vive Pie Neuf!"* The Pope appeared on the balcony to resounding cheers from his soldiers. Pius then prayed aloud, "May God bless my faithful children!" Then all the officers present drew their swords as tears poured down the cheeks of many an old veteran; they then knelt to present arms— when they arose, the Pope had gone in. The Legion of Antibes headed the column, followed by the Swiss carabinieri, the Zouaves, and the native troops, with the artillery bringing up the rear. Trumpets sounded the advance, and the first rank of legionnaires shouted *"Viva Pio Nono!"* a cry taken up by the whole army and the crowd seeing them off. Thus did Pius IX part from his army.

Marching out of the city by the Porta Angelica, the column marched around the walls of the Vatican, arriving at the Porta San Panacrazio, where Cadorna and his staff, with a military contingent made up mostly of Bixio's troops waited. As the pontifical soldiers marched past, the Italian bands struck up martial music and the troops presented arms. The little army marched on to the Villa Belvedere where they laid down their arms (the officers kept their swords, however). Cadorna rode back into the city to make his triumphal entry. On September 29, the Castel Sant'Angelo's garrison turned over their charge to the invaders, and from that day to this the papal domain has been restricted to Vatican City.

The papal army, having divested itself of its weaponry, was to march to the station at San Paolo and take the train to Civitavecchia. But as a large band of Romans had assembled there to bid them farewell, the new authorities—ever mindful of propaganda and already preparing for one of their customary rigged plebiscites—had the army march a further 14 miles to Ponte Galera. The soldiers waited there until dark, when they were crammed into 14 or 15 railway carriages and sent off to the port, arriving at midnight.

Upon disembarking, they were separated by nationality. The English, Irish, Canadians, Dutch, Belgians, and Swiss were herded into prisons, whose inmates—common criminals, not political prisoners—had been sent to Rome to help swell the numbers of the pro-government side in the forthcoming plebiscite. The French (and a few of the Canadians who insisted on staying with them) did not receive water from the authorities until noon the next day; had it not been for the kindness of various Italian soldiers toward their former enemies, the Zouaves and legionnaires would have had a very difficult time indeed.

But the treatment of the native papal troops was worse. Dragoons, chasseurs, infantry, Squadriglieri—all were kept aboard the railway cars they had arrived in. It was intended that they should march to the fortress at Alessandria (ironically named after Pope Alexander III, for his courage in standing up to the Holy Roman Emperor), to the north in Piedmont. Imprisonment in Victor Emmanuel's home country was deemed necessary; it was feared that placing the captives anywhere in territory conquered over the past decade might lead at best to embarrassing demonstrations, and at worst to support of a mass breakout. As they marched through Civitavecchia, the native soldiers of the Pope shouted *"Viva Pio Nono!"* whenever they passed a prison where their foreign comrades were kept. On September 30, the government began releasing them in small parties, finding to their annoyance that the Italian papal soldiers came from every part of the peninsula, not excluding Piedmont. Most embarrassing was the discovery that Prince Salvador Iturbide had been imprisoned with his brother dragoons; the intervention of the Austrian embassy— Emperor Franz Josef took a great interest in his step-nephew, the one living link with his murdered brother—secured his release. But Lauri's Squadriglieri, in violation of the articles of capitulation, were not liberated with the others. Some were held as long as two years after the war ended.

September 22 saw General Courten, Colonels Allet and Charette, the Zouave officers, and a number of the enlisted placed aboard a French frigate in the harbor. When all were safely on the ship, a captain of the Zouaves revealed that he had brought the regimental flag, wrapped around his waist in his uniform sash. It was unfurled and saluted with drawn swords. Charette himself then cut it up into hundreds of pieces that were distributed to all present; these fragments even today remain treasured heirlooms among some of the descendants of the Zouaves. What they did not realize was that the captain of the vessel was mightily impressed by their bearing and behavior. He sent word to his naval superiors in Toulon that—in view of the reverses being suffered by France in the war—the Zouaves might well be a unit worth preserving for the French army.

In the meantime, the Zouaves of other nationalities were being dealt with. The Belgians, Dutch, and Swiss were simply brought by train to the Swiss border and told by the Italian government to go home. The natives of that country dispersed to their own places, after helping their comrades to the German frontier. From there, they marched through a country at war with one that wore similar uniforms to their own; from time to time they were mistaken for escaped French prisoners. Reaching Cologne, the demobilized and exhausted Zouaves slept outside the cathedral. But crossing the Belgian frontier, they were welcomed as heroes, and money was raised to send the Dutch home in honor.

The subjects of Queen Victoria had a somewhat easier return to their homelands. At 8 P.M. on September 22, all 750 embarked on a steamer to take them to Genoa. Although they arrived late the following day, they were kept onboard until the next day. The Irish and Canadians were then transferred to prisons, and the English to the barracks of San Benigo. Interestingly, some of the Italian soldiers based there, who were denied attendance at the Mass through various stratagems of their officers, would come to the rooms of the English to pray with them. From Genoa, starting on October 1, some of the English contingent was sent by the Italian government on steamships to Liverpool.

On October 15, the first large contingent of Canadians—about 290 or so—reached Liverpool, where they were reviewed by the Marquis of Bute, Lord Denbigh, and other members of the British Catholic nobility. In Liverpool, they boarded another ship that arrived in New York harbor on November 4, with 210 Zouaves. In Montreal, a welcome committee was organized that soon made contact with like-minded people in New York; most notable of these was, of course, McMaster, who had unsuccessfully backed Tevis's scheme for an American Zouave unit. When the steamer docked at Battery Park on November 5 and disgorged the Zouaves, they were met by the members of the committee and an enormous number of well-wishers. The 69th New York Infantry, the "Fighting Irish" (a militia regiment that had distinguished itself in the Civil War), were present and formed a guard of honor to escort them to St. Peter's Church on Barclay Street, where a solemn High Mass was offered and the absent archbishop's representative preached a laudatory sermon in their honor. The Zouaves then marched to the Astor House and a banquet, and later to the station for the train to Montreal, where an even more tumultuous welcome awaited.

For the moment, the most dramatic role was reserved for the French Zouaves—both those on the frigate and those left ashore—who were at last dispatched to Toulon on September 25. They were not allowed to disembark for several days while the French government dithered over what to do with them; whatever was to happen, however, the men of the Zouaves did not want to be separated from each other in the combat they were sure faced them.

The France they had returned to was quite different from the one they had left—some as much as a decade before. Most of them were legitimists and fervent Catholics, who had been happy to leave the rule of Napoleon III and felt it a great sin for the usurping emperor to withdraw his troops. They believed that he had shown his true colors and that, with the fall of Rome, the Bonapartist agenda had at last been served.

If that was true, this accomplishment had come at an enormous cost, both to the emperor and the nation he ruled. However much he might have wished to emulate his conquering uncle, the third Napoleon had not the military skill of the first. As we have seen, war was declared by France on Prussia on July 25. Allied with Prussia were both her satellite states of the North German Confederation and the rather more independent Bavaria, Baden, and Wurttemberg, which had nevertheless learned from their defeat by Prussia in 1866. The French and their emperor were confident; had not their veterans fought in Algeria, Mexico, Italy, and in colonial wars across the globe? Did not all the world follow French fashions in uniform and dress (hence the kepi and Zouaves of the American Civil War)? But the Prussians were far more efficient, had more advanced military technology and infrastructure, and had fought well-armed and determined European armies more recently.

From the beginning, things had gone badly as the French mobilization and supply systems proved inadequate to the task. Despite an initial invasion of Prussian territory on July 31 and the seizure of Saarbrucken on August 2, the Prussians and their allies were able to swiftly mass armies all along the border. In the face of this threat, Napoleon III retreated and was badly defeated at Wissembourg in Alsace two days later. The month of August saw victory after victory for the Prussians, as they drove ever deeper into French territory. By August 16, 180,000 French—over a third of the regular army—were trapped in the fortress city of Metz. Attempting to break through to them, Napoleon was defeated at Sedan on September 2 and was captured along with 104,000 of his men.

Two days later, a group headed by Leon Gambetta declared the emperor deposed and constituted themselves as the "Government of National Defense." Since most of the army was either trapped in Metz or in Prussian hands, the new regime called home all French military units from Algeria and the rest of the empire, and asked for volunteers from whatever quarter, domestic or foreign, to try to stave off the invader. The National Assembly swore in General Trochu as president and then decamped to Tours, since nothing stood between the enemy and Paris. By the time Rome fell on September 20, Paris too was under siege. Trochu stayed in Paris to direct the defense, while Gambetta sailed out of Paris in a balloon to direct the government from Tours.

In Tours, a dizzy array of recruits of every ideology and stage of military ability rallied to the government. Garibaldi appeared, ever happy to fish in troubled waters (and hopeful of regaining Nice and Savoy for Italy), and was given command of the Army of the Vosges, to the southeast of the front. Henri de Cathelineau also reappeared. After his unit had been merged into the Zouaves, like a sort of counter-Garibaldi, he surfaced among the Bourbon partisans fighting in the old kingdom of Naples in 1862 alongside other European nobility. In France's current hour of need, he raised a corps of volunteers from the Vendée to come once more to France's aid.

With France in such straits, the Government of National Defense, reflecting the division in the nation's political and religious life (Trochu was a liberal Catholic and Orleanist; interior and war minister Gambetta and Vice President Jules Favre were republican unbelievers), sought help wherever it might be found. For those members who believed in God, the Zouaves were a Godsend; in the end, those who did not believe recognized that France could not afford to do without such men. The Zouaves were allowed to disembark in Toulon on September 29.

All were keen to aid their motherland in her hour of need. One alone could not remain with them. Colonel Allet was a Swiss national and the Swiss had not been allowed to serve in the French army since the dismissal of Charles X's Swiss Guards after the revolution of 1830. From the time of Henry IV in the seventeenth century until that year, members of the Allet clan had been in the French service and their descendant wished bitterly to follow in their tradition— both for the sake of his comrades and for France. But it could not be, and Allet tearfully took his leave and returned to his homeland. In 1860, in order not to offend Napoleon III, it had not been possible to give command of the Zouaves to Charette who had served under Allet ever since. But with his chief's departure, there was no question as to who would lead the Zouaves.

All the Zouaves wished to remain a unit, so Charette made his way to Tours to offer the service of the regiment to the government. While their chief negotiated with the authorities, the Zouaves moved on to the twin towns of Tarascon and Beaucaire. In the meantime, even the revolutionary press praised the Zouaves—a sign of how truly desperate was the hour. A mere ten days after the fall of Rome, the Zouaves were enjoying a peaceful holiday in the south of France, although many took the opportunity to visit friends and family farther afield. The respite would be brief.

At Tours, Charette struck a bargain with the government. The unit would stay together but would alter its name from *Zouaves Pontificaux* to *Volontaires de l'Ouest* (Volunteers of the West). They were also to receive new uniforms but these never did arrive; Pius's would have to suffice. Their organization was to remain intact. With this, after a week in the south, the Zouaves (for such they were still and would always be called) were ordered to Tours. Their train ride via Nimes and Avignon was quite an eye-opener, as they saw the disruption in everyday life and the poverty caused by the war. They also saw the wretched bands of volunteers mustering at various points, whom surviving regular officers would attempt to make into soldiers.

Once all had arrived at Tours, some 300 in number, steps were taken to reorganize them into a fighting unit. Charette was in command; the senior captain, Le Gonidec de Traissan, quickly organized his little battalion of 60 men into three skeleton companies. When the word came of a Prussian advance south of Paris, it was decided to send most of the privates under Le Gonidec via Orleans to Fontainebleau, to help contain the breakout. The rest of the officers and sergeants would remain behind to train new recruits at Le Mans, their new training depot. Both detachments were pleased at leaving Tours, as the comic value of running into Garibaldi and similar men had quickly worn off.

The cadre arrived at Le Mans, where a rapid influx of volunteers would increase their numbers to 1,200. The barracks were established at the Jesuit College of Notre Dame de Sainte Croix of which a few of the Zouaves were alumni. (Although a noted Jesuit institution, it was forced in 1911 by government confiscation to move; the old building became a barracks, the Caserne Mangin, and is now a military school.) Sainte Croix's rector tended to the Zouaves' medical needs himself. The training of new recruits was intensive, to be sure. Theodore Wibaux, the sergeant major, said of Charette in a letter home: "all have to be equipped and instructed; M. de Charette is hard at work in the midst of it all, shouting orders right and left, now scolding angrily, now making good-humored jokes. That man is worth his weight in gold." But sworn to yet another apparently hopeless cause, the men threw themselves ever more strongly into the practice of their religion.

This led to a custom that would be associated with the Zouaves ever after: an intense devotion to the Sacred Heart of Jesus. Used as a symbol in the Vendée, in Carlist Spain, and among other Catholic soldiers, the Sacred Heart represented for its followers the intense love of Jesus for humanity that led to His death on the Cross. Seeing a parallel to their own mission in this, the Zouaves eagerly seized on it as a model for themselves. Starting on Friday (the day dedicated to the Sacred Heart), October 14, the Jesuit Father Marin de Boylesve led them all in the consecration to the Sacred Heart, which reads in part, "Jesus, immortal king of all ages, peoples and kings, wishing to repair the disbelief that in your great generosity in the sacrament of your love and in the person of your vicar, Our Holy Father the Pope, I dedicate to your Divine Heart myself, my family and, as much as it depends on me, France, eldest daughter of the Sacred Heart, and of the Universal Church our mother." He also gave them small cloth badges of the Sacred Heart that rapidly became part of their uniform, and every night conducted a benediction of the Blessed Sacrament. All of this would give them strength for what lay ahead.

Meanwhile, the Zouaves who had been ordered to Fontainebleau were having less pleasant adventures. Upon their arrival at Orleans on October 9, Le Gonidec was informed that they were to go no farther; their original destination had already fallen to the Prussians. Unfortunately, they were at first greeted with suspicion by the local military authorities; because their departure had been so swift, they had not received their military records and their pontifical uniforms were unknown to the garrison. The commander at Orleans, General La Motte-Rouge, said that without their papers, they could not be regarded as regular soldiers; the records must come before the Zouaves could be deployed.

Returning to the hotel where his comrades were dining, Le Gonidec informed them of the problem and sat down at the table to eat. At the other end sat the officers of the 5th *Chasseurs à Pied;* among them, to the enormous surprise of the Zouaves, was a Prussian officer. At first, the two groups did not speak to each other; but then the youngest officers on either side began to talk, and soon the conversation was general. It turned out that the Prussian had been a patient in a Red Cross ambulance that was captured by irregulars. By the rules of war, such wagons were inviolate; so the officer had been able to convince the general that he and it should be returned to the invader's lines. In the meantime, he was staying at the hotel until the affair could be arranged.

As the group chatted, the Zouaves told the Prussian and the Chasseurs of their time in the Papal States. As it happened, the prisoner had had friends and relatives in the Zouaves. Le Gonidec spoke of those who had served under him, such as Kligge, Baron von Berlichingen (who would later die fighting in the Prussian ranks in this war), and Count von Stohlberg. Stohlberg, as it happened, was a friend or relative of the officer. The Chasseurs were convinced that the Zouaves, despite their lack of paperwork, were legitimate French fighters, and shortly after contacted two other officers who had served in the French garrison in Rome and were able to confirm the identity of Le Gonidec and his men. The general made out the proper papers, and the next day saw the Zouaves mustered into the regular forces defending Orleans.

The Zouave leader was extremely unimpressed with procedures in the French army. Where companies had acted like battalions in the papal service, and dash and initiative were demanded of pontifical officers from the most junior on up, the French army was quite different. Used to fighting Arabs in Algeria, French officers almost always waited for instructions from higher up the chain of command. In a situation where that chain was constantly disrupted by the advancing foe, time after time this was a recipe for disaster. Lacking any maps of the area, Le Gonidec went to a bookseller to buy some. The proprietor was quite surprised that an army officer would take such initiative.

But the Zouaves had not arrived a moment too soon; La Motte-Rouge had a total of 30,000 to defend the city against the onslaught of General von der Tann's two army corps—Prussian and Bavarian. On October 10, operations began as the Prussian advance guard of 140,000 men and 100 cannon made contact at Artenay with the French front line, manned here by 8,000 men, mostly militia, and 16 cannon. The Prussians and Bavarians were devastating in their use of rifle and cannon. Having lost 900 killed, wounded, or captured men, the French broke and ran into the forest of Orleans to the south. Von der Tann called a halt, presuming that La Motte-Rouge would evacuate the city and the Prussians could then leisurely occupy the town the next day and claim a great victory.

On the French side, La Motte-Rouge could not afford to give up without a fight. Gambetta had arrived at Orleans, and if the city fell, his own career would come to a disgraceful end. If Orleans was to be saved, the headlong retreat must be covered and the enemy delayed. The newly arrived Zouaves were among the troops selected for the job. They were sent to the Château de la Vallée to overnight.

There, after dinner, Le Gonidec gathered with his officers, and using the maps he had purchased, showed them the difficulty of their situation. They were on the north bank of the Loire, north by northwest of the city, with only a stone bridge or the railway bridge connecting to the city. Once the main body of the army had retreated, these bridges would probably be made impassable. In that event, the Zouaves would either be trapped on the north side or caught in the crossfire if there was sufficient artillery in Orleans. (Not only had Le Gonidec not been issued maps; he had not been informed of the army's strength or tactical plan.) It was decided on consulting the maps they would, after the army was safe, make for either the bridge at Chapelle-Saint-Mesmin, three miles downstream from New Orleans, or the one at Jargeau, the same distance in the opposite direction. Officers and men then retired, though not for long.

Before daybreak they were awakened and ordered to join Colonel Bourgoing's militia battalion for operations in the forest. The staff officer who brought the message told Le Gonidec that, should the army retreat over the river, Zouaves and militiamen were to retreat to the eastern suburb of Chanteau. "Via the bridge of Jargeau," Le Gonidec observed. "Hold on!" the officer replied, "how do you know about that?" The Zouave commander told him that he had a map and about the meeting. Half laughing, the staff officer said, "You hold a council! You form plans! Why didn't you wait for orders?" "And if they had not come?" was Le Gonidec's caustic reply.

The two units moved into the forest. At the first halt, Le Gonidec made sure to show the Zouave uniform to the militia, so that his own men would not be taken for Prussians by their own allies. As the French moved into position in the woods, Bourgoing deployed his battalion in a skirmish line, placing the Zouaves to the left; the Prussians were already approaching as the sun rose. Scouting ahead, Le Gonidec's men observed a Prussian artillery battery setting up; they retreated without betraying their presence. But in the meantime, fearing to extend his line too far, Bourgoing had withdrawn his men to another locale without sending word to the Zouaves. Isolated and without orders, Le Gonidec resolved to withdraw toward the east as previously agreed. To do so, the Zouaves would have to pass through the body of the forest held by other French units. Fortunately, the lines they came to were held by the same unit whose officers had been billeted at the hotel; the Zouave uniforms were recognized, and they were allowed through without being fired upon.

This battalion had received orders to defend a crossing south of the railroad station of Cercottes and the eastward path that led to Chanteau. Le Gonidec was informed by the captain in command that they were all alone in the forest. Showing this officer their exposed position on the map he had brought, Le Gonidec demonstrated how easily they could be cut off by the Prussians if they remained there; moreover, all the troops whose retreat the battalion was supposed to be covering had already passed by. It was between 8 and 9 A.M., and with his binoculars Le Gonidec could already see a battalion of Bavarian reconnaissance advancing. He told the captain that they should retreat along the road to the more defensible crossroads of Quatre-Chemins. There they could hold the enemy, allow more troops to cross over behind them, and finally withdraw themselves to Chanteau.

The officer sadly shook his head, and said, "Do what you want, you are free. For myself, I have been ordered to defend this path before pulling back to Chanteau; I know only my orders." Le Gonidec protested that if the enemy reached Quatre-Chemins, it would be impossible for the captain to get his men to Chanteau. He responded that he was only appointed at the last minute to this command, and that his men were a scratch force put together from soldiers of different units who had escaped from Sedan, and he feared that they would scatter at the first shot. The only thing to do was to hold on as well as he could. Le Gonidec consulted with his officers: On the one hand, time was short and the Zouaves did not want to remain there to be surrounded; on the other hand, they did not want to simply abandon their new companions. Finally, the Zouave commander told the captain that they would fall back toward Quatre-Chemins. But since there were only 160 Zouaves, they could not possibly hold the enemy there. So they would try to delay them, retreating either south toward Orleans or east toward Chanteau, depending on the direction the Bavarians seemed inclined to go. Showing the captain a shortcut through the woods to Orleans on the map, Le Gonidec urged the captain to withdraw his men through it as soon as they either heard firing from the direction of Quatre-Chemins or were attacked themselves. Agreeing that this would fulfill his duty, he bade the Zouaves farewell.

Quickly, the Zouaves move on to Quatre-Chemins. Le Gonidec deployed his men in the woods on the south side of the east-west road and carefully prepared positions on the flanks deeper in the forest; he feared envelopment and attack from the rear. Then he placed four sentries on the road leading south from Cercottes. He stationed himself in the center of the crossroads. All was done in complete silence—the years of chasing Garibaldian infiltrators had served them well.

By a signal, the sentries informed Le Gonidec that the Bavarians were advancing from Cercottes. Soon he could see them. The sentinels were withdrawn, and the captain joined his men in concealment. But the enemy was wary; a voice called out, in perfect French, "Do not shoot! We are French Chasseurs à Pied!" But the Zouaves made no reply, nor did they move. After five minutes in which the troops were drawn up, a voice, in German this time, told the enemy to "fight valiantly for the kaiser!" This was how the Zouaves learned of the proclamation of the German empire two days earlier in the Hall of Mirrors at the occupied palace of

Versailles. Bismarck had finally achieved his goal of uniting the country complete under Prussia—henceforth there were to be no more Prussians or Bavarians—only Germans; thus, at last, had the Iron Chancellor imitated Cavour.

Then the Bavarians began their attack. But the withering fire of the Zouaves soon filled the ditch on the side of the road with enemy corpses. Their comrades shot at the edges of the woods, but by that time the Zouaves had slowly begun their withdrawal deeper into the forest, always silent, always swift. Whenever they came to a clearing, they would race across it, take up positions on the other side, and discharge another fusillade. By the time the foe would recover sufficiently to return fire, the Zouaves would be on the move again. At the same time, other Zouaves pulled back slowly along the sides of the road to Orleans, along which the invaders were trying to advance quickly. But the rifles of Le Gonidec's men insured that the Bavarians could not pass between their fields of fire. After an hour and twenty minutes of this slow withdrawal, Le Gonidec saw off to his left the Bavarian cavalry, which had missed the chance to outflank them. Seeing that they had lost their quarry, the horsemen halted. At that point, the infantry also ceased their pursuit. Either the German commander had reached his goal or he feared a trap; later, it was discovered in the German newspapers that he informed his superiors he had been fighting three regiments of African troops in the forest, instead of three undermanned companies.

Continuing down the road, they came to the path that led back to the place where they had encountered the French troops earlier in the day. Waiting for them were the captain and his officers. He tearfully told Le Gonidec that, as he had feared, his men had fled at the first shot and he envied Le Gonidec his troops. The two central

Zouave companies were drawn up; but the one that had covered the right flank had been delayed, and Le Gonidec could not wait. The Zouaves sped down the road to Orleans, observing the convoys of guns sailing down the Loire. Their delaying action had saved countless French lives.

At the main railroad bridge, as it was prepared for demolition, they waited until the very last for the tardy company, most of whom drifted in, and at last they all crossed into Orleans. (Those who had not arrived at the bridge, had changed into civilian clothes and swum the river, and rejoined their comrades the next day.) In all, the Zouaves lost eight men that day: four had been killed, the other four, captured. These latter were going to be shot as partisans, because of their unfamiliar uniforms and their lack of military identification. But providentially, the Prussian officer they had encountered the evening of their arrival identified them and their lives were spared. The battle of Cercottes was the first bright event the French had seen in a dreary campaign. The reputation of the Zouaves as a unit soared.

But La Motte-Rouge withdrew his army southeast along the Loire to Gien, and Orleans fell to the Germans on the October 13. Le Gonidec and the Zouaves, however, were sent back by rail to Le Mans, where Le Gonidec was promoted to major. As he had feared, La Motte-Rouge was cashiered. But the increasing numbers of Zouaves, now part of the newly formed Army of the Loire, were being trained as rapidly and as well as they could be, given the circumstances. By October 27, they totaled a thousand men; but on that same day, the news arrived that Bazaine had surrendered at Metz. The flower of the French army was in German hands.

Undaunted, the Zouaves continued to train and pray, as Gambetta switched generals and higher formations. By early

November, there were 1,500 in the unit. The government at Tours resolved to try to break through to Paris; the recapture of Orleans was key to this. In early November, the overextended Germans were flung back from the city and the French returned. In preparation for the new offensive, the Zouaves were brought from Le Mans via Nogent to Chateaudun, where they arrived on November 11. They were part of a new formation, the 17th Corps of the Army of the Loire. In a few days their corps received a new commander who not only valued their military prowess but shared their religious views: the illustrious General Louis-Gaston de Sonis, a man very much of the cut of Lamoricière or Charette himself.

Born in the French Caribbean island of Guadeloupe in 1825, Sonis graduated from St. Cyr as a cavalry officer. He soon lost his faith, became an ardent republican, and was initiated in the Grand Orient Masonic Lodge in 1848. After nine months, he became disgusted and returned to Catholicism, in short order becoming increasingly renowned for his devotion. At the same time, his military reputation grew as he served bravely in Algeria, Italy, and Morocco. When he assumed command of the 17th Corps, it was not just that he was proud to have the Zouaves under his command; at last they too had a general—other than their own Charette—that they could respect.

Chateaudun was in ruins; on October 18, it had been the site of fierce fighting between the Germans and French irregulars—many of whom were shot when captured. In reprisal, the town was burned. The Zouaves and their comrades of the 17th Corps waited apprehensively for the order to mount the great offensive against Paris amid evidence of how harsh their opponents could be. The campaign of Orleans that followed is too large and complicated for us to explore in any detail; suffice it to say that it was believed that the army besieged in Paris would try to break out if the Army of the Loire managed to reach Fontainebleau; as a result, all of French strategy was aimed at that goal.

On November 24, the 2nd Battalion of the Zouaves was sent to the northwest of Chateaudun to push the Prussians out of the village of Brou. When the Zouaves arrived opposite the village, the German artillery opened up on them. A number of the Zouaves were killed, but the Prussians evacuated the village after about an hour, and the Zouaves secured it. They were then ordered back to Chateaudun. Over the next few days, other corps of the French army attacked the Germans; the 16th Corps under General Chanzy had driven the Germans back from the town of Loigny. But an enemy counterattack and the flight of some units left a body of Chanzy's troops besieged in Loigny. He called on Sonis to break through to them; the intrepid commander of the 17th agreed to do so.

On the night of December 1, the Zouaves were ordered to advance to Patay, where Joan of Arc had won a renowned victory against the English. Sonis asked Charette, who had no flag of his own, to lend him the Zouaves'. This banner had a curious history. As we saw, the original banner of the unit had been cut up by Charette and the pieces distributed to his men. But in September, the Benedictine nuns of Paray-le-Monial had made a banner bearing a crowned Sacred Heart, with the motto, "Heart of Jesus, Save France." Given the importance of that symbol to the Zouaves when it was made a gift to them in Tours, they heartily embraced it. This was the flag that would lead Sonis's men into battle.

Arriving the next day at Patay, Sonis could not help but contrast the valor of St. Joan and her men with the army he commanded—some of whom were already deserting. He turned to Charette and asked, "O you, at least, my colonel, you will not give up on me like these." "No, no!" answered the Zouave, "Long live Pius IX! Long live France." It was a cry his men would echo and reecho throughout that long and bloody day. In the morning, the men received absolution. At 3 P.M., Sonis rode up to the 1st Battalion of the Zouaves, and shouted, "My friends, two regiments have just run away! Now is the time for you to show these cowards how brave men can fight; hurrah for the Zouaves!"

German infantry and artillery were positioned in the adjacent woods through which they had to pass to reach Loigny. After cheering their general, the Zouave skirmishers began shooting at the enemy positions, but the return fire was too great. Charette ordered them to fix bayonets and storm the woods. With Sonis, Charette, and their senior officers in the lead on horseback, the Zouaves charged. Through the storm of bullets they ran and closed with the foe. General Sonis was wounded in the thigh, and Charette fell, having been shot twice. Captain Montcuit, who had lost an arm at Castelfidardo, was wounded in his stump. One participant, Sergeant Wibaux, wrote of the battle a few days later: "it is impossible to give you an idea of the butchery; the Zouaves literally hacked and hewed as if they were beating butter." The woods were secured and hundreds of Germans taken prisoner. They were about to attack the village when the Prussians realized the very small size of the force with which they were contending and brought up three regiments from their reserve. Sonis's infantry refused to come to the aid of the Zouaves and his artillery was out of ammunition. The Zouaves were forced to retreat as the Germans mauled them with artillery fire and automatic weaponry. The earth was covered with the dead; only 3 out of 14 officers made it back to camp by nightfall. Le Gonidec assumed command; three flag-carriers were

killed in succession, and a wounded fourth returned with the bloodied banner of the Sacred Heart. In one company, only two corporals
were left, all the officers having been killed. Of 300 Zouaves of this
battalion, 218 had been killed. Had the rest of Sonis's command not
broken, they would have won the day.

Back on the battlefield, a strange thing happened. The Virgin
Mary appeared to the wounded General Sonis, assuring him that
all was not lost and that France would survive. At this juncture, it
took an act of faith to believe that. A scattering of soldiers milled
around the former battle; only the Zouaves and a very few other
units retained their order and discipline. The remnant of the 17th
Corps retreated to Poitiers. When the surviving Zouaves reached
this refuge, they were welcomed deliriously by the townspeople.
Deeply saddened by the plight of his former paladins, Pius IX sent
a message to them: "Tell Charette and his heroic sons as speedily as possible that my wishes, prayers, and remembrances constantly follow them wherever they go; that as they were, and still
are, present with me, I am also with them in heart and soul, ever
entreating the God of all mercy to protect and save both them and
their unhappy country, and to bless them as fully and as specially
as I do this day, in His name and with the warmest effusion of my
heart."

But while the survivors of Loigny were safe, their brethren
of the 1st Battalion of the Zouaves, attached to Chanzy's reorganized 16th Corps, were not. On December 4, Orleans fell again to
the Germans, who then turned west toward Le Mans, which was
being defended by Chanzy. He was plagued with all the same sorts
of problems that had characterized the army at Orleans—poorly
trained men, weaponry badly distributed (excellent Springfield
rifles had arrived from America but did not reach the troops—who

did not know how to use them—until the day before the battle).
On January 10, 1871, Chanzy had his troops dig in at the plain
of Auvours, about seven miles east of Le Mans. They repelled the
Germans at first, the Zouaves taking the lead as usual. But in the end,
large numbers of other troops fled and within three days the French
army was routed. For all practical purposes, resistance in western
France evaporated.

The Zouave survivors made their way to Poitiers. To their great
joy, they found that Charette had managed to evade the Germans
and—promoted to General—was presiding over the recuperation
and reorganization of the Zouaves. But the defense of the west, so
far as any could tell, was no longer humanly possible. Charette and
his men prayed for a miracle to stop the Prussian advance; their
prayers were answered.

By January 17, the Germans were at the gates of Laval. The
bishop of St. Brieuc, in Brittany, made a vow to the Virgin Mary,
and the bishop of Nantes separately promised to build a church in
honor of the Sacred Heart if their lands were spared invasion. At
6:45 P.M., in the town of Pontmain, to the north of Laval, the Virgin
appeared to a number of the townspeople. To them, she said, "Pray,
my children; God will aid you in a little while. My Son will be
touched." About that time, the German general received orders to
abandon the occupation of Laval and return to the Paris region.
Ever since, pious Frenchmen have attributed this sudden change in
strategy to "Our Lady of Hope of Pontmain."

The Zouaves, in the meantime, left Poitiers for Rennes. They
continued to attract volunteers, and held themselves in readiness for
whatever might come. On March 1, the government opened negoti-
ations with the Germans; the result was a revolution in Paris and the
city's takeover by radicals, including anarchists and a fair number of

the newly created Marxists. Since they refused to turn over power to the government, it was decided to invade the capital. The result was a week of blood, in the course of which the Communards (as the revolutionaries were called) murdered many of their captives, including the archbishop; many more of them were slain in return. Some of the Zouaves were employed in this business, but Charette refused to participate.

Peace was restored, although on draconian terms—apart from an enormous amount of monetary reparations, Alsace and Lorraine had to be ceded to the German empire. France was shattered economically and politically. As the summer wore on, it was obvious that something had to be done about the Zouaves at Rennes. In July, the minister of war offered to constitute them as a regular regiment in the renascent French army. But Charette declined, explaining to his officers, "Gentlemen, I felt I had not the right to make over our uniform to the French army; this uniform is the property of the whole Catholic world, whose belief we represent; it is the livery of Rome, it is not ours to be disposed of at will, and linked to the fortunes of an unstable government."

On August 13, the regiment attended their last military Mass together in the chapel of the Seminary of Rennes (today the Faculté des Sciences Economiques). Monsignor Daniel, who had been their chief chaplain since 1860, was the celebrant, and when the liturgy ended, he offered a few words of farewell. Then Charette, in front of the altar and in view of their bloodied banner, said, "In the shade of this flag, dyed with the blood of our noble and dear fallen comrades, I, General Baron de Charette, who have had the honor to command you, I devote the legion of the Volunteers of the West, the Pontifical Zouaves, to the Sacred Heart of Jesus, and with the faith of a soldier and all my heart. I say and I ask you to say all with me: Heart of Jesus, save France!" All present repeated his last words.

The men filed out into the courtyard and formed a square. The general declared, "Farewell, dear comrades; it is with heartfelt grief that I now take leave of you, for it is a hard wrench to part after eleven years." In reply, the Zouaves shouted, "Long Live Pius IX!" They were dismissed and went their separate ways. But despite this second dissolution within the course of a year, the story of the Pontifical Zouaves was not yet over.

CHAPTER VIII

Viva Il Papa-Re!

A last salute, 'mid swords upraised,
Linked hands and burning tears,
An oath deep sworn whose purpose rests
In the avenging years,
A long and passionate "farewell!"
And thro' thy silken fold
Swept the bright sword that kept thy fame
On many a field of old,
And scattered wide in severed shreds
Thy web of dusky gold.

—*Katherine Mary Stone, "Our Flag"*

$\mathcal{A}$fter things in Rome settled down a bit, and the Italian government realized that Pius IX was not going to negotiate with them about anything beyond the practical (security around the Vatican and similar matters), they gave up any attempt at conciliation. The laws of 1866 were applied to Rome, and most religious orders were expelled from their monasteries and convents, or in a few cases were allowed to remain as unpaid caretakers. The newly acquired property as well as various papal government offices and buildings were transformed into homes for the new bureaucracy, barracks, and prisons. A "free" plebiscite was arranged in what had become the traditional style and, unsurprisingly, found 99 percent of the population in favor of the annexation.

For his part, Pius IX withdrew entirely to the Vatican, ceasing to appear on the balcony or to give his blessing to the city and the world. The lifestyle of the papal court took on the subdued tone it would possess until 1929. The four remaining corps of the pontifical army—the Swiss Guard, the Noble Guard, the Palatine Guard of Honor, and the Gendarmerie—survived at the Vatican in somewhat reduced numbers, now concerned solely with the immediate security of the Pope. No longer would the Pope himself preside over the liturgies of the Church year in the great basilicas scattered throughout the city. With the proclamation of Rome as the capital of the kingdom, the government moved to the Eternal City from Florence, and the papal palace of the Quirinal became the official residence of the king. The palace chapel was placed under interdict, so the nearby parish church of Santa Maria degli Angeli e Martyri became the center for the Savoy dynasty's religious life: so recently as 2003, Prince Emmanuel Filiberto, grandson of the last reigning King of Italy, was married there.

Despite Pius's nonrecognition of the new state of affairs, he had still to run a universal Church—with virtually no income. The result was the institution of Peter's Pence, the annual collection for the Holy Father from throughout the Catholic world. Although his enemies rejoiced at his downfall, and many predicted the imminent end of the papacy, the Pope's supporters became ever closer to him. He would reign as the "Prisoner of the Vatican" until his death in 1878. His successor, Leo XIII, would inherit this situation, as would successive Pontiffs.

The Pope ordered Catholics to have nothing to do with the new regime—not to vote in its elections, not to serve in its government, not to fight against it. The Roman nobility split: The "whites" accepted a role under the monarchy, the "blacks" did their best to pretend it did not exist and entered into a sort of internal exile. In their palaces, they maintained a shuttered throne room (or at least a throne turned to the wall) in memory of the days when the Pontiff visited socially and in hopes that he would do so again one day.

Although Victor Emmanuel II took up his duties at the Quirinal, he was never happy there; perhaps feeling on some level that it was stolen property, he spent as little time there as he could. Moreover, he did not renumber himself as "the First" of Italy, preferring to keep his Sardinian designation. Perhaps his misgivings about his new palace were correct; he died at the Quirinal on January 9, 1878.

Pius lifted the excommunication just before, so that the king could receive the last rites; the Pontiff himself died less than a month later. Even so, later that year the government abolished the chaplaincy in the Italian military.

Napoleon III, having been taken to Germany after Sedan, never saw France again; he went into exile in England, dying there on January 9, 1873; eventually he would be interred at Farnborough Abbey, the monastery founded in his memory and that of their son (killed fighting the Zulus for the British six years later) by the Empress Eugenie. She would be laid beside them there at her own death in 1920.

Garibaldi did not leave the world gently. He founded the League of Democracy, dedicated to universal suffrage and to the abolition of ecclesiastical property and the standing army in 1879. A year later, he married Francesca Armosino, mother of three more of his children. He died at almost 75 years of age in 1882, with virtually none of his dreams realized; even the unification of Italy did not turn out as he had wished, since it was in the hands of an oligarchy he found obnoxious.

Antonelli, following Pius IX into seclusion in the Vatican, remained his secretary of state. Despite the loss of the Papal States, papal diplomatic activity remained as busy as ever, since then as now the Pope had to deal with foreign governments regarding the local Church in their countries. Antonelli died in 1876. Two years earlier, Archbishop Merode (he was consecrated after retiring as pro-minister at arms), having served as chaplain-in-chief to the Pope after following him into the Vatican, died in Pius's arms.

After 1870, General Kanzler stayed in Rome, organizing relief efforts for impoverished former papal soldiers—not an easy task given the attitudes of the government; he died in Rome in 1888.

After leaving his Zouaves at Toulon, Colonel Allet made his way back to his hometown, Leuk, in Valais, Switzerland, where he died in 1878.

But the passing from the scene of both the major players and the highest papal officers did not mean an end to the Zouaves. The experiences they had in Italy as they risked their lives for both the Church and the Pope—above all, the high idealism these called forth—could rarely be forgotten by them. The survivors in those nations, in which there were enough Zouave veterans to warrant it, formed old comrades' associations with the express purpose of returning to free Rome and liberate the Pope. As time went on and the likelihood of that happening waned, they sought to turn their fervor to other, allied causes in their own countries.

Because the late nineteenth century was a period of great conflict between the Church and various liberalizing, secular governments, and because Catholicism as a whole was undergoing a great revival—both in devotional terms and in exploration of answers to contemporary social problems—opportunities for continuing Zouave action were great.

Until his death in 1911, Charette was recognized as the unofficial "chief Zouave," not only in France but wherever his old comrades could be found. His 11 years of service had left their mark on him, but his return to civilian life was made easier for the widower-baron by his remarriage in 1873. His second bride was a proper match for him: An American from Kentucky, Antoinette Polk was the niece of Leonidas Polk, the "fighting bishop" of the Confederacy. When Union troops occupied her family home, she had ridden out through a shower of bullets (and to various encounters with Union scouts along the way) to warn an approaching body of Southern troops of the trap they were marching into. After that incident, she and her mother wintered in Rome, where they met Charette. They would be wed three years after his last campaign.

On June 20 of the same year, 1873, Charette led 20,000 pilgrims to the Shrine of Paray-le-Monial, where St. Margaret Mary Alacoque had her vision that started the modern devotion to the Sacred Heart. On her tomb, he laid the blood-soaked banner that the Zouaves had carried at Loigny. Less than a month earlier, another devotee of both the Sacred Heart and Henry V, Marshal MacMahon, was elected president of France; the French parliament now had a royalist majority. Charette played a strong role in the events of that time. What he and many others hoped was that a France purified of the evils of the revolution and republicanism would—thanks to the Sacred Heart and the Virgin Mary—rediscover her Catholic soul and regain her king. Thus equipped, she would be strong enough to both retake Alsace and Lorraine from Germany and to restore his territories to Pius IX. As a first spiritual step, 1873 also saw a number of laymen originate and parliament endorse the "national vow": the building of a basilica dedicated to the Sacred Heart in Montmartre.

Unhappily for Charette and his French veterans, things did not go as planned; the eventual building of the basilica was the most concrete realization of their plans. Henry V refused, in 1875, to accept the tricolor—the flag under which his predecessor, Louis XVI, had been murdered—as the national flag. (To be fair, of course, the flag controversy symbolized other problems; Henry did not want to be an ineffectual figurehead.) The republicans and anticlericals gained a majority in parliament in 1877, and the following year MacMahon's term was up. One of the republicans took the presidency.

But amid the gloom, the ex-Zouaves continued to organize. Those in Canada invited Charette to their country in 1882; he visited Montreal, Quebec, and Ottawa, attracting huge crowds wherever he went as well as the acclaim of his old comrades. It was a good memory, and one he would need. The year after the Canadian jaunt, Henry V died. A fissure opened in royalist ranks as two different claimants emerged. Worse still, however, was the distancing of the hierarchy from the activities of the Zouaves in France. The new Pope, Leo XIII, was deeply interested in reconciling the Third Republic to the Church; in pursuit of this ultimately unsuccessful quest, he would, in 1892, order the Catholics of France to abandon the monarchy and "rally to the republic." Many would quietly refuse. But as early as 1885, a sign was given that the Zouaves were no longer automatically favored at the Vatican.

On July 28, 1885, Charette hosted at his château of Kerfily a huge event honoring the twenty-fifth anniversary of the founding of the regiment. Former Zouaves from all over Europe and the Americas came to participate. It was expected that both the nuncio and the local bishop would preside at a Mass in Charette's chapel, in the course of which the old banner would be flown, but both ecclesiastics canceled at the last minute. Undaunted, Charette conducted the ceremonies as planned. It was obvious to all that removing any pretext for the government to claim that the Church was intervening in politics was more important to the hierarchy than honoring a few old warhorses.

Like their leader, the Zouaves of France soldiered on, uncomplaining. Several became high-ranking ecclesiastics while others served as mayors and members of parliament; despite everything, many of them were able to keep the spirit of the Zouaves alive well into the twentieth century. As late as the early 1960s, one still saw in the west of France people dressed as Zouaves lending their dignity to religious processions; many a little boy in that era received his first Communion in that attire.

The situation was quite different in the Netherlands. Although the government revoked the citizenship of the Zouaves (it was only posthumously reinstated after the death of the last Zouave in the Netherlands in 1947), the Church was more forthcoming. Father Hillemons of Oudenbosch, who had recruited so many for the cause, built the gothic-style Basilica of Saints Agatha and Barbara in memory of the Zouaves, complete with a Zouave statue in the square outside. For as long as enough of them were able to attend, they were a constant presence in Church functions. Moreover, many of them were active in organizing Catholic organizations—from the political party to a great many soccer teams—some of which retain "Zouave" in their name today.

In the Catholic kingdom of Belgium, the returning Zouaves were considered heroes, plain and simple. Even today, many towns and villages have monuments to their own lads who went to Rome; indeed, the Zouaves—like the monarchy and the Church herself— were one of the few institutions that bridged the Flemish-Walloon divide. Victor Mousty, who had led the first party of Belgian volunteers, founded the famous Catholic newspaper *La Croix* in Brussels in 1874. To this day, many Belgian Catholic student organizations at various universities still wear the *calotte* (a headdress derived from that of the Zouaves) in token of the contribution made by many ex-Zouaves to their groups' formation. Of course, the contribution of the Zouaves to the Catholic party was enormous.

Great Britain's Zouaves were not so numerous as to have an enormous influence on their homeland after the war, but there were some influential men among them. John Kenyon, who with Charles Buckley and Patrick O'Clery had slipped into Rome to stand with their former comrades at the end, returned home to his family's estate. When he inherited Gillingham Hall, he built the current parish church. O'Clery was made a count by Leo XIII, served in Parliament as an Irish nationalist, and wrote the definitive English-language history of the Italian unification. Charles Menzies Gordon, who had raised the Scottish Zouaves, became a Jesuit and ended his days as bishop of Jamaica. The best known of the British Zouaves was the young hero of Mentana, Julian Watts-Russell.

Pius IX erected a memorial to the victory and the dead of Mentana. When the area fell to the Italians, they removed it and placed it in the Verano cemetery in Rome, where it is today. But they removed another monument as well. A year after Watts-Russell (who by coincidence lies in that same cemetery) was killed, a group of his friends and admirers erected at the very spot he died a sort of small marble tomb containing the young man's heart. When they did so, one cried, "Here is the spot to which Julian pushed on, chasing the enemies of God with fire and sword, passing through a thousand bullets, of which one carried away his cap; and here he fell shot down at point blank." At the same time that the Pope's marker was removed, so was Watts-Russell's which, after being somewhat abused, was dumped in the yard of a nearby tavern. But in 1894 it was found by a Scottish priest, repaired, and set up in the chapel of the English College at Rome, where it may be seen today.

The Zouaves who returned to Canada via New York (leaving two of their number to fight in France) were as marked by their experi-ences as any of their European comrades. In 1871, they founded the Union Allet, an ex-servicemen's association; a number of them founded a town on the banks of Lake Megnatic—Piopolis—named after Pius IX. Others returned to their homes, and still others pioneered settlements in Manitoba. Wherever they went, however, they worked hard to forge a new—and yet traditional—identity for the French Canadians. As in Europe, they intended at first to return to Rome, but as that became ever more unlikely, they too worked to transform their homeland. As mentioned, Charette visited them in 1882; in 1899 the *Association des Zouaves du Québec* was founded: Open not only to former combatants but to descendants and sympathizers, the group supported various Catholic Action initiatives, popularized the feast of St. John the Baptist as the Quebecois national day, and provided uniformed personnel for innumerable civic and religious ceremonies, culminating with the welcome of Pope John Paul II in 1984. But the quiet revolution of the 1960s altered French Canadian society into more secular, American paths, and the organization declined in importance; at this writing the author has been unable to determine whether it still exists.

The position of the Zouaves in the United States was a bit different; of very mixed origins, few in numbers, and unfairly tainted by the memory of Surratt, they became an object of suspicion in many minds. In 1873, when a party of 60 Zouave veterans gathered at St. James' Church in Baltimore to mark the twenty-fifth anniversary of Pius IX's accession, it was widely reported as a semisubversive act marking the beginning of a campaign to overthrow the republic.

But three years later, Major Keogh's death gave a somewhat different impression. After a distinguished record on the Union side in the Civil War, Keogh had remained in the army. Second in command to General Custer at the Little Bighorn, he shared the fate of his superior and their men (Custer's horse, Comanche, was the sole American survivor of the battle). When the Indian braves began desecrating their foes' corpses in accordance with tribal custom, they discovered the medals Keogh had been awarded by Pius IX for gallantry at Ancona. Many of Sitting Bull's warriors being Catholic, they recognized the tiara-and-keys on the medals; instead of abusing Keogh's corpse, they buried it. The other members of St. Patrick's

Battalion who had joined the U.S. Army in 1861 all had distinguished careers in the Civil War. Coppinger stayed in the military
after the war, ending his career as a major general in the Spanish-
American War.

The Confederate veteran Henry Bentivoglio Van Ness Middleton,
having served at the fall of Rome, was one of the few foreign officers in the papal service to accept the commission of the king of
Italy, eventually becoming a court functionary at the Quirinal. His
descendants have remained socially prominent on both sides of the
Atlantic, becoming extinct in the male line in 2002.

The large-scale immigration of French Canadians to New
England after the American Civil War included a number of
Zouaves, of whom the most prominent was Joseph Henri Guillet
(1853–1931), who settled in Lowell, Massachusetts, in 1877. The
first Franco-American lawyer and justice of the peace in his adopted
city, he played a huge role in the creation of institutions serving his
nationality throughout the region: the Jeanne d'Arc Credit Union,
the Franco-American School, l'Alliance Française among them.
Leo XIII made him a papal knight, and he was made a member
of the Academie Française in Paris. In 1884, he organized with his
brother Zouaves in New England (and was elected first president
of) the *Union de Charette*. This in turn contributed to the formation
of various Franco-American shooting clubs that ceased to function
in the 1970s. The beautiful Orpheum Theater in New Bedford,
Massachusetts, was built as a headquarters for them.

Zouaves made their mark farther afield as well. We have seen
how Sir Alphonsus Buckley became a supreme court justice in
New Zealand. George, the youngest of the Collingridge brothers,
whose siblings had distinguished themselves at Mentana, emigrated
to Australia, where he gained renown as an artist, historian, and

photographer. In his as-yet-unpublished papers is a history of the Zouaves.

Despite the stigma attached to them in Italy after 1870, former Zouaves had an effect there as well. The Italian situation was complicated by the withdrawal of activist Catholics from political life; in other countries, they tended to side with the more conservative parties. But in Italy, for many decades, such Catholics concentrated on social questions. Victor Emmanuel's son, Umberto I, was more pious than his father (and his Queen, Margherita, was still more so, contributing gifts to Italian ethnic parishes around the globe), but he also had less say over the conduct of affairs. Although in favor of resolving the Roman Question, he could not, as a constitutional Monarch, do so without the approval of the cabinet —which, needless to say, was not forthcoming. Leo XIII devised a unique way of dealing with the issue. As king of Italy, Umberto was excommunicated, so the elaborate liturgies that characterize most Catholic courts were absent. But as Umberto di Savoia, a private citizen, he remained a Catholic and he attended low Mass daily in his private chapel. Thus, his personal devotion was rewarded without the Pope's surrendering any of the rights he claimed. In this unusual situation, a number of former papal soldiers took up their pens. Most noted of these were Giuseppe Sachetti and Antonmaria Bonetti, who wrote both justifications of the papal position, histories of the unit to which they had belonged, and important works on Catholic social teaching.

Although most of the Zouaves in their various countries were waging the same war with weapons of peace, some few would find other armed conflicts. In 1868, a revolution in Spain overthrew Isabella II, whom the Carlists considered a usurper in any case. She was replaced in 1871 by Amedeo di Savoia; the new king was not only an intruder, he was the second son of Victor Emmanuel II.

A number of the Zouaves began to take notice, the more so because their old comrade, Don Alfonso de Bourbon, was brother to Carlos VII, the Carlist claimant to the Spanish throne—and would doubtless command his army if war broke out. If his old brethren joined him, not only would they be able to give Victor Emmanuel a bit of grief through his son, but Carlos's Spain would doubtless do what it could to regain the Papal States for Pius IX. This latter outcome would become a near certainty if Carlos's cousin, Henry V, regained the French crown.

Captain Savalls, who had refused to surrender at Civitavecchia, resurfaced in his native Catalonia in 1872, leading one of several Carlist guerilla bands in that province. In 1870, from Nice, he had written to a friend, "As his Holiness no longer needs my services, let the King know that I am in Nice, and that I await his orders. I cherish the hope to be one of the first to raise the royal standard in Catalonia, and I shall be found to die sword in hand in the good cause, as my father died before me." Two years later, after going to Rome to receive Pius's blessing, he went on to Spain. Savalls was, to be sure, a clever soldier. When his band was surrounded at one point by government troops, he sent his men away from their position one by one, using goat tracks. The next morning the baffled government troops found that their quarry had vanished.

In February of 1873, Amedeo abdicated and left the country, and Spain proclaimed itself a republic. For the moment—especially since most of the generals had been cashiered—the government forces were in disarray. Don Alfonso returned to Spain and joined Savalls at his camp. In July, Carlos VII crossed the frontier as well. The Carlists controlled most of Catalonia and the Basque country. Don Alfonso had already begun recruiting as many of his old comrades as would join him in a new formation of Papal Zouaves commanded by Savalls. Spanish, Irish, Dutch, and Belgian volunteers (many of them veterans) flocked to his banner. The new (or revived) unit would receive its baptism of fire on July 9, at a town called Alpens, 65 miles from Barcelona. One of the best republican generals, Cabrinety, was in command, of a force of 1,500 armed with artillery and larger than the Carlist detachment of 1,000 men (including the Zouaves). But on the morning of July 9, Don Alfonso decided that the republicans must be attacked. Savalls had misgivings, having tangled with Cabrinety before; still, he would not refuse a direct order. The Carlists were fortunate in that they had captured two of the republican scouts and learned from them the republican plan to pass through Alpens, which had only two mountain passes in and out of the town—and Savalls covered both of them. Cabrinety himself, after the Carlists began their assault in one direction, occupied some of the houses and sent a detachment to secure the path out of town; but the Carlists were ready. For many hours the battle continued, with the Zouaves ever in the thick of things, taking one house after another. When the battle was over, Cabrinety was dead, most of his command killed or captured, and the artillery in Carlist hands. Only a single officer and a few men escaped to tell the tale of this terrible defeat.

On July 11 Baga surrendered; the next town on the road to Barcelona was the fortified town of Igualada. Arriving before the city on July 18, they almost immediately came under fire from the republicans. Here, too, fighting was house to house and over barricades in the streets for 36 long hours; as usual, the Zouaves proved their ability with the bayonet. The lieutenant commanding the Zouaves, a Dutchman named Wills who had served in Rome, ordered their flag with the Sacred Heart symbol unfurled to encourage his men for an assault against a particularly well-manned barricade. As they charged it, the flag-bearer was shot and the banner stained with his blood. Wills grabbed the fallen banner and continued the charge, only to receive three fatal wounds himself. As he stood there, dying, he threw the flag over the barricade and fell. His men swarmed over their opponents and recovered their standard. At last, on July 19 the remnants of the republican garrison in the town surrendered.

Depleted by this action as the Zouaves were, more recruits came to fill their ranks. One of these was Hugh Murray—the first Canadian to serve under Pius IX, he had been wounded and decorated at Mentana. After his return to Canada, he had gone to work for James McMasters' paper in New York. Then as earlier, McMasters was much in favor of Murray's old unit. When Don Alfonso sent out the call, both his editor and his own wishes impelled the intrepid Canadian to answer. Crossing the Spanish border from France on August 23, Murray was made a second lieutenant in the Zouaves. To his great joy, he received a letter of support from Charette, who was organizing monetary support for the Carlist cause. With Henry and Carlos restored to their thrones, his old commander assured him, a "regenerated France and Spain" would soon see Pius's lands restored to him. But shortly after, Murray heard from O'Clery that neither fund-raising nor recruiting was going well in Ireland.

There were many promises of support from various Zouave groups in Great Britain, France, the Netherlands, the United States, and elsewhere. While some money did get through to the Carlists, the lack of artillery made it impossible to attack such centers as Vich or Barcelona. The Carlist columns ranged around the interior of Catalonia, as the 200 or so Zouaves became ever more anxious for decisive action. In lieu of that, they simply acted as guards for Don Alfonso and his wife. But in the field, the royal couple impressed their followers—and especially their guards—with their toughness and tenacity.

A few Irish and Dutch Zouaves were continuing to make their way over the border to join the Carlists. In a border town that Carlos VII made his headquarters, Smith Sheehan, who had been an officer in the Zouaves at Rome and was on his way to the front, met the exiled king. Upon being informed that Sheehan had known his brother while in Rome, Carlos said of Alfonso, "He is in Catalonia now, and has many of your old companions in arms with him. You are serving the same cause here as in Rome—the cause of religion and of order and of legitimate right."

In October and November, a bit of aid trickled in: six recruits and 160 uniforms from Rome, and 14 more Dutchmen under Wills's brother. The spirits of the Zouaves were high, and they distinguished themselves in a number of skirmishes. At last, with the new year, it was decided to take Manresa; on February 4 it was done, and the Zouaves acquitted themselves in their usual manner. Rushing through a breach in the wall, despite a constant barrage from their enemies and fierce hand-to-hand combat, they blazed a bloody trail; victory fell to the Carlists. But among the dead of the Zouaves that day was Hugh Murray.

By mid-1875, the Carlists were masters of the north of Spain and victory seemed imminent. But they were still undersupplied and underfinanced, and in time this would tell. Moreover, an army coup overthrew the republic early in the year, placing Isabella's son, Alfonso XII, upon the throne. While neither a Savoy nor a republic could rally the opposition to the Carlists, another Bourbon could. Although the vast majority of Spain's Catholics preferred the Carlists to the former two alternatives, Alfonso was also a practicing Catholic. The tides of war began to move against Carlos's supporters.

After serving Don Alfonso loyally for four years, the Zouaves went into exile when he did, in February of 1876. But the memory of the Zouaves did not vanish from Spain, any more than did that of the Carlists—indeed, the latter were a major factor in the victory of Franco in the Spanish Civil War. In Catalonia even today, as in Belgium and Switzerland, companies of men dressed as Zouaves take their place in processions in certain towns.

Yet even with the end of the Third Carlist War, the military saga of the Zouaves still had one more adventure in its quiver. In 1868, Cardinal Lavigerie, the archbishop of Algiers, began organizing missionaries to evangelize the interior of Africa. Several failed expeditions and a number of dead clerics and laity convinced him that security was necessary for success. In 1879, he conceived the idea of raising a force of ex-Papal Zouaves to provide this security. Lavigerie appointed Father Felix Charmetant as chief recruiter. In March of 1879, two young Scots volunteered and made their way to Algiers where, with four Belgians, their swords, and a banner of the Sacred Heart were blessed. The six Zouaves, nine priests, and three brothers set off for Uganda. One of the brothers and three of the Zouaves died of tropical diseases before they arrived.

The following year, 14 Belgian Papal Zouaves were recruited, as was one Frenchman, Leopold Joubert (1842–1927). A veteran of Castelfidardo, Mentana, Rome, and Loigny, Joubert went about the Lord's work with a will. Arriving at Mulwewa mission in the present-day Congo in 1880, with his brother Zouaves, he fortified the place and began to train the locals as a home guard to fight Arab slave traders. Joubert had hit upon a winning combination. He built two more such mission forts at either end of the lake, making the slavers' tasks far more difficult. They counterattacked, burning two of his installations. Joubert built new ones, especially the fortress of

Mpala where he trained a new force better than anything the slavers could field. He also married the daughter of a local chief and in time had ten children. Eventually, the Belgians gave him troops and weapons, and in 1898 he defeated the slavers once and for all. He settled down into the life of a lay missionary; two of his sons became priests. Knighted by both the king of Belgium and the Pope, in that faraway outpost he kept up the spirit of the Zouaves—unshakeable piety and a devotion to duty that refused to see any obstacles.

Except perhaps for Joubert's campaign against the slavers, all of the Zouaves' ventures ended in failure. The Papal States were lost, Germany defeated France, and neither Henry V nor Carlos VII, nor any of their descendants, were ever restored to their thrones. The Catholic political parties and organizations that the Zouaves had been instrumental in creating have either folded or were transformed into groups that would be unrecognizable to their founders. Indeed, the philosophies of government and humanity that they fought against in peace and war are completely triumphant; save for a few small countries and some relatively tiny groups, the views of the Zouaves are not merely frowned on but utterly foreign to most people today.

There is a certain romance to most lost causes. Part of it is due to the fact that history's defeated—regardless of what they might have done in their time—are not responsible for whatever evils we enjoy today. Britain's and Ireland's Jacobites presided over neither the British Empire nor its decline; the American Loyalists had no part in the Civil War; French Royalists were victims of, not the perpetrators of, the Terror; the Whites in Russia's Civil War did not create the Gulag. Moreover, although every cause has its idealistic young people, it is those who serve the victors who grow into old, cynical, politicians—save for those of the losers who serve the new regime.

Even someone bordering on the pathetic, such as Pu-yi, China's last emperor, cannot be brought to book for the atrocities of Mao and his successors.

Few today treasure the memory of the Papal Zouaves. Even their fellows in defeat at the hands of the Sardinians, the Neapolitan Bourbons, and the rest boast quite a number of modern apologists and admirers; yet they do not. Why is this? The most obvious reason, apart from the near-universal triumph of the principles of Bismarck and Cavour among today's political classes, is that the Popes, their patrons, having made their peace with the Italian state in 1929 (via the Lateran Treaty, through which the current Vatican City came into existence as a universally recognized sovereign entity), have not chosen to remember them in any significant way. The Pontiffs' examples have been emulated by their followers. If one, for example, visits the Lateran Historical Museum in Rome today, with its collection of uniforms and other memorabilia of the papal court, one is quite literally rushed past the pictures, weapons, and materials of the Zouaves, without any explanation.

After Vatican II, the kind of Catholic militancy associated with the Zouaves fell into disfavor. In 1970, Paul VI not only removed most of the lay positions and ancient ceremonial from the papal court, he also deprived the black nobility of the Vatican citizenship given them in 1929. That Pope further abolished the Noble and Palatine Guards, and deprived the Gendarmerie of both their Napoleonic uniforms and their name (the latter has since been restored).

Apart from the embarrassment that their memory might bring since the Lateran Treaty, this change of attitude toward them on the part of the Holy See also has much to do with the successive Pontiffs' changing views of war and the profession of arms in general. The horrors of the two world wars and subsequent conflicts have shorn armed conflict in most (including papal) minds of any element of the sacred. Modern "holy war" tends to involve acts of terrorism and the mass slaughter of innocents on the basis of their beliefs. Moreover, since many, if not most, Europeans and their descendants no longer believe in Christianity in any form (a proportion that rises steeply among the dominant elements), the idea of fighting for that faith is barbaric at worst, incomprehensible at best. All in all, it would be tempting simply to label the Papal Zouaves complete failures.

But this is a temptation that ought to be resisted. Much more remains of their legacy than a few scattered monuments, museums, and battlefields. Initially, the unique spirituality they developed at worship and on the field became widespread throughout those military establishments where any number of Catholics might be found. General Sonis, himself a sort of honorary Zouave, became an example for Catholics in the French army—particularly in regard to devotion to the Sacred Heart. His cause for beatification has been reactivated and his body is incorrupt. World War I saw this kind of spirituality become very popular, indeed, as the anticlerical government, fearful of another defeat at the hands of the Germans, sanctioned the *Union Sacré*, whereby Catholics were once again allowed full participation in political affairs in return for their wartime support. The completion of Montmartre's Sacre Coeur after the war was the seal of this alliance. During that period, the memory of the Zouaves was constantly invoked by the country's military—as it was by key military elements under both Vichy and Free France during World War II. It would not be until the ideological purging of the French army after the loss of Algeria in 1962 that this invocation would be officially discouraged.

The Zouaves' memory was also venerated by Austrian and German soldiers. The Sacred Heart had been the symbol of the rebels against the French in Napoleonic Tyrol; this stream of tradition merged with that of the Zouaves. It was certainly very much on the mind of the last emperor of Austria, Karl (beatified by John Paul II in 2004). Moreover, although the concept of "Catholic soldierhood" was looked upon askance (to say the least) by Hitler, it animated much of the anti-Nazi resistance in the German army, most notably with such figures as Stauffenberg.

In Spain, the Zouave tradition among the Carlists spilled over into important segments of the Spanish army as a whole—particularly during and after the crusade of the 1930s. Although it has become fashionable to decry the victory of Franco in that conflict, and in recent years his supposed crimes have been recounted with glee, it is forgotten how many thousands his opposition killed. A tour in Eastern Europe should remind one what Spain would be like had the republic prevailed.

Even in Italy, the spirit of the Zouaves began to have an effect within the army during World War I—which conflict saw the government revive the military chaplaincy in 1915. Giosue Borsi, a noted author before the war, writes in his *Soldier's Confidences with God* lines that could have come directly from the pen of those Zouaves whose writings are preserved—lines regarding his relationship with God, the Pope, and the profession of arms.

The growth of veneration of the Sacred Heart of Jesus, in military and civilian circles alike—with its allied devotions to the Precious Blood and the Kingship of Christ—were a direct product of the actions of the Zouaves; in many cases, former Zouaves played a key role in spreading and popularizing them. The twin themes of sacrifice and Catholic transnationalism that played such a large role in the Church's life during the nine decades following the fall of Rome may be laid at their door.

In the last few years of John Paul II's pontificate, and certainly since the election of Benedict XVI, a new spirit has been blowing through the Church—some are already speaking of a "Benedictine reform." Many elements of Catholic life little seen since the 1960s have reemerged—not as an exercise in nostalgia but as a more activist way of engaging the world. Non-English-speaking Catholics, for example, show the beginnings of a revival of interest in the Zouaves. Since the beatification of Pius IX in 2000, his teachings on Church and state, and also of his soldiers, are being reexamined in a more sympathetic way. In Italy, Belgium, and elsewhere, Catholic youth groups dedicated to consciously emulating the Zouaves have begun to emerge—although such youths tend to make their elders as uncomfortable as the latter did their parents and clergy in the 1960s. The annual requiem Mass for the papal soldiers killed in 1870--held in Rome every September 20 but in the last few decades rather sparsely attended—becomes a bigger event every year.

In Italy, the whole question of the Risorgimento is being reexamined for several reasons. The deposition of the House of Savoy in 1946, following a referendum as questionable as any ever mounted by the Sardinians—and with it the legitimacy of the republic itself—finds itself open to scrutiny. The unfortunate results of the centralized state imposed by the victors of 1870—ranging from Mussolini's rule to the instability of postwar cabinets—have led to the formation of various regionalist groups throughout the country. One evidence of this is the popularity of such revisionist books as Cardinal Biffi's 1999 work, *Risorgimento, stato laico e identità nazionale* (Risorgimento, Secular State and National Identity).

Beyond such purely religious and national themes, however, the story of the Zouaves is actually very relevant for all those living in Europe, or her daughter countries in the former colonial world, in the twenty-first century. It presents us with some immediate questions. What, if anything, is worth dying for? If we have a religion or a nationality, is it worth such a sacrifice? If not, how real are those things to us? If we are indeed in the midst of a "clash of civilizations" with radical Islam, these are questions that must be answered, whether one is Christian, agnostic, or atheist, if we are to hope that our descendants will inhabit anything like the culture and civilization that we ourselves enjoy.

On September 20, 2007, Monsignor Ignacio Barreiro, at that year's offering of the requiem for the Zouaves, said: "These soldiers had received from the Church, their reason for living and this why they were ready to sacrifice their own life for her. We are sons of the Church, too, and for her we have to fight the good battle of our time." Others will no doubt have other responses to the questions posed by the story of the Papal Zouaves. Given the issues facing us today, however, they ought to be made soon. Certainly, the Zouaves themselves answered them with a nobility that has seldom been equaled, and never excelled.

APPENDIX I

SONGS OF THE ZOUAVES

MARCHE TRIONFALE PONTIFICALE
Viktorin Hallmeyer (1831–1872)

Salve, Salve Roma, patria eterna di memorie,
Cantano le tue glorie, mille palme e mille altari.
Roma degli Apostoli, Madre guida dei Redenti,
Roma luce delle genti, il mondo spera in te!
Salve, Salve Roma, la tua luce non tramonta,
Vince l'odio e l'onta lo splendor di tua beltà.
Roma degli Apostoli, Madre e guida dei Redenti,
Roma luce delle genti, il mondo spera in te!

Hail, Hail, O Rome, eternal abode of memories,
A thousand palms and a thousand altars sing of your glories.
Rome of the Apostles, Mother and guide of the Redeemed,
Rome, light of the nations, the world hopes in you!
Hail, O Rome! Your light will never fade,
Hatred and shame are conquered by the beauty of your glory
Rome of the Apostles, Mother and guide of the Redeemed,
Rome, light of the nations, the world hopes in you!

INNO DELLA TRUPPA PONTIFICIA DI
PIUS IX—"EVVIVA PIO": (1867)

Al clangore di trombe guerriere
Del più grande dei Regi al cospetto,
Del Soldato s'accende il pensiere,
Del Soldato rinfiammasi il cor.
E sublime s'innalza dal petto
La canzone di fede e di onor.

La Corona che il capo ti cinge
Noi giurammo protegger col brando,
E del giuro che tutti ci stringe
O Signore, terremo la fè.
Sull'arena dei forti pugnando
Noi siam pronti a morire per te.

Re dei Regi, Vicario del Dio,
Che ti guida fra tanta procella,
Il prodigio che n'offri, o gran Pio,
Tutto il mondo spiegare non sa.
Tosto sorgere in cielo la stella
Tutto il mondo stupito vedrà.

Passeranno la terra ed il cielo
Ma di Dio, no, non passa l'accento,
Della Sposa il santissimo velo
No, l'Eterno squarciar non farà:
Ad un guardo ad un soffio a un accento,
La falange d'abisso cadrà.

VIVA PIO! dal mare e dal monte
Sorga il grido dei figli fedeli,

La Corona che cinge sua fronte
Non si strappa...la regge il Signor:
Chi resiste al Monarca dei Cieli?
Cosa è l'uomo d'innanzi al Signor?

The sounding of war's bugles
Impels us to swear loyalty to the greatest of Kings,
Ignites the soldier's thought,
Reignites the soldier's heart.
And raises from deep in the breast
The song of faith and honor.

The crown that encircles your head
We swore to protect with the sword,
And I swear that all of us will hold
O Lord, we will hold the faith.
On the arena where the strong struggle,
We are ready to die for you.

King of Kings, Vicar of God,
Our guide amidst many storms,
The wonder that you offer, O great Pius,
All the world cannot explain.
At once the star will rise in the sky
That all the astonished world will see.

Earth and sky will pass away
But God's voice will not,

From the Spouse [the Church] the holiest veil
The Eternal One will not tear:
To a guard, to a breath, to a voice,
The company of Hell will fall.

LONG LIVE PIUS! From the sea and the mountains
Rises the outcry of his faithful sons,
The crown that encircles his forehead
Is not broken... it is strengthened by the Lord
Who can resist the Monarch of the Skies?
What is man before the Lord?

Source: private correspondence; quoted in Fiorella Bartoccini, *La Roma dei Romani,* Roma: Istituto per la storia del Risorgimento Italiano, 1971, p. 193

CHANT DES ZOUAVES PONTIFICAUX

Vive Lamoricière !
Répétons tous en chœur
Son noble cri de guerre:
Perdre la vie, sauver l'honneur.
[Refrain:]
En avant ! Marchons, (bis)
Zouaves du Pape, à l'avant-garde
En avant ! Marchons, (bis)
Le pape nous regarde
En avant bataillon!

Car notre général,
Qui se connaît en gloire,

Nous mène à la victoire,
A la victoire comme au bal.

Il sera sur nos lèvres,
En bravant le canon,
O noble Becdelièvre,
Le cri de ton vieux bataillon.

Et toi, brave Charette,
Toi, notre commandant,
Toujours à notre tête,
Tu nous conduiras en avant.

Et quand il sera proche
Le moment de mourir,
Sans peur et sans reproche,
Les Zouaves le verront venir.

Vous les vieux camarades,
Si fiers et si vaillants,
Comme aux belles parades,
Chantez encor, malgré les ans.

Et vous, verte jeunesse,
Nos fils et nos neveux,
Répétez sans faiblesse,
Le cri des forts, le cri des vieux.

Ah ! Si jamais l'Eglise
Fait appel à vos bras,
Gardez notre devise :
Le Zouzou ne recule pas!
Pour l'Eglise et la France!

Marchons toujours unis!
C'est là, notre espérance,
Malgré les "bip", nos ennemis.

Long live Lamoricière!
Let us all repeat all in chorus
His noble war cry:
To lose life is to save honor.
[Refrain:]
Forward! Let us march, (repeat)
Zouaves of the Pope, up to the front
Forward! Let us march, (repeat)
The pope looks to us
Forward battalion!

Because our general,
Who knows his glory,
Carries us on to victory,
To victory as to a ball.

It will be on our lips,
By facing the cannon,
O noble Becdelièvre,
The cry of your old battalion.

And you, brave Charette,
You, our commander,
Always at our head,
You will lead us forward.

And when comes
The moment to die,
Without fear and reproach,
The Zouaves will see it coming.

You the old comrades,
So proud and so valiant,
As when on parade,
Sing again, despite the years.

And you, green youth,
Our sons and our nephews,
Repeat without weakness,
The cry of the strong, the cry of the veterans.

Ah! If ever the Church
Calls upon your arms,
Keep our motto:
A Zouave does not retreat!

For the Church and France!
Let us march always united!
That is our hope,
In spite of the rebels, our enemies.

Source: G De Villèle, Charles de La Noüe, *Les français zouaves pontificaux, 5 mai 1860–20 septembre 1870*, Saint-Brieuc, impr. de R. Prud'homme 1903

SONG OF THE ENGLISH ZOUAVES

"Anima mia, anima mia,
Ama Dio e tira via."

Saint George and old England forever !
Once more her sons arm for the fight,
With the cross on their breasts, to do battle
For God, Holy Church, and the right.
Twine your swords with the palm branch, brave comrades,
For as pilgrims we march forth today;—
Love God, O my soul, love Him only,
And then with light heart go thy way.

We come from the blue shores of England,
From the mountains of Scotia we come,
From the green, faithful island of Erin,—
Far, far from our wild northern home.
Place Saint Andrew's red cross in your bonnets,
Saint Patrick's green shamrock display;—
Love God, O my soul, love Him only,
And then with light heart go thy way.

Dishonor our swords shall not tarnish,
We draw them for Rome and the Pope;
Victors still, whether living or dying,
For the martyr's bright crown is our hope;
If 'tis sweet for our country to perish,
Sweeter far for the cause of today;—
Love God, O my soul, love Him only,
And then with light heart go thy way.

Though the odds be against us, what matter?
While God and Our Lady look down,
And the saints of our country are near us,
And angels are holding the crown.

March, march to the combat and fear not,
A light round our weapons will play;—
Love God. O my soul, love Him only,
And then with light heart go thy way.

Source: Joseph Powell, *Two Years in the Pontifical Zouaves*, London: R.
    Washbourne, 1871

APPENDIX II
ZOUAVE SITES

ITALY

REGION OF LAZIO

PROVINCE OF ROME

ROME

Basilica San Giovanni Laterano
Blessed Sacrament Chapel
Monument to Zouaves of all nationalities.

Museo Storico
Palazzo di Laterano
Large number of Zouave paintings, weapons, and uniforms.

Castel Sant'Angelo
The primary papal fortress; its first hall has many exhibits dealing with the papal army in the nineteenth century.

Caserma Serristori
Scuola Pontificia Pio IX
The main Zouave barracks (partially blown up in 1867); a school since 1927.

Palazzo Cimarra
Barracks for both the Zouaves and the Legion of Antibes.

Campo Verano

Major cemetery in Rome; resting place for many Zouaves, including Julian Watts-Russell; location of the papal monument from Mentana, moved here after the conquest in 1870.

Chiesa di San Luigi dei Francesi

Monuments and resting place of many French Zouaves, including Pimodan.

English College Chapel

Monument to Julian Watts-Russell.

Palazzo Salviati

Center High Studies for Defense (CASD); formerly the barracks for papal dragoons, including Prince Salvador Iturbide.

CIVITAVECCHIA

Forte Michelangelo

Site of last stand of papal troops in 1870.

MENTANA

Battlefield

Locale of great papal victory in 1867.

Museo Nazionale della Campagna di Garibaldi

Interesting exhibits, told from the opponents' point of view.

MONTEROTONDO

Rocca Orsini - Barberini

Papal fortress where small force held out against Garibaldi in 1867.

NEROLA

Castella Orsini
Zouave garrison; fighting in 1867.

TIVOLI

Rocca Pia
Zouave garrison.

Villa Gregoriana
Papal residence.

PROVINCE OF VITERBO

CIVITA CASTELLANA

Forte Sangallo
Site of siege of Zouaves in 1870.

MONTEFIASCONE

Rocca dei Papi
Zouave garrison.

VALENTANO

Rocca Farnesiana
Zouave garrison, fighting in 1867 and 1870.

VITERBO

Palazzo Dei Papi
Papal residence.

PROVINCE OF FROSINONE

ANAGNI

Palazzo Bonifacio
Papal residence.

REGIONE OF UMBRIA

PROVINCE OF PERUGIA

PERUGIA

Palazzo dei Priori

Residence of the papal legate (governor).

SPOLETO

Rocca Albornoziana

Garrison of St. Patrick's battalion, siege in 1860.

PROVINCE OF TERNI

NARNI

La Rocca

Papal garrison, skirmish in 1860.

ORVIETO

Fortezza dell'Albornoz

Papal garrison in 1860.

Palazzo del Capitano

Papal residence.

REGION OF MARCHE

PROVINCE OF ANCONA

CASTELFIDARDO

Battlefield

Site of the fight between papal and Sardinian troops in 1860.

LORETO

Santuario di Santa Casa

Site of devotions and hospital for the Zouaves.

Palazzo Apostolico
Papal residence.

SENIGALLIA

Museo Pio IX
Palazzo Mastai
Museum dedicated to the life of Pius IX.

PROVINCE OF PESARO AND URBINO

PESARO

Palazzo Ducale
Residence of the papal legate (governor).

Rocca Constanza
Site of Colonel Zappi's stand.

REGION OF EMILIA-ROMAGNA

PROVINCE OF BOLOGNA

BOLOGNA

Palazzo d'Accursio o Comunale
Residence of the papal legate (governor).

PROVINCE OF FERRARA

FERRARA

Castello Estense
Residence of the papal legate (governor).

PROVINCE OF RAVENNA

RAVENNA

Palazzo dei Governo
Residence of the papal legate (governor).

FRANCE

REGION OF ILE DE FRANCE

PARIS

Musée des Invalides
The premiere French military museum; Zouave information and memorabilia.

Basilique de Sacre Coeur
Launched with financial support and cooperation of numerous Zouaves.

BOULOGNE-BILLANCOURT

Association des descendants des zouaves pontificaux
The association's goal is "to make known, in accordance with the requests of the Sacred Heart, the virtues of Faith and Honor, Fidelity and Courage, Sacrifice and Devotion, heroically illustrated by their ancestors, pontifical and voluntary Zouaves of the west, in the service of the Holy See and France." To meet this goal and to cure the crisis of the civilization of modern times, the association pursues actions of spiritual, historical, cultural and artistic nature.

REGION OF BOURGOGNE

PARAY-LE-MONIAL

Basilique de Sacre Cœur
Scene of numerous Zouave reunions and devotions.
Musée eucharistique du Hiéron
Museum of the Blessed Sacrament founded with the help of Zouaves.

CENTRAL REGION

LOIGNY

Museum of the Battle of Loigny
Monument of Charles d'Albert, duc de Luynes (1845 - 1870) in the Bois des Zouaves.

REGION OF PAYS DE LA LOIRE

YVRE L'EVEQUE

Eglise Saint Germain
Chapel of St. Michael, in honor of the Zouaves killed at battle of Auvours.

NANTES

Cathedrale Saints Pierre et Paul
Cenotaph in honor of Lamoricière.

SAINT PHILBERT DE GRANDLIEU

Eglise Saint Philbert
Tomb of Lamoricière.
Town Square
Statue of Lamoricière.

REGION OF BRETAGNE

ELVEN

Château de Kerfily
Home of Charette and his present-day descendants; chapel in honor of the Sacred Heart and memory of the Zouaves.

Collège-Lycée Saint-François-Xavier

Alma mater of many Zouaves.

Faculté des Sciences Economiques

Formerly a seminary; location of the chapel where the Zouaves had their farewell Mass.

Château de Basse-Motte

Partially ruined home of Charette; chapel in honor of the Zouaves.

Musée Royal de l'Armée et de l'Histoire Militaire

Top military museum in the country; large collection of Zouave memorabilia.

The Arsenal

Former Zouave museum.

Société des Zouaves pontificaux de Jumet

Uniformed society of descendants and reenactors.

Société Royale des Zouaves Pontificaux de Thuin

Uniformed society of descendants and reenactors.

THE NETHERLANDS

OUDENBOSCH

Nederlands Zouavenmuseum
One of the most important collections regarding the Zouaves in the world.

Basiliek van de HH Agatha en Barbara
Basilica in honor of the Zouaves, built after St. John Lateran in Rome.

SWITZERLAND

LEUK

Zuaven-Regiment-Leuk
Uniformed society of descendants and reenactors in hometown of Eugen Allet.

CANADA

OTTAWA

Canadian War Museum
Zouave exhibits.

PIOPOLIS

Quebec village founded by Zouaves in 1871; six-point heritage circuit highlighting their history.

MONTREAL

Cathedral, Marie Reine du Monde
Monuments to the Zouaves.

APPENDIX III

MASS IN MEMORY OF THE POPE'S SOLDIERS

September 20, 2007
Delivered at the church of Corpus Domini, Rome
Monsignor Ignacio Barreiro-Carambula

*I*n this one hundred and thirty-seventh anniversary of the heroic defense of Rome, we offer the Holy Sacrifice of the Mass for the souls of the Pope's soldiers and for all those who sacrificed their own life defending the Faith and the Christian civilization in Italy, in Europe, and all over the world. As Christians, we also pray for the souls of our opponents, wishing that the veil of error will fall from their heart, before their death.

This one hundred and thirty-seventh anniversary—with these numbers: one, three, seven—reminds us of basic truths of the Faith: the uniqueness of God, the Trinity and the Church. The Faith for which our ancestors fought, is the permanent doctrine of the Church, and we wish that it will be preserved in all its fullness for our descendants till the second coming of the Lord. When we talk of the defense of the Faith in our days, it is necessary to speak for a while of its contents, because, unfortunately we can not presume, like our ancestors did, that the Faith is known, after the disappointing results of the Catechesis of the last years.[1]

First of all, let us reflect that God is only one, one for nature, one for substance, one for essence. Only in this God we will find salvation, like God himself says through the Prophet Isaiah: "Turn to me and be saved, all the ends of the earth! For I am God, and there is no other" (Is. 45:22). Here we also see the universal destiny of Christian salvation. Every man is called to become Christian, not anyone is excluded, because this is the only way to salvation, there is no other. Excluding some people or nations from the evangelization would be the worst form of racism. Christ teaches us that we cannot serve two Lords, and that He is the only Lord that has to be loved with all our heart, with all our soul, with all our mind, and with all our strength.

The number one also reminds us, against the relativism and the agnosticism of our days, that there is only one truth. It is not possible to have two omnipotent and two infinite; we cannot have two conflicting truths. One will be true and the other will be false. Unfortunately, this relativism which is the dominant sign of our society in our days, has entered into the Church, as the Holy Father [Pope Benedict XVI] denounced it with a deep perspicacity in his memorable homily that he preached the day before his election. As Archbishop Bagnasco[2] recently recalled: "the society in which we live is afflicted by a strange hatred for itself and considering today's culture, that makes the relativism its own belief, precluding in this way the possibility to discern the truth and to pursue it."[3] This prevailing relativism in society creates a serious obstacle to the transmission of the Faith, as the Holy Father underlined recently: "...precisely in our day educating in the faith is no easy undertaking. Today, in fact, every educational task seems more and more arduous and precarious. Consequently, there is talk of a great educational emergency, of the increasing difficulty encountered in transmitting the basic values of life and correct behavior to the new generations, a difficulty that involves both schools and families…" Later [in his address] the Holy Father adds that "this is an inevitable emergency: in a society, in a culture, which all too often makes relativism its creed—relativism has become a sort of dogma—in such a society the light of truth is missing; indeed, it is considered dangerous and "authoritarian" to speak of truth, and the end result is doubt about the goodness of life—is it good to be a person? is it good to be alive?—and in the validity of the relationships and commitments in which it consists."[4]

The mystery of the Holy Trinity is the central mystery of the Faith of the Catholic life. The revealed truth of the Holy Trinity has been, from the origins, the basis of the living faith of the Church, and we see it first in the baptism that is granted through Christ's mandate in the name of the Father, the Son and the Holy Spirit. The affirmation of the Trinitarian dogma [does not] in any way detract from the magnificent monotheism of the Christian Faith; on the contrary, it enriches it, because we proclaim the existence of one God in three persons. Three divine persons who are really distinct among them. They are not simply names that indicate modalities of the divine being; they are really distinct among them. This Trinitarian God constantly acts in men's history in order to share with us his perfections. It is up to us and to our society to accept the existence of the Trinity. This recognition will give to human society the only possible bases to be strongly built. In the paternity of God we have a model, the exemplar cause of all the human paternity, as Saint Paul strongly affirms in the Letter to the Ephesians. In the Son and the Holy Spirit we have the exemplar cause of love grounded in the truth that is the only cause that can give real life to society.

Number seven makes us think to the perfection of the Church. The perfections of the Triumphant Church in the Book of the Apocalypse are remembered to us by the seven angelical spirits who are in front of God's throne and the seven golden candlesticks representing in a symbolic way, in the eternal celestial liturgy, the Militant Church that works arduously in this world. In the Militant Church, number seven remembers us first of all the seven sacraments, the seven gifts of the Holy Spirit and the seven Christian virtues: three theological (faith, hope, and charity) and four cardinal (justice, fortitude, prudence, and temperance). We have to remember that many of these Pope's volunteers who sacrificed their young lives defending the rights of the Holy See, in some way, fully lived the Christian virtues. If they didn't have these virtues, they wouldn't have had the courage to leave their homes and their families to offer their support to the Holy Father. If they didn't live these virtues, they wouldn't have practiced an extraordinary life as many historical documents show. We have testimonies about the extraordinary prayer life of the Pope's Zouaves. These soldiers had received from the Church their reason for living and this why they were ready to sacrifice their own lives for her. We are sons of the Church, too, and for her we have to fight the good battle of our time. Many of you, have a political and social vocation, and you are fully aware that in politics you cannot leave out the ethical demand of the faith, as unfortunately other people do for opportunism, weakness or other reasons. In some way, these soldiers who died for the Pope and the Church are martyrs and we have to remember that the blood of martyrs cannot be betrayed. It would be a betrayal if we, remembering their heroic deaths, were not willing to live our faith in an integral fashion, in the time in which God has called us to live. We cannot water down the high demands of the Gospel, compromising the doctrinal or moral teachings of the Church.

Thinking to the Church of our days, we have to thank the Holy Father, Benedict XVI, for his efforts to rebuild the Church. Even if we know, from divine revelation, that the Church will never fail, we suffer when we see the long crisis that has been shaking her since the sixties. In front of this long crisis, in the current pontificate, we have a concrete hope that this long and wearing crisis will be solved. We can see many concrete signs of this so-desired restoration that will preserve the identity of the Church. We can talk of many doctrinal reaffirmations like the wonderful affirmation on the need to interpret the twenty-first Council within a hermeneutic of continuity with the tradition of the Church. We can mention the recent answers of the Congregation for the Doctrine of the Faith on the irrevocable rights of sick people who find themselves in the so-called "vegetative state." The reaffirmation of this constant teaching of the Church on this contemporary worrying problem makes me think that it has to be considered part of the ordinary infallible magisterium of the Church on moral matters. We wish that the promulgation of these answers will prevent the recurrence of tragic cases like the death of Terri Schiavo in the United States. In particular, we have to thank the Holy Father for the promulgation of the *Motu proprio Summorum Pontificum* that is most of all meant to "...preserve the riches which have developed in the Church's faith and prayer," as the Holy Father writes in the covering letter of the *Motu proprio*. In front of the difficulties of the present time, we don't have to be afraid, as the Holy Father recently remembered: "if each one of you remains united with Christ, you can accomplish great things.... To anyone who places his trust in God, nothing is impossible."

In order to conclude our prayer, we present ourselves in front of the Immaculate Virgin Mary and the Blessed Pious IX, asking their intercession first of all for the souls of the Pope's soldiers and also for the opponents, so we pray also to live the Faith with the same coherence of these men who sacrificed themselves for God and the Church.

Praised be the Lord.

NOTES

INTRODUCTION

1. Alexander Roberts and James Donaldson, eds., *The Ante Nicene Fathers*, vol. I, "First Apology," St. Justin Martyr (Buffalo: The Christian Literature Publishing Co., 1885) p. 168.
2. Donald Attwater, *A Catholic Dictionary* (New York: The Macmillan Company, 1958) p. 92.
3. Leon Gautier, *Chivalry* (London: George Routledge and Sons, 1891) p. 471.

PRELUDE

1. George S. Pappas, "West Point's Foreign Legion," *Assembly*, July 1991.
2. M. Launay, "De la Bretagne au Congo Belge: le Capitaine Léopold Joubert (1842–1927)," *Omnis Terra*, n. 399, February 2002, pp. 77–84.
3. Charles L. Convis, *The Honor of Arms: A Biography of Myles W. Keogh* (Tucson: Westernlore Publications, 1990).

CHAPTER I

1. For a critical view of the Pontiff, cf. Raffaele de Cesare, *Last Days of Papal Rome, 1850–1870* (London: Archibald Constable, 1909); for the opposite opinion, cf. Fr. Bernard Reilly, *A Life of Pius IX Down to the Episcopal Jubilee of 1877* (New York: P. F. Collier, 1877).
2. Charlotte M. Yonge, "Conversation on Books," *The Monthly Packet*, Third Series, vol. XIV (London: Walter Smith and Innes, 1887) p. 360.
3. TK.
4. John Francis Maguire, *Pius The Ninth* (London: Longmans, Green, and Co., 1878) p. 131.
5. Patrick Keyes O'Clery, *The Making of Italy* (London: Kegan Paul, Trench, Truebner, and Co., 1892) p. 7.

CHAPTER II

1. "The Massacre of Perugia," *Dublin Review*, vol. 47, Old Series, September 1859, pp. 169–264.
2. Pius IX, *Nullis Certe Verbis* (On the Need for Civil Sovereignty), January 19, 1860.
3. Maguire, *loc. Cit.*
4. Imbert de Saint-Amand, *Napoleon III at the Height of His Power*, (New York: Charles Scribner's Sons, 1900) pp. 124–126; Anatole Segur, *The Martyrs of Castelfidardo* (Dublin, M. H. Gill and Son, 1883) pp. 30–41.
5. C. E. Rouleau, *La papauté el les Zouaves Pontificaux*, Quebec, le Soleil, 1905, pp. 160–16; also see his entry in *The Catholic Encyclopedia*, 1908.
6. Henri de Cathelineau, *Le Corps Cathelineau Pendant la Guerre (1870–1871)*, 2 vols., (Paris: Amyot, 1871).
7. Segur, *op. cit.* pp. 60–67.
8. Segur, *op. cit.* pp. 195–222.
9. Ibid.
10. For the Irish volunteers, cf. Berkeley, *Irish Battalion in the Papal Army*; A. M. Sullivan, *New Ireland* (Philadelphia: J. B. Lippincott, 1878), pp. 280–297.
11. For Popiel, cf. Stefan Kieniewicz, Popiel Website, available at http://kingpopiel.tripod.com/english/frames2.htm
12. Glenn Jewison & Jörg C. Steiner, "Fritz Reichsgraf Wolff-Metternich zur Gracht," Austro-Hungarian Landforces 1848–1918, available at http://www.austro-hungarian-army.co.uk/mexican/wolffmetternich.htm
13. For Chorinsky, cf. Hitzig u. Häring, "Die Stiftsdame Julie Ebergenyi von Telekes und der Graf Gustav Chorinsky Freiherr von Lodske," *Der Neue Pitaval*, (n. Premiere serie 1866–77, vol. in). Leipzig, in-8.

CHAPTER III

1. Patrick O'Clery, *The Making of Italy 1856–1870* (London: Kegan Paul, Trench, Trubner, 1892) pp. 199–208.
2. Cf. Anatole, Marquis de Segur, *The Martyrs of Castelfidardo* (Dublin: M. H. Gill, 1883).

CHAPTER IV

1. Maguire, *op. cit.*, pp. 163–164.
2. Rouleau, *op. cit.,* pp. 57–58.
3. Cf. Bernard O'Reilly, *A Life of Pius IX* (New York: Collier, 1877) p. 248 *et seq.*

CHAPTER VII

1. O'Clery, o*p. cit.* p. 529.

APPENDIX III

1. *Catechesis*: Teaching of the Catholic religion.
2. Archbishop of Genoa and The President of the Italian Bishop's Conference.
3. Angelo Bagnasco, *Opening address at the Permanent Council of the Italian Bishops' Conference,* September 17, 2007.
4. Benedict XVI, *Address to the participants in the Convention of the Diocese of Rome,* June 11, 2007.

BIBLIOGRAPHY

X, Barbier de Montault. *L'Anne Liturgique a Rome.* (Rome: Joseph Spithoever, 1862).

Laurent Bart-Loi. *Au Service du Pape et de la France.* (Paris and Lille: Declee et Brouwer, 1901).

Roger de Beauffort. *Histoire de l'Invasion des Etats Pontificaux et du Siége de Rome en Septembre 1870.* (Paris: Victor Palme, 1874).

E. Lef. De Bellefeuille. *Le Canada et les Zouaves Pontificaux : Mémoires sur l'Origine, l'Enrôlement et l'Expédition du Contingent Canadien a Rome, Pendant l'Année 1868.* (Montréal : Le Nouveau Monde, 1868).

G. F. H. Berkeley. *The Irish Battalion in the Papal Army of 1860.* (Dublin: Talbot, 1929).

L. de la Brière. *A Rome: Lettres d'un Zouave Pontifical sur les Fêtes Jubilaires.* (Paris: Jules Gervais, 1888).

"I Crociati di San Pietro." *La Civilta Cattolica.* Tenth Year, Series 1, pp. 170–271.

Fr. Charles Du Coetlosquet, S. J. *Theodore Wibaux: Pontifical Zouave and Jesuit.* (London: Catholic Truth Society, 1887).

Piero Crociani and Massimo Fiorentino. *La Neuvième Croisade 1860–1870: Histoire, organisation et uniformes des unités étrangères au service du Saint-Siège.* (Paris: Tradition Magazine, 2000).

Gustave A. Drolet. *Zouaviana: Etape de Trente Ans, 1868–1898.* (Montreal: Eusebe Senecal et Cie, 1898).

"The Massacre of Perugia." *Dublin Review.* September 1859, vol. 47, Old Series.

Dr. Petra van Essen. *VOOR Pausen Koning.* Oudenbosch, Stiching: Netherlands Zouaven Museum.

John Furley. *Among the Carlists.* (London: Samuel Tinsley, 1876).

Alexis Grochet. *Soldats et Missionnaires au Congo de 1891 a 1894.* (Paris: Desclee, de Brouwer, 1899).

Jean Guenel. *La Derniere Guerre du Pape: Les Zouaves Pontificaux au secours du Saint-Siege 1860–1870.* (Presse Universitaires de Rennes: 1998).

Henri d'Ideville. *Rome and Her Captors.* (London: R. Washbourne, 1875).

Lorenzo Innocenti. *Per Il Papa-Re: Il Risorgimento Italiano Visto Attraverso, La Storia del Reggimento degi Zuavi Pontifici.* (Perugia: Casa Esperia Editrice, 2004).

François Lachance. *Odyssée des Zouaves Canadiens de Rome a Québec.* (Québec: Léger Brousseau, 1870).

Elizabeth Wormeley Latimer. *Spain in the Nineteenth Century.* (Chicago: A. C. McClurg, 1907).

François Le Chauff de Kerguenec. *Souvenir des Zouaves Pontificaux,* 2 vols. (Paris: Librairie H. Oudin, 1890–1891).

Howard R. Marraro. "Canadian and American Zouaves in the Papal Army, 1868–1870."

Canadian Catholic Historical Association Report, 12 (1944–45), pp. 83–102.

John Miley. *The History of the Papal States from their Origin to the Present Day.* (London: T. C. Newby, 1850). 3 vols.

Louis Edmond Moreau. *Nos Croises: ou Histoire Anecdotique de l'Expédition des Volontaires Canadiens a Rome pour la Défense de l'Eglise.* (Montreal: Fabre et Gravel, 1871).

Patrick Keyes O'Clery. *The History of the Italian Revolution: First Period—the Revolution of the Barricades (1796–1849).* (London: R. Washbourne, 1875).

———. *The Making of Italy, 1856–1870.* (London: Kegan Paul, Trench, Trubner, 1892).

Denis O'Donovan. *Memories of Rome.* (London: Catholic Publishing and Bookselling Co., 1859).

John Augustus O'Shea. *Romantic Spain.* (London: Ward and Downey, 1887). 2 vols.

Oscar de Poli. *Souvenirs du Bataillon des Zouaves Pontificaux (Franco-Belges).* (Paris: Chez Tous les Libraires, 1861).

Thomas Canon Pope. *Holy Week in the Vatican.* (Dublin: James Duffy and Sons, 1874).

Joseph Powell. *Two Years in the Pontifical Zouaves.* (London: R. Washbourne, 1871).

L'Abbe Pretot. *Journal d'Un Aumônier Infirmier au Corps Cathelineau.* (Paris: Charles Douniol, 1872).

Piero Raggi. *La Nona Crociata : I Volontari di Pio IX in Difesa di Roma.* (Ravenna: Libreria Tonelli, 2002).

C. E. Rouleau. *La Papauté et les Zouaves Pontificaux.* (Quebec: Le Soleil, 1905).

———. *Souvenirs de Voyage d'un Soldat de Pie IX.* (Quebec: I. J. Demers et Frere, 1881).

Teodoro Salzillo. *Fatti d'arme delle prodi legioni pontificie 1868.* (Senago: La pulce-edizioni di passione, 2004).

Anatole, Marquis de Segur. *The Martyrs of Castelfidardo.* (Dublin: M. H. Gill, 1883).

Mrs. Bartle Teeling. "Memory of Mentana." *Ave Maria Magazine,* Vol, LXI, No. 19 November 4, 1905.

G De Villèle, Charles de La Noüe. *Les français zouaves pontificaux, 5 mai 1860–20 septembre 1870.* (Saint-Brieuc: impr. de R. Prud'homme 1903).

Charles Richard Weld. *Last Winter in Rome.* (London: Longman, Green, Richards, Longman, and Green, 1865).

INDEX

Abd-el-Kader (Arab resistance leader), 24
Academi Française, 206
Acquapendente, 124, 153
Adolf, Grand Duke of Nassau, 88
agnus dei (medallion), 10
Alacoque, St. Margaret Mary, 201
Alban Hills, 118–19, 156, 161–62
Albano, cholera epidemic, 118–20, 124
Albiousse, Major d', 136, 154–56
Albornoz, Cardinal, 70
Alexander III, Pope, 172
Alfonso XII, King of Spain, 211–12
Algeria, 23–24, 51, 175, 180, 215
Allet, Eugene, 58, 100, 110, 137–38, 164, 170, 172, 177, 200
Alliance Française, L', 206
Alsace-Lorraine, 192, 201
Altieri, Cardinal, 119–20
Amedeo di Savoia, 207–8
American Zouaves, 101, 107–10, 120–21, 143–48, 174, 205–6
Ancona, 44, 58
  siege of, 11, 67–69, 73–77, 83–87, 88, 94, 95d, 205–6
Angelino, Major-General, 157
Angioletti, (officer), 153, 156, 158, 161–62, 165
Antonelli, Giacomo Cardinal, 21–23, 25, 65–66, 68, 107, 110, 170, 199
Arab slave traders, 212–13
Argy, Colonel d', 113
Armosino, Francesca, 199
Asian Zouaves, 101
Association des Zouaves du Québec, 205
Australia, 57, 88, 206–7

Austria, 27, 29–34, 48, 51–52, 59, 61, 68, 73–74, 80, 84, 87–88
  revolution of 1848, 30, 32
  Sardinian war of 1859 and, 30, 43–44, 52
Austrian Zouaves, 57–58, 71, 79, 85, 101, 215
Austro-Prussian war of 1866 (Seven Weeks War), 88, 112–13
Azzanesi, Colonel, 124–25, 160, 163

Bach, Sergeant-Major, 127, 128
Bagnorea (Bagnoregio), 107, 124–25, 153
Barberie, cemetery of the, 97
Barreiro, Monsignor Ignacio, 218
Basilica of Saints Agatha and Barbar, 203
Bazaine, General, 150, 186
Beaudiez, Alfred du, 96
Becdelièvre, Count Louis de, 77, 79–80, 99, 100
Beckwith, Paul Edmond, 120–21
Belgian Zouaves, 101, 173, 203, 212–13
Belgium, 13, 23, 203
Benedict XVI, Pope, 217
Berlichingen, Baron von, 180
Berry, Duke de, 52
Berwick, Duke of, 104
Biffi, Cardinal, 217
Bismarck, Otto von, 112–13, 185, 214
Bixio, General, 152–55, 158, 161–63, 165, 171
Blois, bishop of, 97
Bonaparte, Louis (father of Napoleon III), 36
Bonaventure, Saint, 124

Bonetti, Antonmaria, 207
Booth, John Wilkes, 109
Borghese, Prince Camillo, 26
Borsi, Giosue, 216
Bouillon, Godfrey de, 7
Bourbon, Don Alfonso de, 148, 165, 208, 210–12
Bourbons of France, 35
Bourbons of Naples, 22, 30–31, 33, 214
Bourget, Mgr. Ignace, 146
Brazil, 29, 108
"Breach of the Porta Pia," 165, 169
Brigantaggio (guerrilla war in Papal States), 93
Brignone, General, 71, 72, 73
Brisebois, Ephrem, 147
British Parliament, 204
British Royal Navy, 82
British Zouaves, 101, 121–22, 148, 173–74, 203–4
Brittany, France, 35
Brou, batttle of, 188
Buckley, Sir Alphonsus, 206
Buckley, Charles, 203
Buckley, Patrick, 57, 77, 80, 88, 203
Bulgaria, 9
Bute, Marquis of, 148, 174
Byzantine empire, 3

Cabrinety, General, 209
Cadorna, General, 152–53, 156–59, 161–65, 170–71
Cairoli brothers, 131
Calatrava, Order of, 6
California missions, 109, 144
Calvinists, 27
Canadian Zouaves, 9, 101, 146–47, 173–74, 201–2, 204–6, 210
Carbonari, 29, 36
Carlists, 50, 102, 148, 179
   War of 1872–76, 207–12, 216
Carlos VII, Claimant to Spanish throne, 208–13
Carlotta, Empress of Mexico, 145–46
Carmelite order, 6

Castelfidardo, 54, 70, 75
   battle of, 77–82, 93–96, 100–102, 136, 161, 163, 189, 212
   bullet-riddled flag, 100
   Martyrs of, 82, 96–99, 125
Castel Sant' Angelo arsenal, 24, 143, 160, 166, 171
Cathelineau, Henri de, 52, 59
Catholic Action, 205
Catholic Church (Catholics)
   American South vs. North and, 108–9
   Cavour and, 27–28
   Enlightenment and Reformation and, 12–13
   Franz Josef and, 34
   French Revolution and, 13
   Frend political affairs and, 215
   Garibaldi and, 29
   Henry V, count de Chambord and, 35–36
   holidays abolished, 28
   Italian Law of 1866 and, 111
   Napoleon III and, 37–38
   new spirit of reform in, 217
   political life in Italy post-1870, 207
   Pope and worldwide, 4
   property seized by Italian parliament, 112
   Reformation and, 12
   Roman Empire and, 1–2
   "soldierhood" and, 216
   spirituality of Zouaves and, 215
   youth groups, 217
Cavour, Camillo Count di, 17, 25–28, 30–32, 37, 43, 43–44, 48, 61–62, 65–68, 74, 185, 214
   death of, 117
Cavour, Marquis Michele Giuseppe di, 26
Cercottes, battle of, 183–86
Chalus, Count Arthur de, 54–55, 80, 96–97
Chanzy, General, 188, 190–91
Charette, Alain de, 136
Charette, General (of Vendée fame), 51

Charette de la Contrie, Baron Athanase
de, 49, 51–53, 77, 80, 98–100, 104,
125–26, 128–30, 136–37, 139,
153–56, 160, 163, 172–73, 177–78,
187–93, 200–202, 205, 210
Charlemagne, Holy Roman emperor,
3–5, 36
Charles X, King of France, 24, 35, 52,
177
Charles Albert, King of Sardinia, 27–28,
31–33
Charles Felix, King of Sardinia, 31–32
Charmetant, Father Felix, 212
Chateaudun, battle of, 187–88
Chile, 19
chivalry, 5–7, 11, 18
Chivalry (Gautier), 6–7
cholera, 21, 119
Chorinski, Gustav Count, 58, 88
Cialdini, Enrico, 66, 69, 75, 79–80,
84–87
"Civil constitution of the Clergy" (France,
1791), 13
civil marriage, 28, 111
Civita Castellana, battle of, 156–58
Civitavecchia, 74, 130, 133, 152–56, 158
Clarendon, Lord, 33
"clash of civilizations," 218
Clement VII, Pope, 70
Code Napoleon, 37
Collingridge, Alfred, 121, 127–29
Collingridge, Arthur, 121
Collingridge, George, 10, 121, 129,
206–7
Congo, 10, 212–13
Congress of Paris (1856), 43
conscription, 11–12, 28, 60
Constantine, Emperor of Rome, 2
Constantinople, 6, 74
Coppinger, John Joseph, 57, 71, 95,
206
Corpus Christi Mass, 103
Costes, (soldier), 133
Coüessin, Lieutenant, 107
Council of Cardinals of 1870, 152

Courten, Rafael de, 58, 69, 134–35, 137,
172
Couture, Joseph, 147
Crimean War, 9, 28, 33–34, 37, 43, 61,
77, 82
Crusaders (of 1860), 52–53, 59
Crusades, 6–7, 18
Cult of Reason, 13
Custer, Gen. George A., 10, 205

Daniel, Monsignor Jules, 102, 129, 192
D'Arcy, (officer), 77, 79–80
Daudier, Captain, 163
Davis, Jefferson, 108–9, 144–45
Denbigh, Lord, 174
Dufournel, Adeodatus, 107
Dufournel, Emmanuel, 130
Dutch Zouaves, 101, 120, 173, 203, 211

education, secularized, 28, 111
Egptian army, 9
Egypt, 6, 108
Elizabeth, Queen of Austria, 35
Emmanuel Filiberto, Prince of Italy, 198
Enlightenment, 12
Eugenie, Empress of France, 38, 132, 199
Eusebius, Saint, 1

Fanti, General, 61, 70–71, 84–85, 87
Farfa abbey, 112
Farnborough Abbey, 199
Favre, Jules, 176
Ferdinand of Naples, 84
Ferrero, (officer), 153–54, 156, 158, 162,
165
First Foreign Regiment (Swiss), 45
FitzJames, Antoinette de, 104
FitzJames, Jacques, Duke de, 104
Foligno, revolt in, 44–45
Forty Martyrs of Sebaste, 1
France, 9, 13, 19, 27–30, 33–37, 43–44,
48, 53, 68, 173, 201
abandonment of Rome by, 149–51
Armistice of Villafranca and, 48
coup of 1852, 25

France—*continued*
  Government of National Defense, 176
  legacy of Zoaves in, 173, 215
  Mexican war and, 105–6
  Revolution of 1789, 5, 11, 13, 19,
      34–36, 101, 213
  Revolution of 1848, 25, 30, 33, 35–37
  Third Republic, 202
Franciscan order, 6
Francis I, Emperor of Austria (Holy
      Roman Emperor Francis II), 38
Francis II, King of the Two Sicilies, 31
Francis V, Duke of Modena, 52
Franco, Francisco, 212, 216
Franco-Austrian War of 1859, 61
Franco-Belgian Volunteers, 59, 71, 77–80,
      96, 99–100
Franco-Prussian War of 1870, 149–50,
      175–93, 213
Franks, 3
Franz Josef, Emperor of Austria and Holy
      Roman Emperor, 33–35, 57, 84,
      113, 172
freedom, concept of, 12
free France, 215
Freeman's Journal, 145
French, as langauge of command, 102
French Army, 23, 77, 180–81, 215
  garrison in Rome, 60, 67, 104–5
  Mentana and, 133–35, 138–40
  withdrawal from Rome, 106–7,
      112–14, 117–18, 149–50
French Army of the Loire, 186, 188–91
French Army of the Vosges, 176
French-Canadian Zouaves, 49–50, 101,
      146–47, 204–6
French parliament, 38, 176, 201
French Royalists, 202, 213
French Volunteers of the West, 177–93
French Zouaves, 101, 174–93, 199–202
Frosinone province, 107, 122, 153
Fuchman, Major, 79, 80

Gady, Wilhelm de, 86
Gaeta

  battle of 1861, 84
  flight of Pius IX to, 20, 58
Gambetta, Leon, 176, 181, 186
Garibaldi, Giuseppe, 22, 24, 37, 43, 50,
      52, 55, 60, 61, 65–66, 106, 112–13,
      144, 176, 178
  arrest of, 124, 130–31
  background of, 29–31
  battle for Rome and, 118–19, 122–26,
      132–40, 149–51
  Mentana and, 134–35, 137, 139
  old age and death of, 199
Garibaldi, Menotti, 122, 125, 128–29
Garibaldi, Ricotti, 122
Garibaldi Guard (39th New York
      Volunteers), 144
Gautier, Leon, 6–7
Genoa, 82, 88, 94
Gentili, Captain, 125
George, Saint, 1
German states (Germany), 11–13, 33–34,
      148
  Confederation, 112
  unification of, 11, 184–85
German Zouaves, 101, 215–16
Gettysburg, battle of, 10
Ghibellines, 26
Giovine Italia, La, 29
Giustiniani, Giacomo Cardinal, 20
Gleason, John, 57
Good Friday prayers, 38
Gordon, Charles Menzies, 204
Gourgoing, Colonel, 182
Goyon, General, 66, 67
Great Britain (England), 9, 12, 28, 34, 43,
      48, 55, 61, 75, 82, 109, 213
Greece, 3
Gregory II, St. Pope, 3
Gregory XVI, Pope, 20, 36
Guelphs, 26
Guerin, Joseph, 54–55, 96–99, 125
Guerin, Lieutenant (cousin of Joseph),
      125
Guides, 76, 80
Guillemin, Lieutenant, 126–27

Guillet, Joseph Henri, 206
Guttenhoven, Colonel, 80–81

Habsburg family, 32–34, 38, 112
Heliand, Georges, Marquis d', 53–55,
 96, 98
Hellemons, Father, 101
Henry IV, King of France, 177
Henry V, Count de Chambord, 35,
 51–52, 98, 100, 102, 105, 150,
 201–2, 208, 210, 213
Herries, Lord, 148
Heykamp, Nicholas, 125
Hillemons, Father, 203
Hitler, Adolf, 216
Holy Roman Emperor, 4, 38. *See also
 specific individuals*
Holy Roman Empire, 3
Holy Saturday prayers, 38
Howlin, John, 57, 70, 71
Hubert, Saint, feast of, 133
Hughes, Bishop John, 95, 109
Hungarian Zouaves, 101
Hungary, 33–34

Igualada, Spain, battle of, 209–10
Imitation of Christ, The, 89
Imperii Galliarum (Papal bull of 1857), 38
India, 9, 82
Indians, American, 10, 85, 205–6
Irish Zouaves, 55–57, 70, 77–79, 82, 85,
 88, 94–95, 101, 121, 173, 204, 211
Isabella II, Queen of Spain, 207, 211
Islam, radical, 218
Italans in Pontifical Army and Zouaves,
 70–71, 172
Italian army
 2nd Division, 152
 4th Corps, 66–67, 152–53, 156
 9th Division, 153, 156
 12th Division, 153, 156–67
 battle for Rome and, 117–18, 123, 149,
  151–67
 chaplaincy and, 199, 216
 memory of Zouaves and, 216

Italian fleet, 112, 155
Italian Legion (Uruguay), 30
Italian Royal Army, 133
Italian States. *See also specific states*
 Armistice of Villafranca and, 48
 Franz Josef and, 33
Italian unification (Risorgimento), 11,
 28–29, 39. *See also specific battles,
 individuals, and territories*
 aftermath of, 198–200, 204
 reexamination of, 217
Italy. *See also* Italian army; Italian States;
 Naples, kingdom of; Sardinia; Two
 Sicilies, kingdom of; *and specific
 battles, cities, and provinces*
 Napoleonic invasion of, 19, 26
Italian parliament, 111–12
 peace with popes in Lateran Treaty of
  1929, 214
 proclamation of kingdom of, 93
 revolution in, 19, 36
Iturbide, Prince Salvador, 146, 148, 172

Jacobites, 213
Jamaica, bishop of, 204
James II, King of England, 104
Jaquement, Archbishop of Nantes, 97
Jeanne d'Arc Credit Union, 206
Jesuit College of Notre Dame de Sainte
 Croix, 178
Jesuit College of Saint Francois Xavier,
 53–54
Jesuits, 12, 28, 204
Joan of Arc, 188–89
John Paul II, Pope, 205, 216–17
John the Baptist, St., feast of, 205
Jong, Pieter Janzsoon de, 127
Joubert, Leopold Louis, 9–10, 53, 212–13
Juarez, Benito, 88, 105–6, 145
Justin Martyr, St., 1

Kabyles, 24
Kanzler, Hermann, 58, 69, 106–7, 123,
 129–31, 133–35, 137–39, 146,
 149–50, 153, 155–56, 170, 199–200

Karl, Emperor of Austria, 216
Keily, Daniel, 85, 88, 95–96
Kennedy, John F., 109, 203–4
Kenyon, George, 162
Keogh, Myles Walter, 10–11, 56–57, 85, 88, 95–96, 205
Kerguenec, Henri Le Chauff de, 98–99
King, Rufus, 110
Kingship of Christ, devotion to, 216
Kligge, (soldier), 180
knighthood, 5–6, 11
Know-Nothing riots, 144

La Croix (newspaper), 203
La Giustiniana (town), 158–60
Lazaretto forts, 74, 85–86
Lepanto, battle of, 77
Lissa, battle of, 112
Lamoricière, Christophe L. J. de, 24–25, 37, 49–51, 58–60, 66–68, 73–80, 83–85, 87, 89, 99, 106, 187
La Motte-Rouge, General, 179, 181, 186
Lanascol, Hyacinthe de, 98
Lateran Historical Museum, 214
Lateran Treaty (1929), 214
Latin-American Zouaves, 101
Latium province (Lazio), 60, 66, 120
Lauri, officer, 160, 172
Laval, battle of, 191
Lavigerie, Cardinal, 212
Lavigne, Ernest, 147
Law of 1866, 111–12, 152, 197
League of Democracy, 199
Legion of Antibes (Legione Romana), 113–14, 118, 126, 128, 134, 136–37, 170, 181
Legitimist royalists of France, 35, 36, 49, 51, 98, 202
Le Gonidec de Traissan, Major, 125, 136, 178–86, 189–90
Le Mans, defense of, 190–91
Leo IV, Pope, 5
Leo XII, Pope, 19–20
Leo XIII, Pope, 198, 202, 204, 206–7
Leonine Wall, 5, 162–63

Leopold I, King of Belgium, 23
Leotardi, General, 81
Leo the Isaurian, Emperor of Byzantine Empire, 3
Lincoln, Abraham, 109–10, 144–45
Little Big Horn, battle of, 10, 57, 205
Loigny, battle of, 188–90, 201
Loistman, Louis, 88
Loland, (French bugler), 138
Lombardy, 3, 33, 48, 113
Lord of the Rings (Tolkien), 59
L'Ordre (newspaper), 101
Loreto, battle of, 73, 75–82, 87
Louis XIV, King of France, 50
Louis XVI, King of France, 13, 201
Louis Napoleon. See Napoleon III
Louis Philippe, King of France, 35, 51–52
Louth Rifles, 56
Luke the Evangelist, St., 161

MacDonnell, Count Charles, 55
MacMahon, Marshal, 201
Magenta, battle of, 44
Magyars, 34
Manassas, battle of the First, 47
Manresa, capture of, 211
Mao tse-tung, 214
Marches province, 60, 67, 69–70, 93–94
Margherita, Queen of Italy, 207
Marin de Boylesve, Father, 179
Marx, Karl, 108–9, 192
Maryland Volunteer Cavalry, 9
Maurice, Saint, 1
Maximilian, Emperor of Mexico, 58, 88, 105–6, 108, 145–46
Maxwell, Walter Constable, 148
Maze de la Roche, (officer), 157
Mazzini, Giuseppi, 29, 109
McMaster, James, 145, 147, 174, 210
Mentana, battle of, 10, 134–40, 145, 149, 163, 165, 204, 206, 210, 212
Merode, Archbishop Count Xavier de, 21, 23–25, 67, 71, 94–95, 99–100, 102, 107, 199
Mesre de Pas, Mizael, 76

Metz, battle of, 150, 175–76, 186
Mexico, 58, 88, 105–6, 109, 145–46, 175
Middle Ages, 26
Middleton, Henry Van Ness, Count
    Bentivogilo, 108, 206
Milan, 44
military religious orders, 6
Minié ball, 12
missionaries, 4, 10, 19
Miyonnet, Georges, 96
Modena, 33, 44, 48, 62
monasteries, suppression of, 12, 28, 112
Moncuit, Corporal, 99–100
Montcuit, Captain, 189
Montebello, General, 104
Monte Cassino abbey, 112
Monte Libretti, battle of, 126–28
Monte Lupino, battle of, 107
Monte Pelago fort, 85
Monte Rotondo, 107, 125–26, 130,
    132–39
Mousty, Victor, 104–5, 203
Mouzillon, miracle at, 97
Mpala fortress, 213
Muller, Josef Maria, 102–3
Mulwewa mission, 212
Murray, Hugh, 101, 210–11
Muslim pirates, 5
Mussolini, Benito, 217

Nanteuil, Alfred de, 96
Naples, Don Gennaro of, 120
Naples, kingdom of, 30–31, 33, 50, 52,
    60, 61, 65–66, 93, 117
Naples, Queen Mother of, 120
Napoleon, Prince, 44, 45
Napoleon Bonaparte, 26, 32, 36, 38
Napoleon III, Emperor of France (Louis
    Napoleon), 17, 23, 25, 36–39,
    43–44, 48–49, 55, 58, 60, 66, 82,
    99–100, 105–6, 109, 113, 117–18,
    124, 130, 132–33, 145, 149–50,
    174–77, 199
National Committee at Rome, 117, 118
nationalism, 34

"nation in arms," 11–12
Nazis, 216
Neo-Guelphs, 27
Nerola (town), 125–26, 128–29
New Zealand, 57, 88, 206
Ney, (French officer), 37
Nice, 29, 43, 176
Nicotera, (Garibaldi officer), 122
1984 (Orwell), 65
Noble Guard, 197, 214
North Africa, 24
North German Confederation, 175
Noue, General, 67

O'Clery, Count, 84
O'Clery, Patrick Keyes, 121, 162, 203–4,
    210
O'Keefe, Joseph, 57, 85, 88, 95–96
O'Reilly, Myles, 55–56, 71–73
Orleanists of France, 35
Orleans, defense of, 181–91
Orthodox Church, 38
Orvieto, 67, 70, 152
Ospizio Apostolico di San Michele a
    Ripa, 19
Ottoman Empire, 38, 108
"Our Lady of Hope of Pontmain," 191

Paggese, pillage of, 94
Palatine Guard of Honor, 197, 214
Palazzo Serristori bombing, 131
Palestine, 38
Pallfy, Captain, 76
Palmerston, Lord, 48, 55, 61, 75, 82
papal army. See also Pontifical Zouaves;
    and other specific regiments
  first battle of, at Perugia, 45–47
  organization of, 24
papal diplomacy, 4, 199
papal encyclicals, 111
  January 19, 1860 on Papal
    States, 49
papal infallibility, doctrine of, 148–49
Papal States. See also specific battles,
    provinces, and towns

Papal States—*continued*
 birth of, 3–4
 Congress of Paris and, 43
 end of story of, in 1870, 166
 Garibaldi's goal to overthrow Pope in,
  31
 guerrilla war in, after Ancona, 93
 Holy Roman Emperor and duty of
  defending, 33–36
 internal administration of, 20, 22–23
 Italian Army enters last, in 1870,
  152–53, 166
 loss of, 213
 recruits from lost provinces of, 101
 Sardinian war with Austria of 1859
  and, 44–49
 stripped of French garrison, 117
 war of 1860 breaks out, 60, 65–69
Paray-le-Monial
 Benedictine nuns of, 188, 201
 Shrine of, 201
Parcevaux, Paul de, 82
Paris
 Commune of 1871, 191–92
 siege of 1870, 176, 187–88
Parma, 33, 44, 48, 62
Patrician Brothers, 71
Paul VI, Pope, 214
peasantry, 12, 30–31
Pensionaat Saint Louis, 101
Pepin III "the Short," King of the
  Franks, 3
Perkins, (American tourist), 47
Persano, Carlo, 66, 68, 74–75, 83, 85–87,
  89, 112
Perugia, 67, 70
 Massacre of, 44–47, 95
Pesaro, 67, 69, 73
Peter, St., 1
Peter and Paul, anniversary of
  martyrdoms of Saints, 113
Peters, Henri, 120
Peter's Pence, 198
Pettiti, General, 104
Piazza di Colonna bombing, 131

Piccioni, Giovanni, 93, 94
Picou, Rogatien, 99
Picq, Colonel Du, 138
Pimodan, Marquis de, 49, 51, 59, 66, 73,
  76–79, 82, 96
Pinelli, General, 94
Pius VII, Pope, 17, 19
Pius IX (Giovanni Maria Mastai-
  Ferretti), 10
 allies of, 33, 35–39
 Americans and, 108–10, 144–46
 background of, 17–20
 battle for Rome and, 106–7,
  112–14, 120, 132, 134, 151–53,
  161, 164
 beatification of, 217
 death of, 198
 honors bestowed by, 87, 139
 Holy House of Loreto and, 76
 Mentana and, 143, 204
 Mexico and, 106, 146
 ministers and, 21–24
 Neo-Guelphs and, 27
papal infallibility and, 148–49
 surrender of, and withdrawal to
  Vatican, 169–71, 197–99, 201
 seizure of Romagna and, 48–49
 Vatican I and, 118, 148
 Victor Emmanuel II and, 33, 199
 war of 1860 and, 44, 54–57, 60–61,
  66, 68, 99
 Zouaves and, 25, 98, 100, 102–4,
  147–48, 190, 204–5
Poitiers, France, 190, 191
Poland, 34, 57, 87
Polhés, Gen. Baron de, 135, 137
Polish Zouaves, 101
Polk, Antoinette, 200–201
Polk, Leonidas, 200
Pontifical chasseurs, 78–79, 107, 154
Pontifical dragoons, 107, 125, 132,
  134–35, 146, 149, 159, 164,
  172
Pontifical gendarmes, 124–26, 128, 132,
  153, 156–57, 197, 214

Pontifical Zouaves (Army). *See also* specific battles, individuals, and nationalities
Albano cholera epidemic and, 120
American Confederacy and, 10, 107–11
annual requiem Mass for, 217–18
campaign of 1867 and, 120–43
Carlist wars of 1872–76 and, 207–12
chivalry and attitude producing, 6–7
Collingwood's unpublished history of, 207
Congo missionaries and, 10, 212–13
European countries adopt units of, 25
formation and recruitment of, in 1860, 49–62
Franco-Prussian War and, 177–93, 201
legacy of, 213–18
official name, uniforms, and funding of, 99–102
origin of, in Algeria, 24–25
outbreak of war in 1860–62, 67–89, 104–5
Pius IX as chief of, 17–27
recruitment to, 9–11, 36, 54, 98–102, 106–7, 113–14, 120–23, 143–49
religious life in, 102–4, 122, 215
Rome defense of 1870 and, 150–66
Rome surrender and, 164–66, 170–74
Sacred Heart banner of, 188–90, 209–10, 212
25th anniversary of founding of, in 1885, 202
veterans associations and and memory of, 200–218
popes and papacy, 1, 9–10
attitude toward war and, 214–15
make peace Italian state, in 1929, 214–15
sovereignty of, over central Italy and Papal States, 2–5
Popiel, Jan Chosciak, 57–58, 85, 87
Porta Pia (Ancona), 86–87
Porta Pia (Rome), 134, 160, 162–65, 169
Praetorian Camp, 163
Precious Blood, devotion to, 216

prisoners of war, 81–82, 87–88, 94–95
Protestants, 27
Prussia, 34, 47–48, 58, 68, 88, 112–13, 149, 175, 185
Pu-yi, Emperor of China, 214

Quatrebarbes, Count de, 83
Quelen, (soldier), 127–28
Quirinal papal palace, 198, 206

Radetzky, Field Marshall, 33
Rattazzi, Prime Minister, 117–18, 122, 130
Redshirts (Garibaldians, irregulars, guerrillas), 66, 124–26, 131–40, 150–51, 162
Reformation, 12
religious orders, suppression of, 28, 38, 111–12
Resimont, Captain, 157–58
Revolutionary Committee at Rome, 117, 118
Revolution of 1870, 149
Revolutions of 1848, 22, 25, 28, 30, 32–35, 52, 57, 66
Ringard, Lieutenant, 126
Risorgimento, stato laico e identità nazionale (Biffi), 217
Risorgimento (journal), 27
Romagna, 44, 48–49, 51, 60
Roman Empire, 1–3
Roman infantry, 77–79
Roman militia, 3
Roman nobility, whites vs. blacks, 198
Pontificale (liturgical manual), 5
Roman Question, 39, 151–52, 207
Roman Republic of 1848, 66
Rome
annexed to Italy, 197–98
battle of 1867, 113, 117–18, 122–23, 130–40
battle of 1870 and surrender of, 84, 150–66, 212, 217
French garrison in, 48, 60, 66–68, 99–100, 106–7, 113–14, 150–51

Rome—*continued*
  Mentana monuments and, 204
  papal sovereignty over, established, 2–4
  sack of 1527, 70
Rossi, Counte de, 22
Russell, Lord John, 48
Russia, 33–34, 38, 68, 87
  Revolution and Civil War, 213
Russian Zouaves, 101

Saarbrucken, 175
Sachetti, Giuseppe, 207
Sacré, Monsignor, 102
Sacred Heart of Jesus, devotion to, 179,
    191–93, 215–17
  banner, 188–90, 201, 209–10, 212
Shrine of Paray-le-Monial, 201
Sacred Heart (Sacre Coeur) basilica
    (Montmartre), 201, 215
St. Brieuc, bishop of, 191
Ste. Marie, Henri de, 110
St. Patrick, Company of (post Ancona),
    95, 205–6
St. Patrick's battalion (of Zouaves), 11,
    56, 59, 67–68, 70, 71, 77, 84–85,
    88, 94–95
St. Paul's Outside the Walls, sack of 846, 5
St. Pazanne, Mass for Guerin and Chalus
    at, 97
St. Peters Basilica, 5, 20
San Angelo, battle of, 69–70
San Callisto massacre of 1848, 66
San Domenico Osumo monastery, 96
San Frncesco convent, 125
Sangallo, Forte (at Civita Castellana),
    156–57, 158
San Marino, republic of, 30
San Onofrio, Convent of, 159
San Pietro monastery, 46
San Stefano, battle of, 85
Santa Casa (Holy House) shrine at
    Loreto, 75, 76
Santa Maria degli Angeli e Martyri, as
    center of Savoy dynasty religious
    life, 198

Santa Maria in Ara Coeli, Pius IX retreats
    to church of (Rome), 161
Santicci Vineyard, 135, 136
Santo Bambini image, 161
Sardinia, 214
  Armistice of Villafranca and, 48
  Cavour and, 27–28
  Crimean War and, 28, 34, 43
  dukes of Savoy as kings of, 26
  Garibaldi and, 29
  Napoleonic wars and, 26
  revolution of 1821 and, 31–32
  war vs. Austria of 1859, and attack on
      Papal States, 43–48
  war of 1860 and, 61, 65–66
Sardinian army, 60–62, 68–72, 84
Sardinian fleet, 62, 66, 68, 74–75, 83,
    86, 87
Savalls, Captain, 208–9
Savoy, House of, 26, 30–32, 60, 198
Scandanavia, 12
Schiller, 59
Schmid, Antonio, 45–47, 58, 70
Scottish Zouaves, 204
Sebastian, Saint, 1
Sedan, battle of, 175, 183, 199
seminaries
  closed by Italian parliament, 111
  laws governing teaching in, 28
Seminary of Rennes, 192
Senigallia, occupation of, 69–70, 75, 83
September Convention (1864), 106, 113,
    117–18, 149
Serbs, 34
Serra, Colonel, 154–56
Seven Weeks War, 88, 112–13
Seward, William, 95
Sezze (town), 107, 110
Sforza, Constanzo, 69
Shea, Sergeant, 159, 160
Sheehan, Smith, 211
Shields, James, 96
Sicily, 2–3, 30–31
Sisters of Charity, 20, 112–13, 120
Sitting Bull, chief, 10, 205–6

69th New York Infantry (Fighting Irish), 174
slavery, 109
Soldier's Confidences with God (Borsi), 216
Solferina, battle of, 44, 57
Sonis, Louis-Gaston de, 187–90, 215
Spain, 30, 33, 50, 68, 149, 216
  Carlist War of 1872–76, 207–12
Spanish-American War, 206
Spanish Civil War (1936–39), 212, 216
Spanish Zouaves, 101, 148
Spoleto, 20, 60, 158
  battle of, 67, 71–73, 95
Squadriglieri, 172
Stafford, Lord, 56
Stauffenberg, Claus von, 7, 216
Stohlberg, Count von, 180
Stone, Katherine, 129, 139
Sulpician priests, 97
Surratt, John, 109–11, 144–45, 205
Surratt, Mary, 109
Sweden, 12
Swedish Zouaves, 101
Swiss carabinieri, 45, 79, 103, 107, 128, 132, 134, 136–37, 140, 164, 170
Swiss Guard, 160, 197
Swiss pontifical soldiers, 59, 70, 71, 80–81, 101, 107, 134, 173
Swiss Rifles, 77–79
"Swords around the Cross," 49
Sylvester I, Pope St., 2

Tann, General von der, 181
taxation, 28, 60, 111
Templars (Hospitallers), 6
Teramo, ambush at, 93
Testard de Montigny, Benjamin, 101
Teutonic Knights, 6
Tevis, Charles Carroll, 9, 145, 147–48, 174
Thomalé, Captain, 136
Thundering Legion, 1
Tolkien, 59
Tracey, Charles, 121, 162

Trastevere, 5
  battles of, 131–32, 159–63, 165–66
Trochu, General (president), 176
Troussures, Major, 164–65
Tuscany, 32–33, 44, 48, 60–62, 66
Two Sicilies, kingdom of, 30–31, 93
Tyrol, 112, 216

Uganda, 212
Umberto I, King of Italy, 207
Umbria, 44–45, 60, 67–68, 70–73, 93, 100, 152
Union Allet (Canada), 204
Union de Charette, 206
Union Sacré, 215
United States, 9, 110, 143–46, 147–48
  Civil War, 9–11, 47, 85, 88, 93, 95–96, 105, 107–10, 144–45, 174–75, 200–201, 206, 213
  Confederacy and, 107–10, 144–45, 200, 206
Union Army, 9–10, 95–96, 144–45, 200, 205–6
Uruguay, 30

Van der Kerchove, Lieutenant, 164, 165
Vatican City, 5, 160, 166
  Lateran Treaty and, 214
  Pius IX withdraws to, 197–99
  surrender of 1870 and restriction of papal domain to, 169–71
Vatican Gardens, 162
Vatican I (Ecumenical Council of 1869–70), 118, 148–49
Vatican II, 214
Vavasour, Oswald, 148
Vavasour, William, 148
Veaux, Captain de, 126, 136
Velletri, 104–5, 107, 122, 153, 156, 158
Vendée, 35, 49, 51–53, 176, 179
Venetia, 30, 33, 48, 112–13
Verano cemetery (Rome), 204
Vicar, Cardinal, 44
Vichy France, 215

Victor Emmanuel I, King of Sardinia,
    31, 32
Victor Emmanuel II, King of Sardinia,
    23, 25–27, 31–33, 48, 61–62, 65,
    68, 84, 93, 104–7, 112–13, 118, 132,
    135, 149–52, 155–56, 164, 198–99,
    207–8
Victoria, Queen, 57, 88, 173
Villafranca, Armistice of, 48, 58
Virgin Mary, 190–91
Viterbo, 67, 70, 107, 124, 152–54, 156
Volontari Pontifici, 94
Volunteers of the West, 192–93

Wallenstein (Schiller), 59
Watts-Russell, Julian, 121–22, 138, 204

Watts-Russell, Wilfred, 121
Westminthal, Lieutenant, 86
Wibaux, Sgt. Theodore, 178, 189
Wills, Dutch Zouave, 209–10, 211
Wissembourg, battle of, 150, 175
Woelmont, Monsignor, 102
Wolff-Metternich, Count Friedrich Graf
    "Fritz," 58, 87–88
World War I, 214–16
World War II, 214–15

Zambianchi, 65–66
Zappi, Count Giovanni Battista, 69,
    164
Zola, Emile, 38
Zouaoua (Zwãwa), 24